Tales *from 5000 Years* of Chinese History

Volume I

by Lin Handa & Cao Yuzhang

Better Link Press

This book is edited and designed by the Editorial Committee of *Cultural China* series

Managing Directors: Wang Youbu, Xu Naiqing

Editorial Director: Wu Ying

Editors: Zhou Kexi, Patrick Wallace, Sam Meekings

Assistant Editor: Yao Feng

Chinese Text by Lin Handa, Cao Yuzhang

Translation by Yawtsong Lee

Interior and Cover Design: Yuan Yinchang, Xia Wei

ISBN-13: 978-1-60220-112-5

Address any comments about *Tales from Five Thousand Years of Chinese History (I)* to:

Better Link Press

99 Park Ave

New York, NY 10016

USA

or

Shanghai Press and Publishing Development Company

F 7 Donghu Road, Shanghai, China (200031)

Email: comments_betterlinkpress@hotmail.com

Printed in China by Shenzhen Donnelley Printing Co., Ltd.

3 5 7 9 10 8 6 4

CONTENTS

PREFACE 9

BEFORE 2070 BC

1. Emperors Huangdi (the Yellow Emperor), Yao and Shun 11
2. Da Yu Tamed the Floods 14

XIA AND SHANG DYNASTIES (2070 BC–1046 BC)

3. Shang Tang and the Yin Dynasty 17
4. Jiang Taigong the Angler 21
5. Slaves' Rebellion 24

ZHOU DYNASTY (1046 BC–256 BC)

Western Zhou Dynasty (1046 BC–771 BC)

6. The Duke of Zhou—King Cheng's Chief Counselor 27
7. Beacon-fires on Mount Lishan 30

Eastern Zhou Dynasty (770 BC–256 BC)
Spring and Autumn Period (770 BC–476 BC)

8. The Hegemony of Lord Huan of Qi 33
9. Wu Zixu Slipped Through the Gate of Zhaoguan 38
10. The Peripatetic Travels of Confucius 42
11. Gou Jian Slept on Sticks and Tasted Gall 46
12. Fan Li and Wen Zhong 49

Warring States Period (475 BC–221 BC)

13. Mo Zi Took the Scaling Ladder in Stride 53
14. Shang Yang and His Pole at South Gate 56
15. Sun Bin Matching Wits with Pang Juan 60
16. Zhang Yi Undid the Alliance 64
17. King Wuling of Zhao Adopted the Hu Dress and Horseback Shooting 67
18. Meng Changjun's Retainers 70
19. The Quest of King Zhao of Yan for a Capable Man 74
20. Tian Dan's Fiery Bulls Formation 77
21. Qu Yuan's River Sacrifice 81
22. Lin Xiangru Returned the Jade Intact to Zhao 85
23. Lian Po Presented a Stick and Asked for a Flogging 89
24. Fan Sui's Strategy of Allying with Distant Powers and Attacking Nearer Ones 92
25. Zhao Kuo, the Unequalled Military Strategist on Paper 96
26. Mao Sui Recommending Himself 99
27. Lord Xinling Rescued Zhao 102
28. Li Si Advised against the Expulsion of Foreign-born Officeholders 105
29. Jing Ke's Attempt on the Life of the King of Qin 108
30. The King of Qin Conquered the Six States 112

QIN DYNASTY (221 BC–206 BC)

31. Qin Shihuang—the First Emperor of Unified China 116

32. Intrigues at Shaqiu 121
33. The Rebellion of Chen Sheng and Wu Guang 124
34. Liu Bang and Xiang Yu 128
35. Xiang Yu Orders His Army to Smash All its Stoves and Sink All its Boats 132

HAN DYNASTY (206 BC–220 AD)

Western Han Dynasty (206 BC–25 AD)

36. Liu Bang's Contract with the People 136
37. The Banquet at Hongmen 141
38. Xiao He Chases after Han Xin 146
39. Rivalry between the States of Chu and Han 150
40. Xiang Yu Haunted by Chu Chants 154
41. Song of the Rising Wind 158
42. The Oath of the White Horse 162
43. Cao Adopts the Ways of Xiao 166
44. Zhou Bo Wrests Control of the Army 169
45. Zhou Yafu, Martinet of Camp Xiliu 173
46. Li Guang, the "Flying General" 176
47. Generals Wei Qing and Huo Qubing 180
48. Zhang Qian's Mission to the Western Regions 184
49. Su Wu, the Shepherd 188
50. Sima Qian, Author of *Shi Ji* 192
51. Wang Zhaojun Carried off in Marriage by a Xiongnu 195
52. Wang Mang Restores the Old System 198
53. Uprising of the Red Eyebrows and the Army of the Green Woods 202

Eastern Han Dynasty (25 AD–220 AD)

54. Liu Xiu Restores the Han Dynasty 206
55. The Quest for Buddhist Sutras and Statues 210
56. Ban Chao Discovers that the Sword is Mightier than the Pen 213
57. Zhang Heng and His Seismometer 217
58. The Dang Gu Incidents 220
59. Fearless Fan Pang Goes to Jail 225
60. The Yellow Turban Uprising 229
61. Yuan Shao Kills the Eunuchs 233
62. Cao Cao Launches Military Action 237
63. Wang Yun Snares Dong Zhuo 241
64. Cao Cao Discusses Heroes over Wine 244
65. The Battle of Guandu 248
66. Sun Ce Takes Control of Jiangdong 253
67. Liu Bei's Three Visits to the Thatched Hut 256
68. Zhou Yu's Fiery Attack at Red Cliffs 260
69. Guan Yu Swamps the Seven Armies 266
70. Lü Meng Crosses the River in White 270

THREE KINGDOMS (220 AD–280 AD)

71. Lu Xun Torches a 200-mile Chain of Barracks 274
72. Meng Huo's Seventh Capture 279
73. Ma Su Loses Jieting 284
74. Death of a Genius at Wuzhangyuan 288
75. Sima Yi Feigns Illness 293

76. The Ambitions of Sima Zhao 297
77. Deng Ai Sneaks through Jian'ge 300
78. Adou Revels in a Foreign Court and Forgets His Home Country 304

JIN DYNASTY (265 AD–420 AD)

Western Jin Dynasty (265 AD–316 AD)

79. Shi Chong and Wang Kai in a Wealth Contest 307
80. Imbecile of an Emperor 310
81. War of Eight Princes 313
82. A Xiongnu (Hun) Declares Himself Emperor of Han 317
83. Sword Practice at the First Crow of the Rooster 321

Eastern Jin Dynasty (317 AD–420 AD)

84. House of the Simas and the Wangs 324
85. Shi Le Enjoys Han Books 327
86. Zu Ti Knocks His Oar against the Gunwale in Mid-crossing 330
87. Wang Xizhi Writes His Famous "Preface to the Poems Composed at the Orchid Pavilion" 334
88. Huan Wen on a Northern Expedition 337
89. Wang Meng Discusses National Politics While Picking Lice 341
90. Strong-willed Fu Jian 345
91. Xie An Makes a Comeback 349
92. The Battle of Fei River 353

PREFACE

TALES FROM FIVE *Thousand Years of Chinese History* is a collection of stories arranged in chronological order, covering a period from ancient times to the pre-Opium-War Qing dynasty.

The topics were selected by the educator and linguist, Lin Handa (1900–1972), who drew up the outline for the collection and contributed some chapters. Following Lin's death, Cao Yuzhang (1924–1996) took over his mantle and completed the work. This combined effort of two consecutive authors has enjoyed wide appeal by virtue of its historical accuracy, well-structured narrative, fluent writing and distinctive style.

The English edition of *Tales from Five Thousand Years of Chinese History* consists of two volumes. Volume One starts from ancient times and culminates in the last years of the Eastern Jin dynasty (317–420). For the sake of brevity, the original Chinese work has been slightly abridged in this English edition.

BEFORE 2070 BC

1. Emperors Huangdi (the Yellow Emperor), Yao and Shun

ABOUT FIVE THOUSAND years ago, the Yellow River and the Yangtze River valleys were inhabited by numerous clans and tribes. Huangdi was the legendary leader of one of those tribes.

The tribe led by Huangdi originated in the Jishui area in northwest China before migrating to Zhuolu (today's Zhuolu and Huailai in Hebei Province), where the tribesmen settled and started to engage in animal husbandry and farming.

According to legend, Yandi, a contemporary of Huangdi and the leader of another tribe (which had settled in the Jiangshui area in northwest China), had close blood ties to Huangdi's tribe. Yet as the fortunes of Yandi's tribe declined, Huangdi's tribe flourished.

There was at this time a tough leader of the Jiuli tribe by the name of Chi You. Legend has it that Chi You had 81 brothers, all of whom had heads of bronze, foreheads of iron and the bodies of wild animals, and fed on sand and stone. These warriors of uncommon ferocity were said to be makers of a variety of weaponry such as swords, halberds, bows and arrows. They led Chi

You's tribe on frequent raids against other tribes.

It was during one of these raids that Chi You annexed some of Yandi's territory. Yandi put up an armed resistance but proved no match for Chi You, whose marauding hordes quickly routed Yandi's troops. Yandi had no choice but to retreat to Zhuolu, where he requested the help of Huangdi, who had long wanted to eliminate this enemy. He rallied the support of the tribes and put together an army that defeated Chi You in a decisive battle on the plains of Zhuolu. Huangdi gained the loyalty and support of many tribes in the process, but a rift developed between the tribes headed by Yandi and Huangdi, and Yandi lost out in a battle between the two tribes in Banquan (southeast of present-day Zhuolu in Hebei Province). This marked Huangdi's ascendancy to supreme leader of the alliance of tribes in China's Central Plain.

According to legend, the reign of Huangdi coincided with many inventions and discoveries, which have all been credited to Huangdi by posterity. The period also saw the building of many palaces, carts, boats and a growing fashion for colorful clothing.

Legend also has it that Lei Zu, a consort of Huangdi's, took part in a great deal of productive work. Before she taught women in the tribe how to raise silkworms, unwind silk threads from their cocoons and weave them into silk cloth, silk had been unknown in China.

Cang Jie, Huangdi's official historian, reportedly created a written language, though this cannot be confirmed since no vestige of it has survived.

Legends passed down through the ages have exalted Huangdi, who is popularly believed to be the ancestor of the Huaxia race or the Cathay. Since the Yandi and Huangdi tribes shared kinship and eventually merged together, Chinese people sometimes refer to themselves as Yan-Huang descendants. A Mausoleum of Huangdi (the Yellow Emperor) has been erected on Qiaoshan Hills, north of Huangling County of Shaanxi Province, to honor the memory of this legendary ancestor of the Chinese nation.

It is said that after Huangdi died, three famous leaders emerged at different times at the head of tribal alliances. They were, in chronological order, Yao, Shun and Yu, who had been tribal chiefs before becoming leaders of tribal alliances.

In those times, the leader of a tribal alliance always consulted the tribal heads on major issues.

As Yao grew older, he began to give serious thought to the question of succession. He therefore called together all the leaders of the various tribes to discuss the matter.

After Yao explained his thinking, a man by the name of Fang Qi spoke up, "Your son Dan Zhu is an enlightened person. He is supremely suited to the succession."

"No. He has no integrity and is in perpetual argument with others," Yao replied gravely.

Another man, whose name was Huan Dou, then made himself heard, "How about Gong Gong, who oversees irrigation works? He is known for doing a good job."

Again Yao shook his head in disagreement, "Gong Gong has the gift of gab and is glib of tongue. His prudent and polite exterior simply serves as a cover for his duplicitous thoughts. I cannot place trust in that kind of character."

The discussions proved inconclusive and Yao continued to look for a suitable successor. When he called another meeting to consult the tribal chiefs on the question of succession and asked them for recommendations, there was a chorus of support for Shun.

Having listened to glowing accounts of Shun's achievements and qualities, and having closely observed him for a long period of time, Yao came to the conclusion that Shun was indeed blessed with both virtue and competence. He therefore abdicated his throne in favor of Shun. This mode of relinquishing power to a successor is called *shan rang* in Chinese history, meaning abdicating the throne to a deserving candidate. In the era of the clan communes, it was not uncommon for the clans to elect a new leader when their current leader became too old to rule effectively.

After Shun took over the reins, he maintained the people's trust in him by showing his diligence and simple and frugal ways as he labored side by side with them. When Yao died a few years later, Shun proposed to cede his position of alliance leader back to Yao's son Dan Zhu, but the proposal did not meet with wide approval and Shun was therefore formally enthroned.

2. Da Yu Tamed the Floods

DURING THE REIGN of Yao, the Yellow River valley was hit by devastating floods that destroyed crops and houses, forcing the people there to move to higher ground. In many localities people's lives were made more perilous by the poisonous snakes and ferocious wild beasts that were flushed out by the floods.

To try and find a way to tame the wild water, Yao gathered the tribal chiefs of the alliance and asked them to name someone who would be equal to the task of taming the floods. They unanimously recommended Gun.

Yao did not particularly trust Gun, but reluctantly agreed when the chiefs explained that since there was no better candidate available at that moment, he might as well give Gun a try.

Gun spent nine years trying to tame the floods, to no avail. He tried to "bury" the water with earth and build dams, only to see the raging water burst through them to cause even more devastation.

After taking over the reins from Yao, Shun visited the flood zones on a fact-finding tour. He found Gun derelict in duty and had him executed. He then entrusted the mission of taming the floods to Gun's son, whose name was Yu.

In a radical departure from his father's approach, Yu ordered the digging of ditches to divert the overabundance of water, as well as the dredging of heavily silted rivers, all to ensure that the flood water found an unobstructed way to the ocean. He worked side by side with the local people, wearing a straw hat, wielding a spade and carrying excavated earth himself—it is said that he worked so hard that he lost all the hairs on his legs.

After thirteen years of strenuous effort, the flood water was finally channeled to the ocean and the reemerged land could once again be planted with crops.

The recently married Yu was so engrossed in his work that on numerous occasions when he passed by his house in his hectic schedule rushing hither and thither he did not drop in for a visit. Once he passed by his house when his wife Tu Shan had just given birth to their son Qi, but he still resisted the temptation of looking in despite the crying of the newborn baby.

There was at the time a huge mountain in the middle reaches of the Yellow River valley called Longmen (Dragon Gate) Mountain (northwest of today's Hejin County in Shanxi Province). The river channel narrowed as it flowed by, and the water rushing eastward toward Longmen Mountain often overflowed the riverbanks, causing devastating floods. After observing the topography of the vicinity, Yu led his army of workers in an assault on the mountain, and they gouged a channel through it, affording the river an unobstructed path east.

Posterity has celebrated Yu's feat in taming the floods and posthumously bestowed on him the reverential title of Great Yu.

As he aged, Shun followed the example of Yao and began to look for a successor. Yu was a popular choice because of his achievements in harnessing the Yellow River. Yu therefore succeeded Shun as leader of the alliance upon Shun's death.

This was in the late stage of the era of clan communes. As productivity grew, people produced not only enough to sustain themselves and their family, but also a nice surplus. The clan and tribal leaders used their leverage and position to appropriate for themselves the surplus produced by their people, and thus became local nobility. With surplus production, prisoners of war captured in tribal wars were no longer slaughtered but were turned into slaves to work for the nobility. The emergence of the classes of slaves and slave-owners signaled the beginning of the collapse of the clan society.

With Yu's accomplishments in taming the floods, his authority and prestige as the alliance leader grew considerably. It is said that on an eastern tour undertaken in his old age, Yu called the tribal chiefs for a meeting with him near Kuaiji Mountains (near today's Shaoxing in Zhejiang Province). All those who flocked to pay homage to Yu brought jewelry and rare fabrics and performed elaborate rites. One tribal chief called Fang Feng was unfortunate enough to be the last arrival. Considering this a slight, Yu had him beheaded. This shows that by that time Yu had morphed from an alliance leader into a bona fide king.

Yu had a right-hand man called Gao Yao, who helped him with governance. After Gao's death, his son Bo Yi followed in his father's footsteps to become Yu's aide. In the *shan rang* tradition (abdicating to a deserving successor), Bo Yi should have been designated Yu's successor, but upon Yu's death, the nobility of the Xia tribe (from which Yu originated), placed Yu's son Qi on the throne instead.

The election system which was the norm in the clan society was thus officially abolished and replaced by a system of hereditary succession. The Xia dynasty, the first dynasty founded on the slave-owning system in China's history, thus emerged.

XIA AND SHANG DYNASTIES (2070 BC–1046 BC)

3. Shang Tang and the Yin Dynasty

THE REIGN OF the Xia dynasty lasted for around four hundred years. The last ruler of the Xia dynasty in the 16th century BC was Xia Jie, who was a notorious tyrant.

The lower reaches of the Yellow River were inhabited by a tribe called the Shang. Their animal husbandry thrived so much and grew so fast that by the latter years of the Xia dynasty, when Tang became the Shang's leader, they had developed into a powerful tribe.

Noting the corruption and decadence of Xia Jie, Shang Tang dedicated himself to overthrowing the Xia dynasty. While outwardly pledging allegiance to Jie, he secretly built up his own power and strength.

Among the slaves brought to Shang Tang as part of his wife's dowry was a man called Yi Yin. It is said that he started out as a cook after coming to the household of Shang Tang. With time, Shang Tang discovered that Yi Yin was not one of run-of-the-mill slaves. After speaking with him, Shang Tang soon realized that Yi Yin had passed himself off as a dowry slave with the express purpose of meeting Tang. After Yi Yin told Tang his ideas about govenment, Tang immediately promoted him to the position of his advisor.

Shang Tang brought up his idea of an expedition against Xia Jie, whereupon Yi Yin commented, "Xia Jie is still powerful. Why don't we first stop paying him tribute to test the water and see how he reacts?"

Shang Tang stopped paying tribute to Xia Jie, as suggested by Yi Yin. This had the immediate effect of incurring the wrath of Xia Jie, who consequently ordered the nine Yi (barbarian) tribes to attack Shang Tang. Seeing that the Yi tribes still followed the orders of Xia Jie, Shang Tang wasted no time in asking Xia Jie for forgiveness and resumed the paying of tributes.

A year later, after some Yi tribes, fed up with the exactions and exploitation of the Xia dynasty, broke away, Tang and Yi Yin saw that the time had come for a major expedition.

After the accession of Qi to the throne, hereditary succession had been practiced for more than four hundred years and it would therefore be no easy task to overthrow the Xia dynasty. After consultations with Yi Yin, Tang decided to call his troops together, and he addressed them personally before the campaign.

"I would not have dared mount an insurgency save for the many evil deeds of Xia Jie. It was my manifest destiny to eliminate him and I am not one to disobey the mandate of heaven." He then set out his rules of discipline and rewards and punishments.

Shang Tang invoked the gods to motivate his troops, who had long harbored a grudge against Xia Jie. As a result they fought valiantly and routed Xia Jie's army in a battle at Mingtiao (north of today's An Yi Township of Yuncheng County in Shanxi Province).

Xia Jie retreated to Nanchao (southwest of today's Chao County in Anhui Province), with Tang in hot pursuit. Jie was to stay there in exile until his death.

The Xia dynasty was thus replaced by the Shang dynasty. In Chinese history, Tang's expedition against Xia has become known as the *Shang Tang Ge* (change) *Ming* (destiny). The ancient ruling classes considered a change of dynasties to be a change to the mandate of heaven, hence the expression *Ge Ming*, which can be literally translated as "revolution."

At the time of Tang's founding of the Shang dynasty, its capital was Bo (today's Shangqiu in Henan Province).

The Shang was ruled by twenty emperors after Tang before Pan Geng took over the reins. He was an able monarch. In order to restore stability to the country, he decided to move the capital to Yin (today's Xiaotun Village of Anyang in Henan Province), where he got the Shang house in order and revitalized the declining dynasty. The Shang dynasty is thus also known as Yin Shang or the Yin dynasty.

Now, more than three thousand long years later, the capital of the Shang dynasty lies in ruins. The large numbers of archaeological finds excavated in Xiaotun Village of Anyang prove that this was once the site of the ancient capital of the Shang. The village is therefore also known as the Yin Ruins.

The artifacts dug up from the Yin Ruins include more than a hundred thousand fragments of tortoise shell and animal bones bearing inscriptions of unrecognized characters. Assiduous archaeological research eventually succeeded in deciphering the characters. It turned out that the ruling class of the Shang dynasty used tortoise shell and animal bones to divine their fortunes before any sacrificial rites, hunting excursions and military expeditions. After the divination rites, the events and circumstances of the day and the results of the divination were carved on the tortoise shell and animal bones in an ancient language which has come to be known as the *jia gu wen* (shell and bone language). The *jia gu wen* is a precursor of present-day Mandarin.

The relics unearthed at the Yin Ruins also include large numbers of bronze vessels, utensils and weaponry of a wide variety, all of which display fine craftsmanship. Among them is a large square *ding* (ancient cooking vessel) called *si mu wu*, which weighs 875 kg, is 133 cm in height, 110 cm in length and 78 cm in width, and is adorned with elaborate floral designs. A bronze object of this size attests to the high level of technology and artistic achievement attained in the Yin Shang period.

The *jia gu wen* on oracle bones unearthed at the Yin Ruins

affords a solid foundation for a more accurate understanding of the society of the Yin Shang period. It is fair to say that the earliest written records of Chinese history date to the Shang dynasty.

4. Jiang Taigong the Angler

ZHOU, THE LAST emperor of the Yin dynasty (the eleventh monarch after the death of Pan Geng), was, like Xia Jie, interested only in his own pleasures and oblivious of the fate of the common people. He built one palace after another for himself and constructed a luxurious "Deer Pavilion" in his alternate capital Zhaoge (today's Qi County in Henan Province), in which he hoarded all the gold, silver, jewelry and other treasures he had amassed. He also built a huge storehouse called *Ju Qiao* to house foodstuffs that he had taken from his people. He filled a pond with wine and formed a "forest" from the large cuts of meat he ordered hung out. He and his favorite concubine Da Ji led a dissolute and decadent life. He meted out torture and cruel punishments to his subjects, while any nobleman who dared to contradict him could be arrested and roasted to death on a heated bronze pillar. This punishment was called *pao luo*, or cannon roasting.

The cruelty of Zhou hastened the demise of the Shang dynasty. In the meantime, a tribe in the west was flourishing, called the Zhou tribe.

Zhou was an ancient tribe. In the waning years of the Xia dynasty, this tribe inhabited areas that coincide with present-day Shaanxi and Gansu provinces. To get away from the harassment and incursions of the Rong and Di nomadic tribes, the Zhou tribal chief Gu Gong Dan Fu led his people in an exodus to the plains at the foot of the Qishan Mountains (northeast of today's Qishan County in Shaanxi Province), where they settled.

By the time Ji Chang (later assuming the title King Wen of

Zhou), grandson of Gu Gong Dan Fu, had become leader, the Zhou tribe was already a major power. King Wen of Zhou was an able statesman whose lifestyle was in sharp contrast to that of King Zhou of the Shang, who enjoyed drinking, hunting and meting out punishments to his people. King Wen of Zhou banned drinking and forbade the nobility from going on hunting expeditions as these often wreaked havoc on crops. He encouraged his people to raise more cattle and sheep and plant more crops. Furthermore, as a result of his embrace of people with talents, he was able to attract a lot of them to his service.

The rise of the Zhou tribe was perceived as a grave threat by the Shang. Chong Houhu, Shang Zhou's chief minister, told Shang Zhou that King Wen was wielding too much influence, which, if unchecked, would hurt the Shang.

Shang Zhou issued a warrant for the arrest of King Wen, who was subsequently incarcerated in Youli (in the vicinity of today's Tangyin County in Henan Province). The nobility of the Zhou then made a gift of many beautiful women, handsome horses and other treasures to Shang Zhou, while also showering his close advisers with presents.

At the sight of the beautiful women and treasures, Shang Zhou began to grin. "Just one of these items would be enough as ransom for the release of Ji Chang," he said, and promptly set King Wen of Zhou free.

Shang Zhou's incompetence and cruelty steeled King Wen's resolve to attack the Shang dynasty. He needed a wise general to help him wage the war and started to make discreet inquiries to find such a man.

One day, King Wen took his sons and some soldiers in his carriage to hunt on the north bank of the Wei River. On the way he saw an old man fishing by the river, oblivious to the rumbling of the convoy of carriages and horses. His curiosity piqued by the strange serenity exhibited by the lone angler, King Wen descended from his carriage and struck up a conversation with the old man.

He soon learned that the old man's name was Jiang Shang (or Lü Shang, Lü being the name of his ancestral fief) and that he was an expert in the art of war.

"My late grandfather once told me that I would one day meet a great man who would help me make the Zhou tribe great. You are this man! My grandfather had expected you all that time!" King Wen said excitedly. He then invited Jiang Shang to return to the palace with him and the old man accepted.

Jiang Shang was later given the name of Taigong Wang (expected by the grandfather) as he was the man King Wen's grandfather had predicted would help make the Zhou tribe great. In popular lore he is known as Jiang Taigong.

Taigong Wang proved a worthy right-hand man to King Wen. He advocated increased production combined with advanced military training. As the power of the Zhou tribe grew, King Wen one day asked Taigong Wang, "I am thinking of overthrowing a tyrant. Which state do you think we should tackle first?"

"We should go after Mi Xu first," Taigong Wang answered.

Yet another adviser raised an objection, "The monarch of Mi Xu is a tough nut to crack. We may not be able to defeat him."

"The monarch of Mi Xu has lost popular support by his cruelty towards his people. We'd have nothing to fear from him, even if he was ten times tougher," Taigong Wang explained.

When King Wen's expeditionary force approached Mi Xu, the people there started rioting even before battle was commenced. They quickly trussed up their monarch and switched allegiance to King Wen.

Three years later, King Wen sent troops against Chong (east of today's Hu County in Shaanxi Province), which was the largest vassal state on the western borders of the Shang. After subjugating the state of Chong, King Wen erected city walls and established his capital there, naming it Fengyi. In a few years, the Zhou tribe gradually extended its dominion over much of the territory formerly under Shang's ruling as more and more tribes switched over to King Wen's side.

King Wen, however, did not get to see the demise of the Shang dynasty. He died of an illness just as he was preparing to send his troops against Shang Zhou.

5. Slaves' Rebellion

AFTER THE DEATH of King Wen of Zhou, his son Ji Fa acceded to the throne and assumed the title of King Wu of Zhou. King Wu asked Taigong Wang to be his mentor and his brothers, Dan, the Duke of Zhou, and Shi, the Duke of Zhao, to be his assistants as he undertook to improve governance and build up his army in preparation for war against Shang Zhou.

The next year, King Wu marched his troops to Mengjin (northeast of today's Mengjin in Henan Province), where he reviewed the troops, with more than 800 lords from minor states flocking of their own accord to join him. They asked that King Wu lead them on an expedition against the Shang, but King Wu believed that the time was not yet ripe for such action and so returned to Fengyi after the inspection of his troops.

In the meantime, Shang Zhou's rule was going from bad to worse. Princes Bi Gan, Ji Zi and Wei Zi of the Shang were becoming extremely worried and tried to persuade him to change his ways. Their lobbying not only failed to move Shang Zhou but so enraged him that he had Bi Gan killed and sadistically ordered his chest cut open so that he could have a look at what was in his heart. Ji Zi escaped a similar fate by feigning madness, but was instead made a slave. Losing all hope in the Shang, Wei Zi left Zhaoge for good.

In the first year of the eleventh century BC, King Wu received intelligence that Shang Zhou had become a pariah among his people and kin. Concluding that the moment had finally arrived, he mustered a 50,000-strong army and named Taigong Wang, an expert in the art of war, its supreme commander. The army crossed the Yellow River as it thrust eastward, and was joined at Mengjin by the troops of 800 lords of smaller states. At Mengjin, King Wu presided over a ceremony to rally the troops, in which he denounced Shang Zhou's crimes against the people and called for a united fight to overthrow him.

One day, two old men stood in the way of the advancing troops and demanded to see King Wu. They were soon recognized to be the two sons of the head of the state of Gu Zhu (today's Lulong in Hebei Province); the older brother was Bo Yi and the younger Shu Qi. The king of Gu Zhu favored Shu Qi and planned to transfer power to him. Bo Yi had divined his father's intentions and decided to leave Gu Zhu voluntarily. Unwilling to ascend the throne given up by his elder brother, Shu Qi also went into hiding. When King Wen was still alive, the two brothers had immigrated to the state of Zhou and settled there. Upon learning about this expedition against Shang Zhou, they had rushed to meet the troops to try to stop the coming battle.

When King Wu of Zhou received them, they gripped the reins of King Wu's mount and said, "Emperor Zhou is the Son of Heaven and you are a subject of his. How can a subject rise up against the Son of Heaven? That would be an unconscionable perversion!"

The soldiers and officers flanking King Wu were so incensed by these words that they drew their swords, wanting to kill the brothers.

Taigong Wang ordered the soldiers not to harm them however, but simply to ask them to leave, little knowing that they were so traumatized by the experience that they later went up the Shouyang Mountains and committed suicide by starving themselves.

The expeditionary force against Shang Zhou, armed with high morale, sliced through enemy defenses like a sharp axe splitting bamboo, and in no time reached Muye (southwest of today's Qi County in Henan Province), only 70 *li* (1 *li* equals 0.5km) from Zhaoge.

Hearing about the oncoming attack, Shang Zhou immediately

put together an army of 700,000 and led it to Muye to oppose the advance of King Wu's troops. "King Wu has only 50,000 men," he thought, "I cannot imagine how my 700,000 would not defeat the smaller army!"

However, more than a half of the Shang army consisted of hastily armed and insufficiently trained slaves and captives from the eastern Yi tribes, who had suffered grievously under the oppression and abuse of Shang Zhou. They hated Shang Zhou and had no intention of dying for him. When King Wu's troops launched an unrelenting attack at Muye, these slaves turned their weapons against the Shang troops. It did not take long for the Shang army to disintegrate and collapse. Riding on the crest of this victory, Taigong Wang led the Zhou troops on a hot pursuit of the routed Shang army all the way to the Shang capital of Zhaoge.

Having made it back to Zhaoge, Shang Zhou realized that the game was up for him. That very night he ensconced himself in the "Deer Pavilion," set it aflame, and threw himself into the blaze.

After overthrowing the Shang, King Wu of Zhou moved his capital from Fengyi to Haojing (west of today's Xi'an in Shaanxi Province) and founded the Zhou dynasty.

In order to consolidate the rule of the Zhou dynasty, King Wu started the practice of creating fiefs for royal family members and as rewards for people who had made important contributions to the State. Thus Taigong Wang was assigned the fief of Qi, King Wu's brother Dan, the Duke of Zhou, received the fief of Lu, and his brother Shi, the Duke of Zhao, was given the fief of Yan. It is said that between King Wu and his son King Cheng, a total of more than 70 ducal states were created.

Although the Shang dynasty had been extinguished, its nobility and slave-owners still retained some influence in society. In order to pacify these people, King Wu conferred the title of Marquis of Yin on Shang Zhou's son Wu Geng, who stayed in the Yin capital. King Wu also assigned his three brothers Guan Shu, Cai Shu and Huo Shu to Wu Geng, ostensibly to assist him, but in fact to keep him under surveillance. They are therefore sometimes known as the "Three *Jians* (surveillants)."

ZHOU DYNASTY
(1046 BC–256 BC)

WESTERN ZHOU DYNASTY
(1046 BC–771 BC)

6. The Duke of Zhou—King Cheng's Chief Counselor

TWO YEARS AFTER he founded the Zhou dynasty, King Wu died of illness and was succeeded by his son Ji Song, who assumed the title of king Cheng of Zhou. He was then only 13 years old and the recently founded Zhou dynasty had not yet been fully consolidated, so the task of helping the new king govern fell on King Wu's brother Dan, the Duke of Zhou, who became the de facto acting Son of Heaven. Historians have adopted the convention of calling him simply the Duke of Zhou.

The Duke of Zhou's fief was the state of Lu, but he could not stay in Lu because of his many official duties in the capital. As soon as his son Bo Qin was old enough, he sent him to Lu to rule in his place.

Before setting out for Lu, Bo Qin asked his father if he had any instructions or advice for him.

"I am King Wen's son and King Wu's brother. I am also the reigning monarch's uncle. What kind of status do you think I possess?" the Duke of Zhou asked.

"Naturally you have an exalted status," Bo Qin replied.

"Correct! I do indeed occupy a high position. But whenever there is an emergency I have to deal with it straight away. For example, when I am washing my hair, I have to stop washing and rush out with my hand holding my wet hair. Or, for example, if someone asks to see me when I am in the middle of a meal, I must spit out the food already in my mouth and hasten to receive the guest. That way I can be sure that people of talent will gravitate to my side. Remember that you will be only the governor of a state in Lu; you must not become arrogant," the Duke of Zhou said.

Bo Qin nodded at everything his father said and promised to remember his words of wisdom.

The Duke of Zhou dedicated himself to helping King Cheng to govern the Zhou; however, his brothers Guan Shu and Cai Shu started spreading rumors claiming that the Duke of Zhou harbored the ambition of usurping the throne from King Cheng.

Although he had been given the title of Marquis of Yin, Shang Zhou's son Wu Geng felt unhappy with the constant surveillance he was placed under. He wished to return to the throne and restore the Yin regime. In collusion with Guan Shu and Cai Shu, he started an insurgency; he rallied some noblemen of the defunct Shang to his cause, and instigated several eastern Yi (barbarian) tribes to join the action.

The rumors started by Wu Geng, Guan Shu and the company were causing a big stir in Haojing, planting seeds of doubt even in the mind of Shi, the Duke of Zhao. Unable to separate the truth from the lies, the young and inexperienced King Cheng began to waver in his opinion of the uncle who was helping him govern.

Saddened by this turn of events, the Duke of Zhou decided to have a frank talk with Shi, the Duke of Zhao, and assured him that he had no hidden agenda. He asked the Duke of Zhao to take to heart the interests of the state and not to be swayed by the rumors. By pouring out his heart to the Duke of Zhao, the Duke of Zhou was able to dispel the misunderstandings. With domestic tensions defused, the Duke of Zhou led a large army in an expedition to the east.

At the same time, several tribes in the east, such as the Huai Yi and the Xu Rong, had allied with Wu Geng and were spoiling for a fight. The Duke of Zhou issued an order to Taigong Wang, authorizing him to attack any state whose allegiance to the Zhou was in doubt. This enabled Taigong Wang to pacify the east while the Duke could devote undivided attention to dealing with Wu Geng.

After three years, the Duke of Zhou finally succeeded in putting down Wu Geng's rebellion, and had him executed. After Wu Geng's defeat, Guan Shu felt he could no longer face his brother and nephew and therefore hanged himself. After the rebellion was put down, the Duke of Zhou dismissed Huo Shu from office and sent Cai Shu into punitive military service and exile in a remote part of the country.

In the eastern expedition led by the Duke of Zhou, many members of the Shang nobility were captured. Their resistance to the Zhou earned them the appellation of "the recalcitrant remnants." The Duke of Zhou had misgivings about leaving them where they were. With Haojing at the western end of the dominion, it was difficult to exercise effective control over the vast Central Plain to the east. He therefore made the decision to build a new capital in the east. The "recalcitrant remnants" of the Yin dynasty were moved to the new capital Luoyi (today's Luoyang in Henan Province), where they were placed under military surveillance.

From that time onward, the Zhou boasted two capitals: Haojing (also known as Zongzhou) in the west, and Luoyi (also known as Chengzhou) in the east.

The Duke of Zhou's regency, which lasted seven years, consolidated the regime of the Zhou dynasty. He oversaw the creation of an elaborate set of conventions, rites and regulations. When King Cheng reached the age of 20, the Duke of Zhou handed power back to the king.

The reign of King Cheng of Zhou and of his son King Kang spanned half a century, during which the Zhou dynasty saw its power and territory further extended. Historians call it the "Halcyon Era of Cheng and Kang."

7. Beacon-fires on Mount Lishan

THE 12TH KING of the Zhou dynasty was King You of Zhou, who neglected affairs of state and instead spent his time drinking, eating and carousing with beautiful women brought to him from all over his realm. When one of his top ministers, Bao Xiang, remonstrated with King You, he found himself sent to jail.

Bao Xiang was incarcerated for three years, during which time his kinspeople tried every avenue to get him out. They bought a beautiful girl in a remote village, taught her to sing and dance, and then presented her to King You in exchange for the freedom of Bao Xiang. The girl was presented as a member of the Bao clan and given the name of Bao Si.

Elated by the acquisition of Bao Si, King You released Bao Xiang. Despite the fact that King You showering affection and favors on Bao Si, she remained in a constant state of depression and had not smiled once since her introduction to the royal palace. King You tried all kinds of tricks and treats to induce a smile without any success.

Crestfallen, King You posted a reward, declaring that anyone who could make the royal consort smile would receive one thousand *liang* (1 *liang* equals fifty grams) of gold from the king.

A sycophant called Guo Shifu came up with a grotesque idea. To defend against the incursions of the Quan Rong tribe, twenty beacon-fire towers had been erected along the ridges of the Lishan Mountains (southeast of today's Lintong in Shaanxi Province) at intervals of several *li*. When attacked by Quan Rong marauders, defenders at the first beacon tower would light a bonfire, the sight of which would signal soldiers at the second tower to do likewise. This would trigger a chain reaction, sending a ripple effect down the system of beacon towers. As soon as the alert was received by the ducal state near a beacon tower, it would send out reinforcements against the invaders.

"The beacon towers have been in disuse during these years of peace. I'd like to invite Your Majesty and Your Highness for a few days of fun and leisure on Mount Lishan. We can light a bonfire at night to trick the duke in the vicinity into coming to our rescue. When her Highness sees the troops in full battle gear arrive only to find the whole thing a hoax, I guarantee you that she will smile," Guo Shifu said to King You.

King You clapped his hands in approval, "That's a wonderful idea! Let's do it!"

So they went to Mount Lishan and lit a bonfire. Believing the fire to signal an attack by the Quan Rong hordes, the nearby duke rushed over with his troops. When they arrived at Mount Lishan, he and his troops were flabbergasted to find that there was not a single Quan Rong tribesman there. Instead, they heard music and singing wafting down the hills.

King You sent greetings to them, thanking them for their trouble and assuring them that nothing was amiss and that the king and his consort were merely lighting a bonfire for sport. They were told to return to where they had come from.

The duke, realizing that he had been fooled, left with a number of grudges and curses on his lips.

Bao Si could not understand the reason for the gathering of armed men milling about at the foot of Mount Lishan. When she asked for an explanation, King You told her everything and saw a smile blossom on her face.

That smile earned Guo Shifu a thousand *liang* of gold from King You.

In his infatuation with Bao Si, King You eventually deposed the reigning queen and crown prince in order to set up Bao Si as queen and her son Bo Fu as crown prince. This prompted the duke of the state of Shen, father of the deposed queen, to launch an attack on Haojng, with the Quan Rong as ally.

Sent into a panic by the invasion of the Quan Rong, King You ordered that the beacon fire at Mount Lishan be lit immediately. The fires were duly lit but the dukes, having been tricked before by the hoax, ignored the alarm.

Thick smoke spiraled up from the beacon towers by day and fires blazed against the night sky, but no relief materialized.

As a result, large expanses of Zhou's western territory were occupied by the Quan Rong. Fearing the imminent loss of Haojing, King Ping (who had succeeded King You) resolved to move the capital to Luoyi in the east.

In 770 BC, King Ping officially moved the capital to Luoyi. Since Haojing was situated in the west and Luoyi in the east, historians call the era of Zhou rule with its capital at Haojing the Western Zhou period, and the era of Zhou rule after the move to the new capital of Luoyi the Eastern Zhou.

EASTERN ZHOU DYNASTY
(770 BC–256 BC)

Spring And Autumn Period (770 BC–476 BC)

8. The Hegemony of Lord Huan of Qi

THE EASTERN ZHOU period, which began when King Ping of Zhou moved the capital to Luoyi, is subdivided into the Spring and Autumn Period and the Warring States Period. In the Spring and Autumn Period, the House of Zhou underwent a decline. While the Son of Heaven of the Zhou exercised authority over the states in name, in reality he only possessed the power of a king of a secondary ducal state. After more powerful states annexed smaller ones, and major states engaged in perennial wars of territorial expansion, the monarch of the victorious ducal state would gain the allegiance of all the other states and be chosen as leader of the ducal states.

The first hegemonic state in the Spring and Autumn period was Qi (with its capital at Linzi, today's Zibo in Shandong Province). Qi was the fief of Taigong Wang, King Wu's most trusted strategist. Its large territory, successful exploitation of coastal resources and higher productivity accounted for its superior national strength.

In 686 BC, the state of Qi was plunged into internal strife, during which its monarch, Lord Xiang of Qi, was killed. He had two surviving brothers, one of whom was Gongzi Jiu, who was at the time in the state of Lu (with its capital in today's Qufu in Shandong Province); the other was Gongzi Xiao Bai, who was at the time in the state of Ju (with its capital in today's Ju County in Shandong Province). Each of them had a mentor. Gongzi Jiu's mentor was Guan Zhong, while Gongzi Xiao Bai was under the tutelage of Bao Shuya. Upon learning of the death of Lord Xiang of Qi, both desired to go back to Qi to claim the vacated throne.

Lord Zhuang, the monarch of the state of Lu, wanted to personally accompany Gongzi Jiu back to Qi. Guan Zhong said to Lord Zhuang of Lu, "Gongzi Xiao Bai is in Ju, which is geographically much closer to Qi. If he were able to enter Qi first, we would be in trouble. Let me take some men with me to intercept him."

As predicted by Guan Zhong, Gongzi Xiao Bai was rushing back to Qi under the protection of Ju. On the way he was met by the party led by Guan Zhong. Guang Zhong armed his bow with an arrow and shot it at Xiao Bai, who emitted a cry and fell back into his carriage.

Thinking he had killed Xiao Bai, Guan Zhong escorted Gongzi Jiu back to Qi in an unhurried fashion. Little did he know that the arrow had actually hit Xiao Bai's belt buckle and his falling with a cry was just a ruse. By the time Gongzi Jiu and Guan Zhong entered the state of Qi, Xiao Bai and Bao Shuya had already outflanked them by taking a shortcut. Xiao Bai acceded to the throne and became Lord Huan of Qi.

Once enthroned, Lord Huan of Qi defeated the state of Lu in a military campaign and directed Lord Zhuang of Lu to kill Gongzi Jiu and extradite Guan Zhong to Qi for criminal prosecution. Lord

Zhuang of Lu had no choice but to obey.

As soon as Guang Zhong was placed in a pillory and carted back to Qi, Bao Shuya recommended Guan Zhong to Lord Huan of Qi.

"Guan Zhong tried to kill me with an arrow. How can I trust him?" Lord Huan of Qi said angrily.

"He was Gongzi Jiu's mentor at the time. His shooting an arrow at you just shows his loyalty to Gongzi Jiu. His abilities surpass mine. If Your Majesty aspires to greatness, Guan Zhong is someone you can depend upon to help you achieve it," Bao Shuya replied.

Lord Huan of Qi, who had a generous disposition, allowed himself to be persuaded by Bao Shuya. Instead of prosecuting Guan Zhong, he named him his chief minister in charge of helping him govern Qi.

Guan Zhong helped Lord Huan of Qi improve and reform the working of the government, develop production and diversify the economy. Under his guidance, the extraction of iron ores was expanded, which led to the manufacture of more farming implements and improved agricultural techniques. He also encouraged the large-scale mining of salt from sea water, and recommended fishing in the ocean. Those states situated far from the sea thus had to depend on Qi for their table salt and sea food. People could do without a lot of things, but salt was a necessity and Qi grew in wealth and power on the strength of its salt production.

Lord Huan of Qi never for a moment gave up his ambition to become the leader of all the states, knowing that his orders would be then universally obeyed and all the ducal states would pay tribute and pledge their allegiance to him. "Now that we have superior military strength and abundant food, isn't it time to call together the leaders of all the ducal states to sign a pact of alliance?" he said to Guan Zhong.

"What's your rationale for convoking the dukes? We are all dukes under the emperor of the Zhou dynasty, and which duke is going to voluntarily defer to any other duke? While the Son of Heaven has seen his authority weakened, he is after all still the

Son of Heaven and therefore outranks the rest of us. It would be another matter if my Lord could, by order of the Son of Heaven, rally the dukes and conclude a pact with them that calls for unity under the Son of Heaven against alien tribes. Under the pact any party that encounters difficulties will be helped by the other parties, and those that make trouble will be put in their place by the others. When that happens, you will be acclaimed leader by the others even if you try to decline the honor," Guan Zhong replied.

Lord Huan of Qi agreed, "You are right. But how do we go about it?"

"I have an idea. With King Xi of Zhou recently now on the throne, my Lord can send an envoy to congratulate the new Son of Heaven and take the opportunity to call his attention to the turmoil in the state of Song (with its capital south of today's Shangqiu), the precarious position of its new lord and social unrest. The envoy could hint at an edict from the Son of Heaven affirming the authority of the Lord of Song. When you had such an edict in hand, it could serve as a rallying point for convoking the dukes of the realm. No one could refuse then," Guan Zhong replied.

Lord Huan of Qi nodded his approval as Guan Zhong developed his idea, and decided to follow his advice.

By that time, the Son of Heaven of Zhou had seen his real power severely reduced. Absorbed in countless wars of territorial expansion, the leaders of the ducal states had long stopped bothering paying homage to the Son of Heaven, so when the freshly enthroned King Xi of Zhou saw an envoy from a powerful state like Qi bringing tribute and congratulations, he was greatly pleased and entrusted Lord Huan of Qi with an edict affirming the authority of the Lord of the state of Song.

In 681 BC, by order of King Xi of Zhou, Lord Huan of Qi called all the leaders of the ducal states to a conference at Beixing (north of today's Dong'a County in Shandong Province) on the southwestern border of Qi. At that meeting, the dukes signed a pact of alliance and elected Lord Huan of Qi leader of the alliance. With Guan Zhong's help, Lord Huan of Qi finally saw the fulfillment of his ambition of becoming leader of the ducal states.

The Spring and Autumn Period saw the emergence of five leaders of the ducal states, who were in chronological order: Lord Huan of Qi, Lord Wen of Jin, Lord Xiang of Song, Lord Mu of Qin and King Zhuang of Chu, who are therefore known in Chinese history as the "Five Leaders of Spring and Autumn."

9. Wu Zixu Slipped Through the Gate of Zhaoguan

BY THE TIME King Ping of Chu (grandson of King Zhuang) ascended the throne, the state of Chu was already in decline.

In 522 BC, King Ping decided to depose his crown prince Jian. At the time, the crown prince and his mentor Wu She were on garrison duty in Chengfu (west of today's Xiangcheng in Henan Province). To preempt any opposition on the part of Wu She, he called him back and confronted him with the fabricated story of the crown prince's plot to overthrow the monarch.

Although Wu She adamantly denied everything, he was then immediately thrown in jail.

As King Ping dispatched an assassin to kill the crown prince Jian, he forced Wu She to write to his two sons Wu Shang and Wu Zixu asking them to return, with the clear intention of eliminating them as well. The older son, Wu Shang, returned to Yingdu (northwest of today's Jiangling in Hubei Province), where King Ping had both him and his father Wu She murdered. When the crown prince Jian got wind of the turn of events, he sought asylum in the state of Song, taking with him his son, Gongzi Sheng.

Wu Zixu, the other son of Wu She, also escaped from Chu and quickly met up with the crown prince Jian in Song. However, it was a bad time in Song, which was then filled with civil strife. Wu Zixu took the crown prince Jian and Gongzi Sheng to the state of Zheng for asylum and tried to enlist the state's help in avenging them. But Lord Ding of Zheng, the monarch of Song, did not give his assent.

Obsessed with the idea of avenging himself, the crown prince Jian ended up colluding with some high officials of Zheng in a failed plot to overthrow Lord Ding of Zheng, and was subsequently executed. Wu Zixu had to take Gongzi Sheng on the road again, this time to seek asylum in the state of Wu (with its capital in today's Suzhou in Jiangsu Province).

King Ping of Chu had posted a reward for the arrest of Wu Zixu and a portrait of him was displayed at all city gates throughout the state of Chu. There were also strict orders for local authorities to search and inspect all suspect subjects.

After making their way out of Zheng, Wu Zixu and Gongzi Sheng had to hide themselves during the day and continue their flight under cover of night. When they came to Zhaoguan (north of today's Hanshan County in Anhui Province) on the border between Wu and Chu, they found the searches at the city gates were extremely thorough. It is said that Wu Zixu was so worried that he could not fall asleep for several nights and that his hair soon turned completely white. Luckily, however, they had the good fortune of running into a kind-hearted man by the name of Dong Gao Gong, who took Wu Zixu in out of compassion. A friend of Dong Gao Gong who happened to bear a resemblance to Wu Zixu was asked to present himself at the city gate to draw suspicion away from Wu Zixu, who was unrecognizable since his hair had turned white. The guards at the gate took the false Wu Zixu into custody while the real article managed to slip away unnoticed.

After slipping through the gate of Zhaoguan, Wu Zixu began to run for fear of being pursued by the guards. However, he soon found a wide river in the way. As Wu Zixu fretted in anguish, an elderly fisherman brought his small boat toward him and ferried him across.

The grateful Wu Zixu took down his sword and gave it to the fisherman, saying "This sword was a gift from the Lord of Chu to my grandfather and is worth a hundred *liang* of gold. I am giving it to you as a token of my gratitude."

"The Lord of Chu has offered a reward of fifty thousand *dan* (one volume unit that roughly equals 100 liter) of grain for your head and has promised high office to whoever denounces you. If I was not tempted by the monetary reward or the promise of high office, why would I accept this sword from you?" the elderly fisherman replied.

Wu Zixu immediately apologized to the old fisherman for his rudeness, put his sword away and bade farewell to his savior.

Wu Zixu arrived in the state of Wu at a time when Gongzi Guang, a nephew of King Liao of Wu, was plotting to overthrow the reigning monarch. With Wu Zixu's help, Gongzi Guang killed King Liao of Wu and set himself up as monarch, assuming the title of King He Lü of Wu.

After his accession to the throne, King He Lü of Wu made Wu Zixu his top aide. He also enlisted the help of General Sun Wu, an expert military strategist. With the assistance of Wu Zixu and Sun Wu, the king of Wu was able to build up his army and annex several smaller neighboring states.

In 506 BC, King He Lü of Wu promoted Sun Wu to supreme commander and named Wu Zixu deputy commander of the army that he personally led in a campaign against the state of Chu. With a series of victories he routed the army of Chu and marched all the way to Yingdu.

Meanwhile, King Ping of Chu had died and his son King Zhao of Chu had deserted his throne and fled. In bitter hatred of King Ping of Chu, Wu Zixu had the king's corpse exhumed from his tomb so that he could whip the dead body.

With Wu troops occupying Yingdu, Shen Baoxu of Chu fled to the state of Qin and requested its help. At first, Lord Ai of Qin did not agree to send troops to help Chu. Shen Baoxu would not give up and stayed in front of the Qin palace, wailing night and day for a whole week. Moved by his persistence, Lord Ai of Qin finally said, "To be sure the authorities of Chu were a bunch of scoundrels but they have such a great minister as Shen Baoxu! I can't very well sit on my hands as Chu teeters on the brink of extinction."

Lord Ai of Qin sent reinforcements to Chu and defeated the Wu army, forcing King He Lü of Wu and his troops to retreat home.

Once back in the capital of Wu, King He Lü credited the merits mainly to Sun Wu. However, uninterested in public office, Sun Wu retired to a life of seclusion in his home village. He bequeathed to posterity *Sun Zi's Art of War*, which is China's earliest masterpiece of military doctrine.

10. The Peripatetic Travels of Confucius

WITH THE HELP of Wu Zixu and Sun Wu, King He Lü of Wu routed the state of Chu. As his power grew, even some major states in the Central Plain began to feel worried, among which Qi faced the most immediate threat. Since the death of Lord Huan of Qi, the state of Qi had been marked by perennial instability. However, when Lord Jing of Qi took over the reins he nominated the able Yan Ying as his prime minister, who set Qi on the path to political renaissance and economic prosperity.

In 500 BC, Lord Jing of Qi and Yan Ying sought to rally the support of the neighboring state of Lu, as well as dukes of the Central Plain, for a renewed effort to carry on the ambition of the late Lord Huan of Qi. To this end, a letter was sent out to Lord Ding of Lu, inviting him to a meeting at Jiagu on the border between Qi and Lu.

At that time, it was common practice for leaders of ducal states to bring along a minister called *xiang li* to a meeting of dukes as personal adviser. Lord Ding of Lu decided to bring his *si kou* (secretary of justice) Kong Zi (aka Confucius) with him as his *xiang li*.

The actual name of Confucius (Kong Zi, or Master Kong) was Kong Qiu. He came from Zouyi (southeast of today's Qufu in Shandong Province). His father was a low-ranking military officer, who died when Confucius was three years old. His mother took him to Qufu and raised him there. It is said that since he was a child he had been fascinated with rites, etiquette and conventions. He would often arrange plates and dishes to imitate the rites of sacrifice to the gods or ancestors performed by the adults.

The young Confucius was an assiduous student. He had great admiration for the Duke of Zhou, who set down political systems, prescribed rules of etiquette, conventions and rites, and developed musical accompaniments in the early years of the Zhou dynasty. He developed a deep knowledge of ancient etiquette and rites and was proficient in all the six classical arts that a man of learning was expected to master, namely, rituals, music, archery, riding, writing and arithmetic. He was always meticulous and conscientious in performing his duties. Early in his career, he served as a petty official in charge of a storehouse. During his tenure there was never any stored item missing. When he later became a low-ranking official in charge of animal husbandry, his flocks of cattle and sheep proliferated. By the time he was thirty years old, his reputation had spread far and wide.

As some people expressed the wish to study under him, he decided to found a *si shu* (private classroom) and started accepting students. On his deathbed, Meng Xizi, a high official of Lu, directed his two sons Meng Yizi and Nangong Jingshu to study ritual and etiquette under Confucius. Upon Nangong Jingshu's recommendation, Lord Zhao of Lu sent Confucius to Luoyi, the capital of the state of Zhou, to study the rites and ritual music of the ancestors.

When Confucius turned 35, Lord Zhao of Lu was driven from his throne by three of his top aides, Ji Sun Shi, Meng Sun Shi and Shu Sun Shi. Confucius went to the state of Qi, and asked for an audience with Lord Jing of Qi in order to expound his political ideas. Lord Jing of Qi was very courteous to him, and even watched to enlist him in his service. But he changed his mind, when his prime minister commented that Confucius's ideas were impractical. Confucius returned to Lu to carry on teaching, and soon saw a steady increase in the number of his followers.

In 501 BC, Lord Ding of Lu named Confucius governor of Zhongdu (today's Wenshang County in Shandong Province); the next year he was designated *si kong* (official in charge of public works) and from that position he went on to become *si kou* (Secretary of Justice).

When Lord Ding of Lu told Confucius about the proposed meeting with Qi at Jiagu, Confucius said, "Given Qi's track record of incursions into our territory, it is prudent to go to the meeting with armed protection. Please consider taking both the right and the left ministers of war with you."

Lord Ding of Lu agreed with Confucius and brought the two top generals and a military contingent with him to Jiagu.

At the Jiagu meeting, Confucius acquitted himself well as *xiang li*, helping to ensure a diplomatic success for the state of Lu. After the meeting, Lord Jing of Qi decided to give back territory previously taken from Lu in three areas in Wenyang (southwest of present-day Tai'an in Shandong Province).

Li Chu, a top official in the state of Qi, considered Confucius a liability to Qi if the continued to serve Lu. He suggested that Lord Jing of Qi send a group of female musicians to Lord Ding of Lu. Lord Jing of Qi was persuaded and sent eighty female singers to Lu.

After accepting this gift of singers, Lord Ding of Lu started indulging himself in drinking, gluttony and merry-making and consequently neglected important affairs of the state. Although Confucius wished to persuade him to change his ways, the monarch kept avoiding him. Deeply disappointed, Confucius told his students, "The monarch of Lu is uninterested in serious business. Let's leave!"

Confucius left the state of Lu and embarked on a series of travels through the various states, accompanied by a group of his students, in search of an opportunity to realize his political visions. However, in that period the larger states were obsessed with their wars for hegemony, and the smaller states faced the ever present threat of invasion; the whole country lacked stability. There was therefore no interest in Confucius's proposition of restoring the system of rites and ritual music prevalent in the early years of the Zhou dynasty.

Confucius' travels took him to the states of Wei, Cao, Song, Zheng, Chen, Cai and Chu, but none of the monarchs in those states offered him public office.

Once, when Confucius was in the vicinity of the states of Chen and Cai, King Zhao of Chu sent for him. Believing that it would not be in their interest for Confucius to serve Chu, the ministers of Chen and Cai sent soldiers to intercept Confucius, who was therefore left stranded for days without food. He was saved only after Chu sent troops to rescue him.

After seven or eight years of constant traveling through the states and being repeatedly snubbed, Confucius was getting on in age. He finally returned to Lu and devoted the rest of his life to education and to sorting through and editing ancient literature.

In his old age, Confucius edited important ancient classics such as *shi jing* (*The Book of Songs*), *shang shu* (*Book of Documents*) and *chun qiu* (*The Spring and Autumn Annals*). *Shi jing* is China's earliest collection of songs and verse, containing 305 songs and poems from the Western Zhou and the Spring and Autumn Period. Many of them are folk songs describing the daily life of people in ancient times, and therefore form a vital part of the history of Chinese literature. *Shang shu* is a compilation of China's historical texts dating back to antiquity. *Chun qiu* is a book of history based on the historical records of the state of Lu, covering major events from 722 BC to 481 BC.

Confucius died in 479 BC. His theories and ideas, passed down by his disciples after his death, eventually formed the basis of the Confucian school of thought. The legacy of Confucius' thoughts and scholarship has greatly influenced succeeding generations, and has earned him the well-deserved title of the premier thinker and educator in China's history.

11. Gou Jian Slept on Sticks and Tasted Gall

KING HE LÜ of Wu became leader in the south after defeating the state of Chu. Wu had long been at loggerheads with the neighboring state of Yue (with its capital at today's Shaoxing in Zhejiang Province). Gou Jian acceded to the throne of Yue in 496 BC. The king of Wu took advantage of the recent death in the house of Yue to attack. A major battle was fought between them at Zuili (southwest of today's Jiaxing in Zhejiang Province).

Though he anticipated an easy victory in the battle, King He Lü of Wu actually found himself defeated. Gravely wounded by an arrow, the aging monarch died soon after his return to Wu.

After the death of King He Lü of Wu, his son Fu Chai took the throne. On his deathbed, He Lü said to Fu Chai, "Don't forget to avenge our humiliation by the state of Yue!"

Fu Chai remembered these last words and asked those close to him to constantly remind him of them. At the entrance of his palace, his subordinates would cry at the top of their lungs, "Fu Chai! Have you forgotten that the king of Yue killed your father?"

"No, never!" Fu Chai would reply in tears.

He ordered Wu Zixu and another minister, Bo Pi, to intensify military training in preparation for an attack on Yue.

Two years later, King Fu Chai of Wu personally commanded a large army in a military operation against Yue. At that time, there were two very able ministers at the Yue court, called Wen Zhong and Fan Li. Fan Li said to Gou Jian,"The Wu army has been in intensive training for three years. They are now bent on revenge and exhibit unusual ferocity. We should try to defend the city without engaging them in a frontal fight."

Dismissing the suggestion, Gou Jian pitted his army against the Wu attackers in a fight-to-the-death battle. The two armies met near Tai Lake and, not surprisingly, the Yue army was routed.

King Gou Jian of Yue retreated with his five thousand remaining troops to Kuaiji, where they were encircled by the Wu troops.

At the end of his tether, Gou Jian said to Fan Li, "I regret not having heeded your advice and having gotten us into this mess. Now what can I do?"

"We must sue for peace now!" Fan Li replied.

Gou Jian sent Wen Zhong to the Wu camp to initiate peace talks. Wen Zhong explained that Gou Jian was ready to surrender. King Fu Chai of Wu was on the point of agreeing when Wu Zixu voiced his opposition.

Wen Zhong thus went away with his aim unreached. Later, after learning that Bo Pi of the state of Wu was a corrupt and lecherous man, he privately offered beautiful women and jewelry to Bo Pi in return for him putting in a good word about Yue in front of Fu Chai.

With the lobbying of Bo Pi, King Fu Chai decided to accept the peace offer of Yue, over Wu Zixu's objections. One condition, however, was that Gou Jian was to be transported to Wu.

Getting the results of the negotiations from Wen Zhong, Gou Jian, entrusted the governance of Yue to Wen Zhong and went to Wu, accompanied by his wife and Fan Li.

When Gou Jian arrived in Wu, Fu Chai told him that he and his wife would live in a stone hut by the tomb of King He Lü. Fu Chai gave Gou Jian the chore of feeding his horses, while Fan Li served as valet and servant. Every time Fu Chai took his carriage on a trip, Gou Jian would be the groom that held the bit. Two years later, believing that Gou Jian had finally become submissive, Fu Chai sent him back to Yue.

Once back in his own land, Gou Jian planned to revenge his

disgrace. Worried that the return to a life of luxury might sap his determination, he hung a gallbladder by his dining table. At every meal, before he ate he would first taste the bitter gall to remind himself of his bitter humiliation at Kuaiji. He also had his sleeping mat removed and replaced with bedding consisting of sticks. This is the origin of the much-quoted Chinese idiom "sleeping on sticks and tasting gall."

Determined to achieve greatness for Yue, Gou Jian went into the fields to work on the land himself, and asked his wife to spin cloth, in an effort to raise productivity by their example. To counter a sharp decline in population brought about by war, he instituted a system of incentives for having larger families. He delegated the authority of governance to Wen Zhong and military training to Fan Li, while devoting himself to the task of gleaning wisdom from others and lifting his people out of poverty. The people of the state of Yue were thus greatly motivated to do the utmost to transform their downtrodden country into a strong power.

12. Fan Li and Wen Zhong

AS KING GOU Jian's efforts at good government and increased productivity paid off in ever-growing national strength, he began to discuss the matter of launching a military campaign against Wu with Fan Li and Wen Zhong.

Having attained the position of leader of the ducal states, King Fu Chai became arrogant and began to indulge himself in a decadent lifestyle. At Wen Zhong's suggestion of presenting a beautiful woman to the king of Wu as tribute, King Gou Jian of Yue sent out scouts to find the most beautiful woman in the kingdom. The woman they found was Xi Shi, from Zhuluo hill (south of today's Zhuji in Zhejiang Province). Gou Jian then sent Fan Li as envoy to present Xi Shi to King Fu Chai.

Fu Chai was struck by Xi Shi's beauty and showered her with favors, comparing her to an angel sent from heaven.

In a year of bad harvest, Wen Zhong was sent to plead before the king of Wu, "Yue had a terrible harvest and is suffering from widespread famine. We beg to borrow 10,000 *dan* (a unit of measure for dry grain, equals 50kg) of grain from Wu. It would be returned after the spring." To please Xi Shi, Fu Chai immediately agreed to the loan.

After the spring, Yue harvested a record crop and Wen Zhong personally returned the 10,000 *dan* of grain to Wu.

Fu Chai was pleased that Yue had made good on its promise of repayment. When he scooped up a handful of the Yue grain, he found that the kernels were big and fat. "The Yue grain has bigger kernels than ours. Give the 10,000 *dan* of grain to the farmers as seeds!" he said to Bo Pi.

Bo Pi distributed the grain to the farmers, ordering them to plant the seeds in their fields. When spring came, the seeds were planted. Weeks later, the seeds still hadn't germinated. Thinking that perhaps good seeds took a longer time to germinate, the farmers waited patiently, only to find a few days later that the seeds had all rotted. By that time, it was too late in the season to replant the fields with their own seeds.

As a result, Wu was devastated by a widespread famine that year and the people of Wu turned their wrath on Fu Chai, little knowing that they had fallen victim to Wen Zhong's ploy. The 10,000 *dan* of grain had actually been boiled and then redried before delivery to Wu, and therefore would never have germinated.

Upon learning of the famine in Wu, Gou Jian wanted to send his army into action.

However, Wen Zhong said, "It's not time yet. First of all the famine has just started and Wu's coffers are not yet empty. Moreover, Wu Zixu is still in office and will be a tough opponent."

Gou Jian saw Wen Zhong's point, and went back to intensive military training and preparation.

When King Fu Chai of Wu expressed the desire to attack the state of Qi in 484 BC, Wu Zixu immediately went to see him. "I've heard that Gou Jian is steeling himself by sleeping on sticks and tasting gall. He appears to be bent on revenge against Wu. If he is not eliminated now, he will become a big liability in the future. I hope you will consider eliminating Yue first."

Ignoring Wu Zixu's advice, King Fu Chai went ahead with his campaign against Qi, and duly won the battle. When he returned in triumph to universal praise and congratulations from all the government officials, Wu Zixu raised the lone voice of criticism. "The defeat of Qi is only a minor gain. The greater peril lies in the potential destruction of Wu by Yue."

This only further increased Fu Chai's resentment of Wu Zixu. With Bo Pi keeping on malign Wu Zixu, it was therefore not long before Fu Chai gave Wu Zixu a sword and ordered him to kill himself.

Before his death, Wu Zixu told the messenger angrily, "Don't forget to gouge out my eyes and place them at the east gate of the Wu capital so that I can see how Gou Jian enters the city at the head of his troops."

Fu Chai named Bo Pi his chief minister after the death of Wu Zixu.

In 482 BC, King Fu Chai of Wu invited Lord Ai of Lu and Lord Ding of Jin to meet with him at Huangchi (southwest of today's Fengqiu County in Henan Province) in order to form an alliance. He took all his elite troops to the conference, leaving only old and weak soldiers behind to man the defenses of the capital.

By the time Fu Chai returned in high spirits from Huangchi, troops commanded by King Gou Jian of Yue had already fought their way into the Wu capital, Gusu. Tired from the long march home from Huangchi, the Wu troops proved no match for the well-trained and highly motivated Yue army and were quickly routed in the battle.

Fu Chai had no choice but to send Bo Pi to sue for peace. After consulting Fan Li, Gou Jian agreed to a temporary truce and withdrew his troops.

In 475 BC, having been fully prepared, King Gou Jian of Yue launched a large-scale campaign against Wu, in which Wu suffered one setback after another. The Yue troops laid siege to the Wu capital for two years until Fu Chai, at the end of his tether, declared, "I will be ashamed to show my face in front of Wu Zixi in the underworld," and committed suicide.

After destroying Wu, Gou Jian led his army across the Huai River and invited the leaders of the ducal states in the Central Plain to a meeting at Xuzhou. The Son of Heaven of the Zhou dynasty also sent an envoy bearing a gift of sacrificial meats for Gou Jian. After that, the Yue troops enjoyed control of the southeast, and all the states recognized Gou Jian as leader.

On his triumphant return to Yue, Gou Jian hosted a grand celebration to reward all those who had contributed to the successful campaign. Fan Li, however, was conspicuously absent. Legend has it that he had taken Xi Shi with him to another state to live in seclusion under a false name.

Before his departure, Fan Li left a letter addressed to Wen

Zhong, in which he warned, "When all the birds have been hunted out of the sky, the good bows and arrows will be put away, and when all the rabbits have been hunted down, the hunting dogs will be roasted for food. The king of Yue is someone with whom you can share hard times, but not good ones. You would be wise to leave as soon as possible."

Wen Zhong did not believe these words. When Gou Jian sent a messenger to present him with a sword, Wen Zhong immediately recognized it as the one that Fu Chai gave Wu Zixu to commit suicide with. Regretting not having heeded Fan Li's advice, he took his own life.

The struggle for hegemony between Wu and Yue took place toward the end of the Spring and Autumn period. With increased productivity and a succession of slave rebellions, the slave society was beginning to burst at the seams. In 475 BC, the Warring States period began, marking China's transformation into a feudal society.

WARRING STATES PERIOD
(475 BC–221 BC)

13. Mo Zi Took the Scaling Ladder in Stride

IN THE EARLY years of the Warring States period, King Hui of Chu, was planning to restore the hegemony of Chu. To this end he started a military buildup in preparation for an attack on the state of Song.

King Hui had one of the ablest craftsmen of the time in his service. This man was Gongshu Ban, from the state of Lu, known more popularly by posterity as Lu Ban (Ban of Lu). Gongshu Ban could use an axe better than any other craftsman. It would have been the highest hubris for anyone to compare himself to Lu Ban in worksmanship, hence the popular Chinese admonition against "showing off one's skill with an axe in front of Lu Ban."

King Hui of Chu invited Gongshu Ban into his government as a minister. Gongshu Ban then designed a device for storming a walled city. This device acquired the name of *yun ti* (cloud ladder) because it gave the impression of reaching the clouds.

King Hui of Chu ordered Gongshu Ban to speed up the

construction of these scaling ladders as preparations were being made for an attack on Song. When news of these scaling ladders began to spread, the leaders of the ducal states became worried. The state of Song in particular was filled with a sense of doom in anticipation of an attack by Chu.

The planned attack on Song was not without its critics, however. The man who most vehemently opposed the invasion was Mo Zi (Master Mo).

Mo Zi was the founder of the Mo school of thought. He opposed waste and extravagance and advocated frugality. He instructed his disciples to wear shorter tunics and straw shoes, and encouraged them to engage in physical labor. He espoused the view that hard work is one of the noblest virtues of man.

Mo Zi also opposed the perennial wars of territorial expansion, which only brought misery to the common people. When he heard about Chu's plan to invade Song with the aid of scaling ladders, he immediately set off for Chu. When his feet got blistered and bloody he would simply rip off a piece of clothing to bandage them, and march on.

When he finally arrived in the Chu capital of Yingdu, after having marched constantly for ten days and nights, Mo Zi went directly to Gongshu Ban in order to dissuade him from helping the king of Chu attack Song.

But Gongshu Ban said, "There's nothing I can do now. I've already promised King Hui of Chu that I will help."

At the request of Mo Zi, Gongshu Ban took him to see King Hui of Chu. In a passionate plea, Mo Zi said to the king of Chu, "Chu possesses a vast territory spanning five thousand *li* as well as rich resources, while Song is only one tenth the size of Chu. Furthermore, Song is mostly comprised of poor land which yields few resources. Why does a monarch possessing elegant carriages want to take a poor man's rickety cart? Why are you throwing out your wardrobe of embroidered brocade robes to steal a pair of ragged breeches?"

Although King Hui of Chu saw Mo Zi's point, he had no intention of shelving his plan to attack Song. Gongshu Ban also had full confidence in the ability of his scaling ladders to help break city walls.

"You may attack a city with the ladders, but I can parry the attack and you will not gain any advantage," Mo Zi said bluntly.

He then unbuckled his belt and placed it on the ground to simulate a walled city. He found a few pieces of wooden planks to serve as battering rams to break down the city's defenses. He then dared Gongshu Ban to match wits with him in a war simulation.

Every offensive operation launched by Gongshu Ban triggered a defensive tactic from Mo Zi. When a scaling ladder was employed, it would be met with burning projectiles. When a battering ram was used to try to break down a gate, it would be crushed with a shower of rocks and heavy wooden rollers. When a tunnel was dug, it would be filled with smoke.

Even when Gongshu Ban had exhausted all nine tactics of offense, Mo Zi still had many more defensive tricks up his sleeve.

Gongshu Ban was stymied but would not concede defeat. "I've though of a way to deal with you, but I will not say what it is," he said.

"I know how you intend to deal with me, but I will also not say what it is," Mo Zi riposted with a faint smile.

Baffled by the cryptic exchanges between the two men, King Hui of Chu asked, "What on earth are you two talking about?"

"Gongshu Ban's intention is none other than to kill me, thinking that if I am dead, no one will be able to help the state of Song to defend its capital. He miscalculates, for I have already sent 300 of my disciples, including Qin Huaxi, to help defend the Song capital. Every one of them has mastered my tactics of city defenses. Chu would not derive any advantage from my death," Mo Zi replied.

After hearing this exposé and witnessing the demonstration of Mo Zi's defensive tactics, King Hui of Chu realized that he had no hope of defeating Song. "You are right. I've decided to rethink my plan to attack Song," he said.

Thus a war was averted thanks to Mo Zi's intervention.

14. Shang Yang and His Pole at South Gate

IN THE AFTERMATH of the perennial wars for hegemony throughout the Spring and Autumn Period, many smaller ducal states were swallowed by larger powers.

As a result, the states of Han (with its capital at today's Yu County in Henan Province, later moved to what is now Xinzheng in Henan Province), Zhao (with its capital first situated southeast of today's Taiyuan in Shanxi Province, later moved to today's Handan in Hebei Province) and Wei (with its capital northwest of today's Xia County in Shanxi Province, later moved to today's Kaifeng in Henan Province) became major powers in the Central Plain. Along with the states of Qin, Qi, Chu and Yan, they formed the "Seven Giants of the Warring States Period" in China's history.

Among the Seven Giants, Qin was politically, economically and culturally less developed than the other ducal states of the Central Plain. Its neighbor, the state of Wei, was stronger than Qin and had taken large tracts of its land to the west of the Yellow River.

In 361 BC, Duke Xiao of Qin came to the throne. Determined to make Qin stronger, he made the recruiting of talented men in all fields his highest priority. He issued an edict that declared "Any citizen of Qin or foreign visitor who can devise a way to make Qin stronger and more prosperous will be invited to serve in my government."

Duke Xiao of Qin's rallying call attracted many talented people to his realm. Since his talents were unrecognized in Wei, Gongsun

Yang (later known as Shang Yang), a member of the Wei nobility, decided to go to Qin and obtained an audience with Duke Xiao of Qin.

"To make a country stronger and more prosperous, attention must be paid to developing agriculture and motivating the military. Good government requires an effective system of incentives and disincentives. If rewards and punishments are perceived to be quick and certain as well as just, the government's authority and credibility will be enhanced and reforms will go through more easily, " Shang Yang said to Duke Xiao of Qin.

Shang Yang's ideas had the full endorsement of Duke Xiao of Qin, but met with stiff resistance from some members of the nobility and high officialdom. In the face of so much opposition, Duke Xiao of Qin, who had only recently ascended the throne and was wary about the possible chaos that might result from the proposed reforms, decided to put them on the back burner.

Two years later, when Duke Xiao of Qin felt more secure, he named Shang Yang his *zuo shu zhang* (an official title in Qin bureaucracy ranking the tenth in status), declaring "The *zuo shu zhang* will be in charge of reforms from now on."

Shang Yang soon drafted a reform law. However, as he was concerned that the people might not have enough trust in him to abide by the law, he first had a ten-meter-high wooden pole erected at the south gate of the capital. He declared that anyone who would take this pole to the north gate would receive a reward of 10 *liang* of gold.

Very soon a throng of people gathered at the south gate and began to trade comments about the reward. "This pole is light enough for anybody to carry. Why would they offer 10 *liang* of gold for it?" some people wondered. "The *zuo shu zhang* must be pulling our legs!" others concluded.

The people at the scene looked at each other, but none had the courage to take up the challenge.

Realizing that the public still did not believe his offer, Shang Yang raised the reward to 50 *liang* of gold. However, the higher the reward, the more incredulous the public became, and still no one stepped up.

Finally, a man came forward and offered to take up the challenge. He pulled up the pole and carried it all the way to the north gate.

Shang Yang immediately sent someone to deliver 50 *liang* of gold, not a penny less, to the man who had carried the pole to the north gate.

The news spread quickly, creating a national sensation. "The *zuo shu zhang* keeps his promise," the public said.

Knowing that the experiment had worked, Shang Yang put the new law that he had drafted into practice. The new law set forth clear rules on rewards and punishments. It also stated that the hierarchical ranking of official functions and titles would be determined on the basis of distinguished military service. It noted that no honorific title or knighthood would be conferred on members of the nobility who made no contributions to the war effort. Compulsory community service would be exempted for productive food growers and fabric makers. Anyone who fell into poverty on account of mismanaging his business or because of laziness would be, together with his wife and children, pressed into service as servants in residences of government officials.

As a result of the implementation of Shang Yang's reforms, agricultural production and military strength grew in Qin. Qin troops then attacked the state of Wei from the west and crossed the river to take its capital, Anyi.

In 350 BC, Shang Yang announced his second round of reforms, whose highlights included:

1. Abolition of the "Nine Squares System" of tillage (in Yin and Zhou times, tracts of farm land were divided into nine squares) and reclamation for farming purposes of the access roads that used to border the farm fields. These roads were then leveled and planted with grain. Berms, wasteland, woods and gullies that used to serve as boundaries were also reclaimed for farm use. Whoever reclaimed unused land would then own it and land became tradable.

2. Creation of a new administrative division called the *xian* (county), which integrated cities, towns and villages and was directly administered by a mandarin appointed by the state. The powers of the central authorities thus became more concentrated.

3. The move of the capital to Xianyang. To facilitate an eastward expansion, Qin moved its capital from Yongcheng (today's Fengxiang County in Shaanxi Province) to Xianyang (northeast of today's Xianyang in Shaanxi Province), north of the Wei River.

Such radical reforms understandably triggered bitter infighting, with many members of the nobility and many high officials expressing hostility to the changes.

Once, when the crown prince of Qin got into trouble with the law, Shang Yang said to Duke Xiao of Qin, "The law of the land must be obeyed by all, high and low. If those in high office do not obey the law, the government will lose public trust. When the crown prince violates the law, his mentors should be punished."

In the end, Shang Yang meted out punishments to the crown prince's two mentors Gongzi Qian and Gongsun Jia. One had his nose cut off and the other had his face branded. This quickly stopped the nobility and high officialdom from challenging the new law.

Ten years of reforms saw Qin's power and prosperity steadily grow. Qin's new prominence prompted the Son of Heaven of the Zhou dynasty to send an envoy with sacrificial meats to Duke Xiao of Qin and to confer on him the title of *fang bo* (Regional Earl, the regional leader of the ducal states). The ducal states of the Central Plain also sent congratulations to the state of Qin. The state of Wei saw no alternative but to cede to Qin its territory west of the river and move its capital to Daliang (today's Kaifeng in Henan Province).

15. Sun Bin Matching Wits with Pang Juan

KING HUI OF Wei, emulating Duke Xiao of Qin, was also on the lookout for talented advisors in the same league as Shang Yang. He spent huge sums on efforts to recruit talented men from all corners of the country. When Pang Juan, a citizen of Wei, requested an audience with him to explain his ideas on creating national wealth and increasing Wei's military might, King Hui of Wei was impressed and appointed Pang Juan his top general.

Pang Juan soon proved his worth. He put his troops through rigorous daily training and carried out several successful military campaigns against small neighboring states. After defeating the powerful state of Qi, he won increasing trust from King Hui of Wei.

Although Pang Juan had a very high opinion of himself, he knew that Sun Bin, a citizen of Qi, who he had gone to school with, was more able than him. It is said that Sun Bin was a descendant of General Sun Wu of the state of Wu, and was therefore the only person privy to *Sun Zi's Art of War* passed down from generation to generation in the Sun clan.

King Hui of Wei had also heard about the reputation of Sun Bin, and so he brought up the subject with Pang Juan. Pang Juan sent for Sun Bin and invited him to join the Wei government. However, Pang Juan had an axe to grind and, in front of King Hui of Wei (yet behind Sun's back),often falsely accused Sun Bin of secretly colluding with the state of Qi. In a rage, King Hui of Wei slapped criminal charges on Sun Bin and had his face branded and his kneecaps gouged out.

However, it so happened that an envoy from Qi was in Wei at the time; he snuck Sun Bin out of jail and took him back to Qi.

Having heard about the military talents of Sun Bin, Tian Ji (a top general of Qi) recommended him to King Wei of Qi, who was also committed to making his country strong and prosperous through reforms. After discussing the art of war with Sun Bin, the monarch was deeply impressed and regretted not having met him sooner.

In 354 BC, King Hui of Wei ordered Pang Juan to lead an attack against the state of Zhao. The Wei troops duly laid siege to the Zhao capital of Handan (southwest of today's Handan in Hebei Province). The following year, Zhao sought help from King Wei of Qi, who wanted Sun Bin to be the commanding general. However, Sun Bin declined, saying "I cannot accept it. I am physically disabled because of the punishment I have received. If I were named commanding general, I would be a laughing stock. Please give the honor to Minister Tian!"

King Wei of Qi therefore named Tian Ji the commanding general and Sun Bin the chief strategist of the troops that would go to Zhao's rescue. From inside a covered wagon, Sun Bin dispensed advice to Tian Ji.

"Wei has sent all of their elite troops to Zhao, leaving only old and frail soldiers to defend the country. Why don't we attack Daliang, the capital of Wei, which is now thinly defended? When Pang Juan gets wind of the attack, he will surely give up Handan and rush back. We will then cut him off midway, dealing him a heavy blow. We will defeat him there," Sun Bin said to Tian Ji.

Tian Ji carried out this stratagem. When Pang Juan, whose troops had already taken Handan, was told of Qi's unexpected assault on Daliang, he immediately ordered a withdrawal of his troops. When his troops reached Guiling (northwest of today's Changyuan in Henan Province), they were met by the Qi army. Pang Juan was roundly defeated.

The Qi army thus returned triumphantly and the siege of

Handan was lifted.

In 341 BC, the state of Wei launched an attack against the state of Han, who also sought help from Qi. King Wei of Qi had recently died, so his son King Xuan of Qi sent Tian Ji and Sun Bin to relieve Han. Again, Sun Bin used his tested tactic of attacking Wei instead of rushing to Han's aid.

Receiving an urgent appeal for help from his capital, Pang Juan had to abort his military campaign and rush home. By that time, the Qi troops had marched into Wei.

Wei's crown prince Shen led a large force in an attempt to repel the Qi invasion. After the retreat of the Qi troops, Pang Juan inspected the ground where the Qi troops had been camping. He found the Qi army had pitched their tents in a vast area, and when the cooking pits were counted it was estimated that they could feed 100,000 soldiers. Pang Juan was rendered speechless.

The next day, when Pang Juan came with his troops to the next campsite of the Qi troops in their retreat, he counted only enough cooking pits to feed 50,000 men.

On the third day of the pursuit, when they came to the third campsite of the Qi army, they found only enough cooking pits to feed 20,000 men. Pang Juan felt finally reassured. "I knew the Qi soldiers were cowards. They were 100,000 strong soldiers when they came into Wei. In only three days, more than half of them have deserted." He ordered his troops to continue the pursuit by retracing the steps of the retreating Qi troops, without even stopping to rest for the night.

The pursuit took them all the way to Maling (southeast of today's Daming County in Hebei Province). The roads in Maling were very narrow and strewn with obstacles. Burning with a desire to catch up with the Qi troops in one bound, Pang Juan ordered his troops to continue marching despite the darkness of night. Suddenly a scout from the advance party ran back to report that their advance was blocked by wooden objects.

When Pang Juan surveyed the scene, he found that the trees on both sides of the road had been cut down, with only the largest tree left standing. Upon closer scrutiny, he could see that it had been partially debarked, leaving a bare strip of bole on which some characters could vaguely be discerned. However, the darkness prevented a clear reading.

Pang Juan ordered a torch to be brought to him. By its light the characters on the tree trunk could now be clearly made out: "Pang Juan will die under this tree!"

Shocked, Pang Juan ordered an immediate evacuation from the site, but it was too late. Countless arrows flew toward the Wei troops like swarms of locusts, and battle cries erupted from Qi troops suddenly appeared around them.

Pang Juan had fallen into a trap laid by Sun Bin, who had deliberately decreased the number of cooking pits to encourage Pang Juan to continue his pursuit. Calculating accurately that the Wei troops would reach this spot at this hour, he deployed an ambush of archers, ordering them to shoot the moment they saw torch light under the tree. Driven into a corner, Pang Juan drew his sword and committed suicide.

Riding the crest of victory, the Qi troops routed the Wei army and captured Wei's crown prince Shen.

After that, Sun Bin's reputation spread through all the ducal states and his work *Sun Bin's Art of War* has been preserved to this day.

16. Zhang Yi Undid the Alliance

AFTER SUN BIN'S routing of the Wei army, Wei's influence waned while Qin grew in strength. After the death of Duke Xiao of Qin, his son King Huiwen of Qin took over the reins and steadily expanded Qin's influence, causing panic among the other six states. How would they defend themselves against the attack of Qin? Some political activists proposed the idea of uniting the six states to resist Qin's inroads. This strategy was called *he zong* (vertical or north-south alliance). Other political activists lobbied various states on Qin's behalf, urging them to come under Qin's protection and attack other states. This was called *lian heng* (horizontal or east-west alliance). These political activists had no deep political convictions; they had no loyalty to any particular leader or ideology and served anyone who offered them high office.

The most famous among these activists was Zhang Yi, a citizen of Wei. To escape poverty, he left Wei and went to Chu to make his political fortune. He failed to obtain an audience with the monarch of Chu, but was instead taken in by Ling Yin as a retainer. One day, a rare and expensive piece of jade was found missing in Ling Yin's household, and suspicions immediately fell on Zhang Yi. He was consequently given a thrashing that nearly killed him.

Zhang Yi returned home in dejection. "If you had not studied so much for the purpose of seeking high office, you would not have suffered this ignominy," his distressed wife said to him.

Zhang Yi opened his mouth and asked his wife, "Is my tongue still there?"

"Of course it's still there!" his wife replied.

Zhang Yi was relieved. "As long as I still have my tongue, I will go places."

Eventually, Zhang Yi went to Qin, where by virtue of his gift of gab he won the trust of King Huiwen of Qin, who made him prime minister. At that time, the six states were working toward an alliance (*he zong*). In 318 BC, the states of Chu, Zhao, Wei, Han and Yan organized a joint force and attacked Hangu Pass in the state of Qin. Disagreements among the five prevented a true unity of purpose, and the coalition force disintegrated in the face of the Qin counterattack.

Of the six states, Qi and Chu were major powers. Zhang Yi believed that in order to realize his strategy of east-west alliance (*lian heng*), the alliance between those two states must be undone first. He presented a plan to King Huiwen of Qin and was sent to Chu.

Once in Chu, Zhang Yi brought expensive presents to King Huai of Chu's favorite minister Jin Shang, asking him to arrange an audience with the monarch.

Impressed by Zhang Yi's reputation, King Huai of Chu received him courteously and sought his advice on various issues.

"The monarch of Qin entrusted me with the mission of improving relations between our two countries. If you sever relations with Qi, my monarch will not only maintain permanent peace with you, but is also willing to make a gift of 600 *li* of territory in the Shangyu area (southwest of today's Xichuan County in Henan Province) to your country. By agreeing to this, you will not only weaken Qi's influence but also win Qin's trust. This is to our mutual advantage," Zhang Yi told him.

King Huai of Chu was swayed by Zhang Yi's lobbying. "If Qin could do that for me, why would I cast my lot with Qi?"

When King Xuan of Qi heard that Chu had severed relations with Qi, he immediately sent an envoy to King Huiwen of Qin to discuss a joint attack against Chu.

When Chu's envoy went to Xianyang to take possession of Shangyu, Zhang Yi denied having made any commitment. "There's no such thing! Your monarch must have misheard. How can Qin give away territory like that? What I said was six *li* not 600 *li,* and furthermore I was talking about land in my personal fief, not state land."

When the envoy reported back to King Huai of Chu, he was furious. He decided to send one hundred thousand troops to attack Qin. However, King Huiwen of Qin met the invading force with his own hundred thousand men, augmented by reinforcements from Qi. Chu was routed in the battle and saw its 100,000 men decimated, leaving only 30,000 survivors. In addition to the failure to obtain the 600 *li* of land in Shangyu, Chu lost 600 *li* of land in its Hanzhong area to Qin. King Huai of Chu was forced to sue for peace, and Chu's strength was greatly sapped as a result.

Zhang Yi had subdued Chu by deceptive means. He later shuttled between Qi, Zhao and Yan to persuade them to join his scheme of "east-westl alliance" (*lian heng*) with Qin and succeeded in undoing the six-state north-south alliance (*he zong*).

17. King Wuling of Zhao Adopted the Hu Dress and Horseback Shooting

WHILE CHU WAS being deceived by Qin, Zhao in the north was meanwhile on an ambitious drive to develop the state. Its monarch, King Wuling, was a visionary and bold reformer.

One day, King Wuling of Zhao was speaking to his minister Lou Huan, "We have the states of Qi and Zhong Shan (ancient state) to our east, the states of Yan and Dong Hu to our north, and Qin, Han and Lou Fan (ancient tribe) to our west. If we do not grow stronger, we might be subjugated any moment. To be strong we need radical reforms. Our national attire, characterized by loose-fitting long robes, is unsuitable for work or battle, in sharp contrast to the style of the Hu minorities (northern tribes), who wear short tunics with short sleeves and leather boots. They move about more agilely in those clothes. I intend to adapt our costumes so that they are similar to those of the Hu. How does the idea strike you? "

Lou Huan agreed, saying "Perhaps if we dress like the Hu minority, we will also be able to master their battle skills."

"You are right! We have a heavy reliance on infantry and horse-drawn carriages but are unfamiliar with the skills involved in fighting on horseback. I intend to adopt the Hu style of clothing precisely because I want our troops to learn how to shoot arrows while riding a horse, just as the Hu tribesmen do," King Wuling said.

However, many high officials began to voice opposition to this plan, so King Wuling of Zhao consulted another minister Fei Yi. "I want to change a custom of ours by promoting the clothing and fighting skills of the Hu tribesmen, but there is widespread resistance to the idea. What should I do?"

"Hesitation is the enemy of great initiatives. If you hesitate, no initiative will succeed, no matter how noble. Since you consider the idea beneficial to the country, there's no need to be concerned about public opinion," Fei Yi replied.

King Wuling of Zhao was pleased with this line of reasoning. "In my view, those who deride the idea are fools. Any sensible person would agree my idea," he said.

The next day, when King Wuling of Zhao presided over the daily assembly of his ministers and top officials, he did wear Hu clothes. The ministers were startled by his short tunic and narrow sleeves. King Wuling of Zhao presented his idea of adapting the national dress code, but the ministers were reluctant to come on board, feeling that the change would be too humiliating. When Gongzi Cheng, an uncle of the monarch and an influential minister, heard about the monarch's intention to change the national dress code, he feigned illness in order to cease reporting for duty.

Undeterred, King Wuling of Zhao made up his mind to implement his reforms. Realizing that to pave the way for the new measure he must first bring his old uncle around to his way of thinking, he paid a personal visit to Gongzi Cheng. He went over the advantages of the Hu style of clothing and the benefits of learning to shoot arrows on horseback, and finally convinced him. King Wuling of Zhao immediately gave a Hu outfit to Gongzi Cheng.

When the other ministers saw Gongzi Cheng was also wearing Hu clothing, their resistance melted and they too followed suit.

Seeing that the conditions were now ripe, King Wuling of Zhao formally issued an edict on dress reform. Soon after, the citizens of Zhao, rich or poor and regardless of their social standing, all adopted the Hu style of dress.

King Wuling of Zhao followed this with another edict, this time calling on his people to learn how to shoot arrows from horseback. In less than a year, a powerful calvary had been formed. In 305 BC, King Wuling of Zhao defeated the neighboring Zhong Shan and brought Dong Hu and several nearby tribes into his fold. Seven years after Zhao's adopting the Hu style of dress and learning how to shoot from horseback, Zhong Shan, Lin Hu and Lou Fan had all been brought under Zhao, whose territory was thus significantly expanded. King Wuling of Zhao was now eager to challenge Qin.

King Wuling of Zhao spent most of his time in military conquests away from home and therefore entrusted domestic governance to his son. In 299 BC, he formally abdicated in favor of his son, who became King Huiwen of Zhao, with King Wuling receiving the title of *Zhu Fu* (King Father).

Having made prudent arrangements for the smooth running of the country, the King Father of Zhao, in his quest to defeat Qin, decided to travel to Qin to study its terrain and to observe the actions of King Zhaoxiang. Disguising himself as an envoy from Zhao, he took a few men with him on his expedition.

Once in Xianyang, the King Father of Zhao called on King Zhaoxiang of Qin in the capacity of a Zhao envoy, and informed him of the abdication of King Wuling of Zhao.

King Zhaoxiang of Qin, however, thought that the envoy showed unusual grace and authority and started to have suspicions about him. A few days later, King Zhaoxiang of Qin sent for him again, but the "envoy" had departed without notice, leaving only one of the men who had accompanied him to Qin. When he was brought before the monarch, King Zhaoxiang of Qin was startled to learn that the "envoy" had been none other than the famous King Father of Zhao. He immediately ordered his general Bai Qi to take his best men on a manhunt to find him. By the time the pursuing party reached Hangu Pass,however, the King Father of Zhao was long gone.

18. Meng Changjun's Retainers

IN ORDER TO drive a wedge between Qi and Chu, who were close allies, King Zhaoxiang of Qin employed two tactics. He was tough toward Chu, but was friendly and gentler with Qi, Upon learning that the most influential minister in Qi was Meng Changjun, he issued an invitation to Meng to come to Xianyang, offering him the position of prime minister.

Meng Changjun was a member of the Qi nobility. In order to consolidate his position, he surrounded himself with many talented people that he had taken in as *men ke* (house guests) or *shi ke* (table guests); these retainers were given room and board by Meng. It is said that Meng Changjun had 3,000 retainers, many of whom were freeloaders with no real talents or skills.

When Meng Changjun departed for Xianyang, he brought along a large retinue of his retainers. He was personally received by King Zhaoxiang of Qin, to whom Meng Changjun presented a robe made of pure white fox fur. King Zhaoxiang of Qin was very pleased, and had it stored in the royal vault.

King Zhaoxiang of Qin had intended to aske Meng Changjun to be his prime minister, but some of his advisors warned, "Meng Changjun is a member of the Qi nobility and has a large power base. If he were made prime minister, he would owe first allegiance to Qi. That would surely put Qin's interests at risk."

"Then perhaps we should just send him back," King Zhaoxiang of Qin said.

"He's been here for a long time now and knows Qin inside out. How can we simply let him go home?" they replied.

King Zhaoxiang of Qin therefore put Meng Changjun under house arrest.

Meng Changjun was very anxious, so when he found out that there might be a way of getting assistance from a favorite concubine of the Qin monarch, he asked her for help through an intermediary. The concubine sent word that she would intercede for him with the monarch on condition that she be given a robe made of silver fox fur.

Meng Changjun consulted his retainers, "The only silver fox robe had been given to the Qin monarch. There is no way I could ask him to give it back."

"I have an idea," one retainer said.

That same night the retainer snuck into the palace grounds under cover of night, found the vault and stole the fox fur robe.

Meng Changjun sent the robe to the favorite concubine of King Zhaoxiang of Qin, who in return went to the king and interceded for Meng Changjun, urging his release. King Zhaoxiang of Qin agreed, and had the requisite documents issued to expedite the return of Meng and his retinue.

With the documents in hand, Meng Changjun hurried toward Hangu Pass. Fearing that the Qin monarch might change his mind, he assumed another name and altered the identity in the visa documents. The group arrived at the pass at about midnight. According to Qin regulations, the gate would be opened to let people through only when cocks started crowing. While the group waited anxiously for daybreak, one retainer started to imitate a cock crowing. As he did so, one local cock after another joined in the chorus.

The gatekeepers duly opened the gate and let Meng Changjun through after checking his altered papers.

When King Zhaoxiang of Qin changed his mind and sent his men after Meng, he was already beyond capture.

After returning to Qi, Meng Changjun became prime minister, and even more retainers sought his patronage. He established a hierarchy among his retainers: the first-class retainers got to ride in a carriage when they went out; the average retainers were given meat and fish for their meals, while the lower-ranking retainers had to content themselves with more simple fare.

A famished, impoverished old man called Feng Xuan was driven to seek help from Meng Changjun and became a "table guest." Meng Changjun asked one of the staff, "What skill does this man have?"

"He claimed not to have any skill," the staff member replied.

Amused, Meng Changjun said, "Let him stay."

The staff member knew what Meng Changjun meant and entered Feng Xuan in the category of low-ranking retainers.

A few days later, Feng Xuan, leaning against a column and tapping his sword, started to sing, "Sword, sword, let's go home! I don't get any fish to eat here. "

When staff reported this to Meng, he said, "Give him fish! Feed him the regular fare!"

Five days later, Feng Xuan once again started tapping on his sword and singing, "Sword, sword, let's go home! I don't get to ride in a carriage when I go out."

When Meng heard about this, he instructed the staff, "Get him in a carriage! Give him the first-class treatment!"

Another five days later, Meng asked staff whether Mr. Feng had any more complaints. "He's singing again, this time complaining that he does not have enough money to keep his family alive," the staff replied.

Upon inquiries, it was learned that Feng Xuan had an elderly mother at home. Meng sent food and clothes to Feng's mother. Feng Xuan's singing then finally stopped.

Meng Changjun's salary was not large enough to cover the room and board for so many retainers. He had to foot the huge bill by charging interest on loans he made to people in his fief, Xuecheng (southeast of today's Teng County in Shandong Province).

One day, Meng Changjun sent Feng Xuan to Xuecheng to collect interest due on some loans. Before setting off, Feng asked Meng Changjun, "What do you want me to buy for you on my way back?"

"You be the judge. Get whatever you think I do not have enough of!" Meng Changjun replied.

Once in Xuecheng, Feng Xuan called together all the debtors

and asked to check the IOUs. The debtors, unable to repay the loans, became nervous, but Feng Xuan announced a decision falsely attributed to Meng Changjun. "If you can't repay your debt, it will be forgiven."

Seeing the crowd not quite convinced, Feng Xuan torched all the IOUs.

Upon his return to Linzi, Feng Xuan faithfully reported the whole affair to Meng Changjun, who soon became incensed. "With the IOUs gone up in flames, how am I going to feed my three thousand retainers?"

"Before my trip you told me to buy whatever I thought you did not have enough of. In my estimation, you have enough of everything except for the hearts and minds of the people. That is why I bought you hearts and minds," Feng Xuan replied.

Unappeased, Meng Changjun said, "Enough of this!"

As Meng Changjun's good name spread far and wide, King Zhaoxiang of Qin started to worry about the trust Meng enjoyed at the Qi court. The Qin monarch therefore sent people to Qi to spread the rumor that Meng Changjun had been working to win the hearts and minds of the people and would soon claim the throne. King Min of Qi was persuaded by the rumor to believe that Meng Changjun's growing popularity was threatening his position. He therefore decided to ask Meng Changjun to surrender the seal of the prime ministership. There was nothing for the ousted Meng to do but to return to Xuecheng.

By that time, most of the 3,000 retainers had dispersed, leaving only Feng Xuan, who drove his master to Xuecheng. When his carriage was within 100 *li* of Xuecheng, he was greeted by the entire townspeople.

Deeply touched by what he was witnessing, Meng Changjun said to Feng Xuan, "I can finally see the hearts and minds you bought for me."

19. The Quest of King Zhao of Yan for a Capable Man

AFTER MENG CHANGJUN had been relieved of the post of prime minister, King Min of Qi subjugated Song with the help of Chu and Wei. This success fed his arrogance and he became all the more obsessed with the idea of becoming the Son of Heaven by annexing other states. This alienated the leaders of the ducal states, particularly Yan (to the north of Qi), as their leader had been waiting for an opportunity to avenge all the mistreatments the state had received from Qi.

Yan had been a major power until the reign of King Kuai of Yan, who had been persuaded to abdicate the throne in favor of his Prime Minister, Zi Zhi, in emulation of the legend of Yao passing his throne to Shun. As a result, Yan was thrown into chaos when Yan's generals and the crown prince, Ping, moved against Zi Zhi. On the pretext of putting down the internal strife, Qi sent troops into Yan, which would have lost its sovereignty were it not for the robust resistance led by Ping, who had been set up as monarch with the backing of the people and the military. They succeeded in driving out the Qi forces.

Ping then assumed the title of King Zhao of Yan. He was dedicated to rebuilding Yan's strength and was determined to bring in people with good leadership skills to help him govern. However, he had no luck in finding suitable candidates until an advisor reminded him that the elderly minister Guo Wei was an experienced statesman renowned for his knowledge.

King Zhao of Yan paid a visit to Guo Wei and said to him, "I will never forget the humiliation of Qi's invasion during the turmoil of our civil unrest. However, Yan is still too weak to avenge itself. If a capable man could help me remove this stain on our honor, I am willing to be his servant. Is there someone you can recommend?"

Guo Wei stroked his beard and thought the question over for a moment. "I don't have any ready names, but please allow me to tell you a story."

"In ancient times, there lived a king who was obsessed with finding a flying horse. He sent people to look for one everywhere, but in three years of searching they found nothing. A court attendant heard about the existence of a rare flying horse in a distant place, and told the monarch that he could surely bring it back for 1,000 *liang* of gold. When the court attendant got there, however, he found that the horse was already dead. Loath to return empty-handed, the attendant paid half of the gold for the horse's bones.

"When the attendant presented the bones to the monarch, he was furious. 'I sent you to get me a live horse; I never authorized you to spend money on these useless bones.' Unperturbed, the attendant said: 'When word gets about that you were willing to pay good money for a dead horse, people will soon come to you with live ones.'

"Although only half persuaded, the monarch let the attendant off the hook. Yet soon the story traveled around the kingdom, showing people that the monarch really cared about finding a flying horse. Before the year was out, several flying horses were presented to the monarch by people from all corners of the world.

"If you are determined to find someone of high caliber to help you govern, why not try using me as the horse bones?" Guo Wei concluded.

Greatly inspired by the story, King Zhao of Yan soon had an elegant house built for Guo Wei and invited him to be his mentor. Learning of King Zhao of Yan's desire to recruit talented men, people with unusual skills and capabilities came to Yan in droves asking for interviews. Among them the most famous was Yue Yi from the state of Zhao, who was named deputy prime minister by King Zhao of Yan, and charged with improving the government and military. From this time on, Yan's strength steadily grew.

Meanwhile, King Min of Qi was becoming increasingly arrogant and unpopular. King Zhao of Yan said to Yue Yi, "The failings of the monarch of Qi give us a good opportunity to have our long-awaited revenge. I intend to launch an all-out attack against Qi. What do you think?"

"Qi has superiority in the size of both its territory and population. We may not be able to defeat it on our own. If you want to attack Qi, you must work with allies," Yue Yi replied.

King Zhao of Yan sent Yue Yi to Zhao, in order to secure King Huiwen of Zhao's support. At the same time, he sent other envoys to Han and Wei to rally their support. The state of Zhao was also asked to bring Qin into the alliance. All those states were willing to join forces with Yan against Qi.

In 284 BC, King Zhao of Yan made Yue Yi the supreme commander of the allied armies of the five states, which he then led in a major attack against Qi.

King Min of Qi panicked at the news of the attack. He assembled all his troops to engage the coalition forces west of the Ji River. As a result of Yue Yi's excellent command, and the high morale of the coalition forces, the Qi army was routed and King Min of Qi was driven back to Linzi.

In the wake of the victorious campaign, the troops of Zhao, Han, Qin and Wei occupied several Qi cities, where they decided to stay and rest. Only Yue Yi and the Yan troops pressed on in a straight drive toward Linzi, and finally took the capital of Qi. King Min of Qi was forced to desert his capital and was killed in Jucheng.

King Zhao of Yan credited Yue Yi for bringing about the glorious victories. He personally congratulated the troops on the banks of the Ji River and distributed rewards and medals, before making Yue Yi the Prince of Chang Guo.

20. Tian Dan's Fiery Bulls Formation

IN SIX MONTHS of their campaign, the troops commanded by Yue Yi took more than 70 cities in Qi, leaving Jucheng (today's Ju County in Shandong Province) and Jimo (southeast of today's Pingdu County in Shandong Province) still in Qi's hands.Qi's minister from Jucheng declared the monarch's son the new king, with the title of King Xiang of Qi. However, when Yue Yi's troops attacked Jimo, the minister defending the city rode out to battle the attackers and received wounds that later killed him.

Jimo was thus left without a strong leader, and pandemonium threatened. At this time, there was a distant relation of the royal family by the name of Tian Dan, who had commanded troops before. By popular demand, he was made the commanding general in charge of the defending forces.

Tian Dan shared weal and woe with the soldiers and enlisted members of his clan and his immediate family into the forces fighting against the Yan troops, thus earning the admiration of the local people and boosting the troops' morale.

Yue Yi laid siege to Jucheng and Jimo for three years without being able to take them. Some people back in Yan who were jeaslous of Yue Yi said to King Zhao of Yan, "Yue Yi was able to take more than 70 cities in six months. Why is he unable to take these two cities after three years of siege? It is not that he is incapable of doing it. He is trying to win the hearts and minds of the people of Qi. Once he succeeds in winning them over, he will set himself up as the monarch of Qi."

Yet King Zhao of Yan's faith in Yue Yi remained unshaken. "Yue Yi has made an invaluable contribution to the country. Even if he became the monarch of Qi, he would fully deserve it. How can you malign him like this?" he said.

King Zhao of Yan then sent a messenger to Linzi to proclaim Yue Yi the monarch of Qi. Yue Yi was deeply grateful to King Zhao of Yan, but adamantly declined the honor.

As a result, the stature of Yue Yi grew considerably.

Two years later, King Zhao of Yan died and his crown prince succeeded him, assuming the title of King Hui of Yan. Hearing the news, Tian Dan considered this the break he had been waiting for. He secretly sent people to Yan to spread the rumor that Yue Yi would have become the ruler of Qi a long time ago but had refused the title in order to keep the favor of the late monarch of Yan. Now that a new monarch has ascended the throne, Yue Yi planned to stay in Qi to be its ruler. If Yan sends another commander to replace Yue Yi, therefore, Jucheng and Jimo will surely fall.

King Hui of Yan had long harbored ill feelings about Yue Yi and was thus easily swayed by this rumor into deciding to send General Qi Jie to replace Yue Yi as commander. Yue Yi therefore returned to his place of origin in the state of Zhao.

Qi Jie was promoted and took over the command of the expeditionary force. The officers and soldiers were unhappy with the change of command, but had to keep their feelings to themselves.

Qi Jie soon ordered an attack against Jimo, surrounding it with layers of troops. However, inside the city Tian Dan had already completed preparations for a decisive battle.

A few days later, Yan troops began hearing concerns voiced by the local residents. Some observed, "General Yue was a wonderful man. He treated prisoners well and the city residents had nothing to fear from him.If the Yan troops start cutting the noses off captured enemy soldiers, nobody in Qi will have the heart to go on fighting."

"My ancestral burial grounds are outside the city walls. What if the Yan troops start to desecrate the graves?" others asked.

These comments reached Qi Jie's ears, and he went on to cut off the nose of any Qi soldier captured by his troops and ordered all the tombs outside the city walls to be destroyed.

The people inside Jimo were in an uproar upon hearing of the treatment of prisoners by the Yan troops. They immediately enlisted in the forces under Tian Dan's command and vowed to fight to the death.

Tian Dan then sent several people disguised as wealthy gentry from Jimo to see Qi Jie in secret and offer him gold and silver. "The city is running out of food. The residents are sure to surrender in a couple of days. When your troops enter the city, can you please protect our families against any harm?" they said to him.

Qi Jie gladly accepted the gift and gave them his word.

The Yan troops were thus lulled into thinking there would be no more fighting and that they could just wait for the people of Jimo to surrender.

Meanwhile, Tian Dan picked 1,000 bulls and covered them with blankets painted in colorful, outlandish patterns. Sharp knives were fixed to their horns and reeds soaked in oil were tied to their tails.

Late one night, Tian Dan ordered dozens of openings made in the city walls through which the bulls were herded out of the city. When their tails were lit, the 1,000 bulls became so maddened that they stampeded toward the Yan encampment, followed immediately by 5,000 Qi soldiers wielding spears and swords.

In the city, the locals climbed up on the battlements and started to make a deafening racket with their copper pots and pans.

The Yan troops were suddenly roused from their slumber by the cacophony of battle cries mixed with drumbeats and the clanging of copper pots and pans. Before their sleepy eyes had a chance to fully adjust, the strange fiery beasts with daggers growing from their heads were already inches from them. Many soldiers were so scared that they were frozen to the spot and so offered no real resistance.

Many of the troops were killed by the daggers fixed on the

horns of the 1,000 bulls, while many others were hacked to death by the 5,000 Qi soldiers. Furthermore, some Yan soldiers were crushed to death by their own comrades in the stampede following the attack.

General Qi Jie tried to flee on his chariot but was surrounded and killed by Qi troops.

The Qi army counterattacked on the strength of their victory, sending a ripple through the entire country. Troops and civilians in cities still under Yan occupation were inspired to rise up against the occupiers. Where Tian Dan's troops advanced, the people there rose up in revolt. In a few months, Qi took back the 70 cities previously occupied by Yan, Qin, Zhao, Han and Wei.

Tian Dan escorted King Xiang of Qi back to Linzi, knowing that Qi had narrowly averted the fate of losing its sovereignty.

21. Qu Yuan's River Sacrifice

SINCE CHU'S DEFEAT at the hands of Qin, it had endured constant humiliation and bullying. This prompted King Huai of Chu to revisit the idea of entering into an alliance with Qi. Upon taking the throne, King Zhaoxiang of Qin wrote a courteous letter to King Huai of Chu inviting him to a meeting at Wuguan (southeast of Danfeng County in Shaanxi Province) in order to conclude a pact.

King Huai of Chu did not know what to do. If he refused, then he risked offending Qin. However, going to the meeting could be dangerous. Therefore, he sought the views of his ministers.

One of his ministers, Qu Yuan, said to King Huai of Chu, "Qin is like a ferocious jackal and we have suffered at its hands more than once. If you go to the meeting, you will be walking into a trap."

However, King Huai's son Gongzi Zilan approved of King Huai of Chu going to the meeting. "Antagonizing Qin has brought us nothing but high casualties and loss of territory. Now that Qin has shown a willingness for reconciliation, how can we justify not accepting the offer?"

Following Gongzi Zilan's urgings, King Huai of Chu traveled to Qin.

As feared by Qu Yuan, as soon as King Huai of Chu set foot in Qin's territory at Wuguan, he immediately found himself surrounded by Qin ambushers. In the meeting, King Zhaoxiang of Qin pressured King Huai of Chu to cede territory in the Qianzhong area to Qin, but King Huai of Chu would not agree.

King Zhaoxiang of Qin therefore had King Huai of Chu taken to Xianyang and put under house arrest. The ministers of Chu were then told to cede the territory in order to ransom their monarch.

When they learned of the detention of their monarch, the ministers of Chu set up the crown prince as the new monarch and refused to cede any territory. The new monarch assumed the title of King Qingxiang of Chu, while Gongzi Zilan became Chu's new prime minister.

King Huai of Chu was detained in Qin for over a year. In one attempt to regain his freedom, he fled Xianyang but was quickly recaptured by the Qin troops sent after him. Depressed and beset by illness, he died in Qin soon after.

The people of Chu were deeply upset by the mistreatment of King Huai of Chu by Qin and his death in an alien land. Qu Yuan was particularly incensed by this event. He urged King Qingxiang of Chu to invite more men of merit into the government and to insulate himself against men of dubious character. He advocated intensified military preparation and boosting troop morale in order to avenge the country and King Huai.

These words of advice, however, fell on deaf ears. Instead, they had the opposite effect of antagonizing Prime Minister Zilan and Jin Shang, who maligned Qu Yuan whenever they had a chance in front of King Qingxiang.

"You should know that Qu Yuan is very critical of you. He likes to tell people that you are not a dutiful son because you have forgotten our grievance with Qin. He questions the loyalty of the ministers simply because they do not advocate resisting Qin. According to him, this is a recipe for the country's downfall," they said to King Qingxiang of Chu.

King Qingxiang of Chu duly sacked Qu Yuan and sent him into exile in southern Hunan.

Qu Yuan was deeply distraught that his enthusiasm for the revitalization of the country and improving the lot of the people had only earned him the fate of being edged out by other ministers. While in exile in the south of Hunan, he was often seen roaming the banks of the Miluo River singing sad songs.

The local farmers knew that he was a patriotic minister and

sympathized with his plight. One fisherman plying his trade on the Miluo River had great admiration for Qu Yuan's integrity, but disapproved of his melancholy.

One day when Qu Yuan ran into the fisherman on the riverbank, the latter said to him, "Weren't you a minister of Chu? How did you end up here?"

"Many were the unclean, I alone am spotless; many were the intoxicated, I alone am sober. That's why I have been ostracized to this part of the world," Qu Yuan replied.

"Why set yourself apart by emphasizing your purity when you see corruption all around you? If you find yourself surrounded by drunkenness, why insist on being the only one who remains sober?" the fisherman said disapprovingly.

"I've heard that people who have just washed their hair always take care to dust their hats before wearing them, and that people who have just taken a bath shake the dirt from their clothes before putting them back on. I would rather throw myself in the river and become fish food than compromise my purity by jumping into a muddy mire," Qu Yuan replied.

Thus on the fifth day of the fifth month in 278 BC Qu Yuan threw himself into the Miluo River and drowned.

The local peasants rowed their boats toward the scene in an attempt to rescue him, but he was nowhere to be found. They spent long hours trawling the Miluo River without ever finding his remains.

Saddened by the tragedy, the fisherman scattered rice from bamboo containers into the river as sacrifice to Qu Yuan.

When the fifth day of the fifth month came around the next year, the local people remembered the anniversary of Qu Yuan's death and once again rowed their boats to the middle of the river to scatter rice as an offering to Qu Yuan. The bamboo containers holding the rice evolved over time into *zong zi* (cooked glutinous rice wrapped in large dried leaves) and the boat trips became dragon boat races. This is how the celebration of Qu Yuan has gradually developed into a national custom; May 5 of the lunar calendar has since been designated as the Dragon Boat Festival.

Qu Yuan left some memorable verses to posterity, the most

famous of which is *Li Sao*. In his verses, he lambasted those unprincipled officials who betrayed the country's interests and described his deep concern for the well-being of his country and people. His poetry was marked by a profound attachment to Chu. Qu Yuan is now considered an outstanding patriotic poet of ancient China.

22. Lin Xiangru Returned the Jade Intact to Zhao

IN 283 BC, an envoy dispatched by King Zhaoxiang of Qin presented his credentials to King Huiwen of Zhao. He conveyed the Qin monarch's offer of 15 cities to Zhao in exchange for a priceless stone in Zhao's possession called *He Shi Bi* (the Jade Disc of He, so named in honor of its discoverer, Bian He).

King Huiwen of Zhao consulted his ministers about the matter. If he were to agree to the exchange, he might be tricked into losing the jade disc and getting nothing in return. If he rejected the offer, however, he would antagonize Qin.

Someone mentioned the name of Lin Xiangru, who was considered very knowledgeable and experienced, so King Huiwen of Zhao duly summoned Lin Xiangru for consultation.

"Qin is powerful and Zhao is weak. There's no choice but to agree to their offer," Lin Xiangru advised.

"What are we to do if upon obtaining the jade disc Qin refuses to give us the promised cities?" King Huiwen of Zhao asked.

"The price of 15 Qin cities for a piece of jade is high enough. If Zhao refuses the offer, the fault lies with Zhao. If Qin does not keep its part of the bargain after Your Majesty hands over the jade, then the fault lies with Qin. It would therefore be in our interest to agree to the offer and let Qin bear the fault," Lin Xiangru replied.

"Then I will send you on the mission to Qin. But what am I to do if Qi does not fulfill its promise?" King Huiwen of Zhao said.

"If Qin cedes the cities to Zhao, I will leave the jade disc in Qin.

However, if Qin should renege on the offer, I promise to bring it back undamaged to Zhao," Lin Xiangru replied. (This is the origin of the Chinese expression "returning the jade intact to Zhao.")

Lin Xiangru then traveled to Xianyang with the incomparable jade disc. The elated King Zhaoxiang received him in one of his palaces, and Lin Xiangru presented the jade disc to the Qin monarch.

King Zhaoxiang of Qin took the jade disc and examined it. Quite satisfied, he passed the piece to the beautiful ladies and the attendants around him for a closer look. All those present congratulated King Zhaoxiang.

Waiting in the reception hall for a long time, Lin Xiangru saw no sign that the monarch of Qin was going to mention the offer of the cities. He soon came to the realization that King Zhaoxiang of Qin did not really mean to give the cities in exchange for the jade disc. However, the jade was now already in the king's hands. How was he going to retrieve it?

An idea flashed through his mind. He took a few steps toward King Zhaoxiang of Qin and said, "Although this is a priceless piece, it is not without minor imperfections which are not obvious to the eyes. Allow me to point them out to Your Majesty."

King Zhaoxiang of Qin told an attendant to hand the jade disc to Lin Xiangru.

With the jade in his hands, Lin Xiangru stepped back to lean on a massive pillar. "Your Majesty sent an envoy to Zhao with an offer of 15 cities in exchange for this precious piece of jade in Zhao's possession. The king of Zhao sent me in good faith to deliver the jade, but the good faith has not been reciprocated by Your Majesty. The jade is now in my hands. If Your Majesty makes a move against me I am ready to dash my head and this piece of jade against this pillar." Suiting action to word he made as if to hurl the jade against the pillar.

Afraid that Lin would destroy the jade disc, King Zhaoxiang of Qin immediately offered his apologies. "There's been a misunderstanding. I will keep my promise."

He ordered his ministers to bring him a map, on which he pointed out to Lin Xiangru the 15 cities earmarked for Zhao.

Cautioning himself against being tricked a second time, Lin Xiangru said, "Before sending the jade disc to Qin, the king of Zhao fasted for five days and held a solemn ceremony in the royal hall. I will only deliver the jade disc when you have likewise fasted for five days and held a ceremony to formally receive it."

Thinking that he now had Lin Xiangru under his control, King Zhaoxiang of Qin said, "All right, I agree." He then had Lin Xiangru escorted to a guesthouse.

At the guesthouse, Lin Xiangru gave the jade disc to an aide disguised as a tradesman, who hid it under his coat and snuck back to Zhao via back streets and alleyways.

Five days later, King Zhaoxiang of Qin gathered his ministers in Xianyang to attend a ceremony to receive the jade disc. When Lin Xiangru was summoned to the hall, he walked with great composure toward King Zhaoxiang of Qin and saluted him.

"Now that I have completed five days of fasting, it is time for you to hand over the jade disc," King Zhaoxiang of Qin said.

"From Duke Mu of Qin to the present day, none of the twenty odd monarchs of Qin has ever shown good faith. I was afraid of being tricked into losing the jade disc and abusing the trust of the king of Zhao, so I have sent the piece back to Zhao. I am ready to accept your punishment," Lin Xiangru replied.

"Did you trick me or did I trick you?" King Zhaoxiang of Qin asked in fury.

"Please do not be angry. Let me finish what I have to say. All the ducal states know that Qin is a major power while Zhao is very weak. Only powerful states can bully weaker ones, not the other way round. If Your Majesty really wants the jade disc, please cede the 15 cities to Zhao first, before sending an envoy to come for the stone. When Zhao receives the 15 cities, it will not have the audacity to deny you the jade disc," Lin Xiangru replied.

Finding it hard to argue with the convincing case being made by Lin Xiangru, King Zhaoxiang of Qin said, "It is just a piece of jade after all. We should not let it come between our two countries."

Lin Xiangru was finally allowed to return to Zhao.

Upon his return to Zhao, King Huiwen of Zhao elevated him

to the rank of *shang da fu* (Senior Grand Master) for successfully accomplishing the mission. It turned out King Zhaoxiang of Qin had not really intended to trade 15 cities for the jade disc but had merely wanted to test Zhao's strength. After the safe return of the jade disc to Zhao, the Qin monarch never again expressed an interest in the exchange.

23. Lian Po Presented a Stick and Asked for a Flogging

BENT ON SUBJUGATING Zhao, King Zhaoxiang of Qin mounted numerous cross-border attacks against them and even occupied Zhao's territory. In 279 BC, he invited King Huiwen of Zhao for a meeting at Mianchi (west of today's Mianchi County in Henan Province). King Huiwen of Zhao's first reaction was to decline the invitation for fear of being detained in Qin. However, his generals Lian Po and Lin Xiangru believed that not accepting the invitation would only be seen as a sign of weakness.

King Huiwen of Zhao therefore decided, despite his misgivings, to take the risk. He asked Lin Xiangru to accompany him to Qin, leaving Lian Po in Zhao to help the crown prince run the country.

As a precaution, King Huiwen of Zhao ordered his general Li Mu to bring 5,000 men as an escort, and asked his Prime Minister Lord Pingyuán to ensure security by stationing tens of thousands of troops near the border crossing.

On the appointed day, the monarchs of Qin and Zhao met in Mianchi and attended a banquet at which they drank and chatted together.

After a few glasses of wine, King Zhaoxiang of Qin said to King Huiwen of Zhao, "I understand that the king of Zhao is an excellent zither player. Can I ask the king to play a tune for the enjoyment of the company?" He then had a zither brought in.

Considering it bad form to refuse, King Huiwen of Zhao

reluctantly played the guests a tune.

The official historian of Qin immediately recorded what happened and read it aloud, "At the banquet in Mianchi the King of Qin ordered the King of Zhao to play a tune on the zither."

King Huiwen of Zhao was livid with rage. At this moment Lin Xiangru produced a *fou* (an earthen percussion instrument) and fell on his knees in front of King Zhaoxiang of Qin. "The king of Zhao understands that the king of Qin is an expert player of Qin's musical instruments. I have an earthen instrument with me and would appreciate it if Your Majesty would condescend to play it for the merriment of the company."

King Zhaoxiang of Qin blanched with anger and ignored him.

His eyes glaring with anger, Lin Xiangru said, "Your Majesty went too far this time. Qin may possess a powerful army, but I am five steps from you and could easily spill my blood on Your Majesty."

Startled by this violent reaction, King Zhaoxiang of Qin beat a few desultory notes on the *fou* to placate Lin Xiangru.

Lin Xiangru turned toward the official historian of Zhao and asked him to record what had happened, dictating to him, "The king of Zhao and the king of Qin met at Mianchi and the king of Qin played on the *fou* for the king of Zhao."

The ministers of Qin found it hard to stomach Lin Xiangru's audacity in embarrassing their monarch. One of them stood up and said, "I propose that the king of Zhao make a gift of 15 cities to Qin as a birthday present for the king of Qin."

"I propose that the king of Qin cede Xianyang to Zhao as a birthday present for the king of Zhao," Lin Xiangru in turn replied.

King Zhaoxiang of Qin was becoming worried that the situation would soon become dangerous, since he had found out that large numbers of Zhao troops had been deployed near the location. He silenced his ministers, saying "Let's have no more of this! This is supposed to be a friendly meeting between the sovereigns of our two countries."

Thus the meeting of Mianchi ended on a positive note.

On two separate missions outside his country, Lin Xiangru spared Zhao from humiliation, rendering a great service to his country. Placing total trust in Lin Xiangru, King Huiwen of Zhao elevated him to the rank of *shang qing* (Senior Minister), above that of General Lian Po.

Lian Po was unimpressed. "I am Zhao's top general, with a great number of victorious battles under my belt. What has Lin Xiangru done to deserve this promotion above me? Next time I see him, there will be trouble."

When Lin Xiangru got wind of this, he began to feign sickness in order to stop attending the daily royal audience.

One day, when Lin Xiangru left home in his carriage accompanied by some retainers, he noticed Lian Po's retinue coming his way. Desperately looking for a way to avoid a confrontation, he told the driver to back the carriage into a narrow alley to allow Lian Po's party to pass.

Lin Xiangru's retainers were very upset by the incident and criticized Lin for his faintheartedness.

"Who do you think is more powerful, General Lian or the king of Qin?" Lin Xiangru asked them.

"The king of Qin of course!" was the reply.

"Correct. All the sovereigns fear the king of Qin, but I dared to confront him in order to protect the interests of Zhao. So why do I appear to be afraid of General Lian? Because after giving some thought to the matter, I have come to the conclusion that the reason Qin has not dared to invade Zhao is the presence of General Lian and myself in the government. If Qin senses a grudge between us, it will be emboldened into invading our country. This is the reason for my deference to him," Lin Xiangru explained.

This was brought to the knowledge of Lian Po, who was so ashamed of himself that he bared his upper torso and carried a stick to Lin Xiangru's residence to beg for forgiveness. When he saw Lin Xiangru he said to him, "I am a crude, ignorant and meanspirited person, but you have been generous to me. I am ashamed to face you. Please punish me!"

"Both of us are ministers of Zhao. I'm already very grateful to you for being so understanding. You have no need to apologize," Lin Xiangru said.

Both were moved to tears and they became the closest of friends.

24. Fan Sui's Strategy of Allying with Distant Powers and Attacking Nearer Ones

THE UNITY OF Lin Xiangru and Lian Po in defending Zhao acted as a deterrent against invasion by Qin. However, Qin instead annexed large parcels of land from Chu and Wei. At that time, real power in Qin was in the hands of the queen mother and her brother Wei Ran (the Marquis of Rang). In 270 BC, the Marquis of Rang decided to send an expeditionary force against Qi.

Meanwhile, King Zhaoxiang of Qin received a letter signed by a man called Zhang Lu asking to see him on an urgent business.

Zhang Lu was originally from Wei, and had originally been called Fan Sui. He had been a retainer in the household of a minister called Xu Gu, who once took Fan Sui with him on a mission to Qi. Having heard about the talents of Fan Sui, King Xiang of Qi sent a messenger to offer him money and gifts to persuade him to join the Qi government, but Fan Sui refused.

This incident aroused Xu Gu's suspicion that Fan Sui was in secret collaboration with Qi. Upon their return to Wei, Xu Gu denounced Fan Sui to Wei's prime minister Wei Qi, who subjected Fan to torture that nearly killed him. Wei Qi then had him wrapped in an old bamboo mat and thrown in a latrine.

When dusk fell, Fan Sui gradually came to and saw a soldier standing over him. He sought the help of the guard, who eventully let him go and told Wei Qi that he had died.

Fan Sui then changed his name to Zhang Lu so that he would not be caught by Wei Qi.

An envoy from Qin happened to be in Wei at the time, so Fan Sui went to see him. The envoy then took him to Qin.

After arriving in Qin, Fan Sui was summoned to a meeting by King Zhaoxiang of Qin.

On his way to the palace, Fan Sui came upon the carriage of King Zhaoxiang. Fan pretended not to know who was in the carriage and did not move aside for the procession.

"The king is here!" the imperial guards shouted.

"What? Does Qin have a king?" Fan Sui said casually.

King Zhaoxiang approached and heard Fan Sui saying "I've heard of the queen mother and the Marquis of Rang in Qin, but never of a king!"

This touched a nerve with the king of Qin, who immediately took Fan Sui into his palace and ordered his attendants to leave them alone.

"I sincerely wish to seek your advice. You can speak out without fear about anybody, from the queen mother to the officials of my court," King Zhaoxiang said.

"Qin has a vast territory and valiant soldiers. It would have been easy for it to dominate the other states, yet it has made no headway in the last fifteen years. It has to be said that the Marquis of Rang has not done his best for Qin. Furthermore, the king is also not without fault," Fan Sui said.

"What, in your opinion, is my fault?" King Zhaoxiang asked.

"Qi is far from Qin, with Han and Wei sandwiched between them. If you were to send an expeditionary force against Qi, you would never be able to join it with Qin, even if you were to defeat it. I believe it is in your best interest to implement a strategy of allying with distant powers and attacking nearer ones. You should maintain a stable relationship with Qi, since it is far from Qin, while defeating the states that are closer. This will steadily expand Qin's territory. Once Han and Wei are annexed, Qi's days will be numbered," Fan Sui replied.

King Zhaoxiang nodded in approval. "If Qin can one day defeat the six states and unify the Central Plain, it will be thanks to your strategy of allying with the distant states and attacking the closer ones."

King Zhaoxiang immediately invited Fan Sui into his government and shifted the main focus of his military campaigns to Han and Wei.

Several years later, King Zhaoxiang of Qin sacked the Marquis of Rang and barred the queen mother from interfering with the affairs of state. Fan Sui, meanwhile, was made chief minister.

The king of Wei was alarmed by what was happening in Qin. When Wei Qi heard that Qin's chief minister was originally from Wei, he dispatched Xu Gu to Qin to sue for peace.

When Fan Sui learned of Xu Gu's arrival in Qin, he changed into rags and went to the guesthouse to see him.

Xu Gu was startled to see Fan Sui still alive. "What do you do now?" he asked.

"I am a valet," Fan Sui replied.

When he saw Fan Sui shivering in his flimsy clothes, Xu Gu gave him a silk robe and asked him to stay for supper.

"I understand that the king of Qin has entrusted weighty responsibilities to his chief minister Zhang Lu. I would very much like to see him. Do you know of anyone who can introduce me to him?" Xu Gu asked.

"My master knows the chief minister. If you want to see the chief minister, I can take you to him," Fan Sui replied.

At the entrance to the chief minister's residence, Fan Sui said to Xu Gu, "Please wait here for a moment while I go in to announce your visit."

Soon after Fan Sui went in, a voice inside summoned Xu Gu. Xu Gu asked the man guarding the door, "Why has Fan Sui who just went in not come out yet?"

"I don't know any Fan Sui. It was the chief minister who just went in," the doorkeeper said.

Xu Gu shook in his boots as he realized that the chief minister Zhang Lu was none other than Fan Sui. Once in the reception hall, he fell on his knees and crawled to where Fan Sui sat. "I must be blind not to have recognized the chief minister. I've offended the chief minister. Please punish me!" he begged.

After severely reprimanding Xu Gu, Fan Sui said, "You gave me this robe today at our earlier meeting. It means you still have some goodness left in you. I am sparing your life on this account." He then asked Xu Gu to take a letter to the king of Wei telling him that only when he had Wei Qi killed would Wei be allowed to cede territory to Qin in exchange for peace.

Upon his return to Wei, Xu Gu reported Fan Sui's terms to the king of Wei. The king of Wei agreed to cede territory in exchange for peace, and Wei Qi was left with no choice but to kill himself.

After Wei sued for peace, Qin attacked Han in accordance with Fan Sui's strategy of allying with distant powers and attacking closer ones.

25. Zhao Kuo, the Unequalled Military Strategist on Paper

IN 262 BC, in an attack ordered by King Zhaoxiang of Qin against Han, the Qin army occupied Yewang (today's Qinyang in Henan Province) and cut Shangdang Prefecture (with seat in today's Changzhi in Shanxi Province) off from the Han capital. Yet the generals of Shangdang garrison refused to surrender to Qin, and instead sent an envoy to offer Shangdang to Zhao.

King Xiaocheng of Zhao (son of King Huiwen) thus sent troops to take over Shangdang. Two years later, however, Qin again sent troops under the command of Wang He to lay siege to Shangdang.

When King Xiaocheng of Zhao learned of the siege, he immediately sent Lian Po with two hundred thousand men to relieve Shangdang. However, by the time they reached Changping (northwest of today's Gaoping County in Shanxi Province), Shangdang had already fallen to the Qin attackers.

As Wang He poised his troops for a march to Changping, Lian Po dug in and ordered fortresses, trenches and foxholes built, in preparation for a prolonged standoff between the two armies.

Wang He repeatedly challenged the Zhao troops to a battle, but Lian Po persistently refused to engage the Qin army. Wang He then sent word back to King Zhaoxiang, saying "Lian Po is a seasoned veteran general. He cannot easily be provoked into engaging our forces. Our troops are far from home. If this standoff lasts much longer, we may soon have problems replenishing our supplies. What should we do? "

When King Zhaoxiang asked Fan Sui for advice, he said, "If we want to defeat Zhao, we must first of all cause Lian Po to be recalled to his capital."

"How will that be possible?" King Zhaoxiang wondered.

"Leave it to me!" Fan Sui replied.

A few days later, King Xiaocheng of Zhao overheard one of his attendants speaking. "Qin is afraid that the young and vigorous Zhao Kuo will be given the command of the Zhao army. Lian Po is past his prime after all. It looks like he is on the point of surrendering."

Zhao Kuo was the son of a famous general of Zhao by the name of Zhao She. Zhao Kuo had studied the art of war since he was a child and enjoyed discoursing on military doctrine and strategies. He believed that no one in the world was more intelligent than himself, including his father.

The king of Zhao immediately sent for Zhao Kuo and asked him whether he had any confidence in beating back the Qin assault. "If Qin had sent Bai Qi to command its forces, I would need to think carefully about how to deal with him. But Wang He is more in the league of Lian Po. It goes without saying that if I were to be named commander of the Zhao forces, I would defeat him easily," Zhao Kuo replied.

Pleased by what he heard, the king of Zhao made Zhao Kuo commander, replacing Lian Po.

"Zhao Kuo may have read all his father's books on the art of war, but he lacks the ability to adapt tactics to changing circumstances. He is not qualified for top command," Lin Xiangru said to the king of Zhao. However, the king of Zhao was in no mood to heed Lin Xiangru's advice.

Zhao Kuo's mother also asked the king of Zhao to reconsider her son's appointment. The king of Zhao summoned her to explain the reason for her request. "Before his death, Zhao Kuo's father reminded me time and again that our son Zhao Kuo treats the business of war as if it were a child's game. It would be better if the King did not entrust him with any serious responsibility. If he is given a top military position, the Zhao army will likely be ruined under his command. That is why I implore you not to name him commander," she explained.

"The decision has already been made. Stay out of it!" The king of Zhao replied.

In 260 BC, Zhao Kuo arrived in Changping at the head of 200,000 men, and relieved Lian Po of command. Lian Po then returned to Handan.

Now at the head of an impressive army, Zhao Kuo ordered the dismantlement of the entire system built up by Lian Po. "When the Qin troops challenge us to fight again, we must go out immediately to drive them back. We must take no prisoners."

When Fan Sui learned about the replacement of Lian Po by Zhao Kuo, he knew his ploy of sowing discord in the enemy camp had succeeded. He then secretly promoted Bai Qi and named him commander of the Qin forces. When Bai Qi arrived in Changping, he prepared ambushes and deliberately lost several battles. Not knowing that he was being set up, Zhao Kuo led his forces in hot pursuit. Bai Qi lured the Zhao forces to where he had laid an ambush and ordered 25,000 men to cut off their retreat. Another 5,000 cavalrymen were sent straight into the main encampment of the Zhao army, separating the 400,000-strong Zhao army into two unconnected parts. Zhao Kuo was now realized the Qin army was a tough opponent and the only thing he could do was dig in and construct defenses while he waited for the arrival of reinforcements. However, Qin troops soon cut off Zhao's supply routes.

Zhao Kuo's troops were now running out of rations and fodder, with no reinforcements on the horizon. After 40 days of being holed up, the troops started complaining bitterly and lost any appetite for battle. Zhao Kuo led his troops in an attempt to break out of the encirclement, but was killed in a barrage of arrows from Qin archers. When the Zhao troops learned of the death of their leader, they threw down their weapons and surrendered. This was how the huge Zhao army of 400,000 men was wiped out under the command of Zhao Kuo.

26. Mao Sui Recommending Himself

QIN THEN LAUNCHED a large-scale operation against Zhao's capital, Handan. Zhao put up a stiff resistance, but its strength had been failing since its disastrous defeat at Changping. King Xiaocheng of Zhao therefore asked Zhao Sheng (Lord Pingyuan) to seek help from Chu. Zhao Sheng was Zhao's prime minister and the king's uncle. He decided to travel to Chu to discuss the possibility of an alliance against Qin with the king of Chu.

Zhao Sheng planned to travel to Chu with a retinue of 20 men with both administrative and military expertise. Although he had 3,000 retainers, it was not easy to find such talented men. After careful vetting, 19 were picked from the 3,000.

As Zhao Sheng fretted, a retainer sitting at the back of the room got to his feet and recommended himself, "Can I be the twentieth?"

Surprised, Zhao Sheng asked, "What's your name? How long have you been my retainer?"

"My name is Mao Sui and I have been here for three years," the retainer replied.

Zhao Sheng shook his head. "A talented person is like an awl in one's pocket. It would not be long before its sharp tip pierces the pocket and thrusts itself into view. Why have I never heard about your skills though you have been here three years?"

"It is because I chose to show you the awl only today. If you had put it in your pocket sooner, it would have pierced through a long time ago. Are you interested only in the tip showing?" Mao Sui replied.

The 19 retainers picked for the mission thought Mao Sui was bragging, and looked at him with contempt. Zhao Sheng, however, was impressed by Mao Sui's audacity and eloquence and decided to make him the twentieth member of the group. They bade farewell to the king of Zhao the same day and set off for Chu.

While Zhao Sheng discussed the proposal of a coalition against Qin with King Kaolie of Chu in the royal council chamber, Mao Sui and the 19 other retainers waited outside. The talks started in the morning and by noon Zhao Sheng had lobbied so hard that his mouth had become parched. Yet the king of Chu remained dead set against attacking Qin.

The retainers waiting at the foot of the steps were getting impatient, but none of them knew what to do. Someone remembered the wild boasts of Mao Sui back in Zhao, and whispered to him, "Mao Sui, this is your opportunity to show off your talents."

Cool and composed, Mao Sui went up the steps carrying his sword and in a loud voice said, "Do you want an alliance or not? This matter can be settled in a few words. Why have you been unable to come to a conclusion after talking from morning till noon?"

The king of Chu was very upset at this intrusion. "Who is this man?" he asked Zhao Sheng.

"He is Mao Sui, one of my retainers," Zhao Sheng replied.

Upon hearing that he was only a retainer, the king of Chu became even angrier. He upbraided Mao Sui, saying "We are discussing weighty matters of state, who are you to interrupt us? Leave us now!"

Mao Sui took another step forward while putting his hand on his sword. "Stop bullying people just because you are powerful! Why do you attempt to upbraid me in front of my master?"

Seeing the sword he carried and hearing the vehemence of his protests, the king of Chu switched to a more conciliatory tone. "What do you have to say then? Go on, I am listening."

"Chu boasts a territory of 5,000 *li* wide and an army of 1,000,000 men. Chu used to be a major hegemonic power but with the rise of Qin, Chu has suffered a string of defeats and one of its monarchs even became a prisoner of Qin and died there. No humiliation is greater than this for your country. Bai Qi of Qin, who is not noted for any great talents, was able to take Yingdu, the capital of Chu, in one battle, forcing the king of Chu to move its capital. Even we, the people of Zhao, feel shame for you. Yet Your Majesty does not seem to desire revenge, to want to remove this stain on the honor of your country. My master is discussing an alliance against Qin with you not so much for Zhao's sake, but more importantly, for Chu's sake," Mao Sui said.

Every word Mao Sui spoke felt like a sharp stab at the King's heart. Red-faced, he kept repeating, "You are right! You are right!"

Mao Sui, relentless, pressed him. "So the matter of the alliance is settled!"

"It is settled!" The king of Chu replied.

Mao Sui wasted no time; he immediately asked the attendants of the king of Chu to bring some chicken, dog and horse blood to him. Holding a bronze basin, he knelt down in front of the king of Chu and said, "Your Majesty is the supreme leader of the alliance, so please swear a blood oath first." (In ancient ceremonies to conclude an alliance, animal blood was rubbed on the mouth as a token of good faith.)

After the king of Chu had sworn a blood oath, Zhao Sheng and Mao Sui did the same. Following the creation of the alliance between Chu and Zhao, King Kaolie of Chu sent Huang Xie (Lord Chunshen) with 80,000 troops to rush to Zhao's rescue.

27. Lord Xinling Rescued Zhao

WHILE CHU SENT troops to Zhao's aid, Wei also received Zhao's call for help. Thus King Anxi of Wei sent General Jin Bi with troops to aid Zhao.

When King Zhaoxiang of Qin learned that Wei and Chu had sent troops to relieve Zhao, he went to Handan to personally direct the campaign. He sent word to King Anxi of Wei, saying "It is only a matter of time before Handan falls to Qin. Whoever dares go to its aid should know that once I have annihilated Zhao I will turn on him." This threat succeeded in frightening King Anxi of Wei, who immediately sent someone after Jin Bi, ordering him to stop the advance of his troops. Jin Bi therefore billeted his 100,000 men in Yecheng (southwest of today's Linzhang County in Hebei Province) and waited for further orders.

Zhao sent an envoy to Wei urgently requesting it to order its troops into action. King Anxi of Wei, however, was afraid to antagonize Qin. Yet, if he kept the troops in camp, he would antagonize Zhao. So his troops stayed put, neither advancing nor returning home. King Xiaocheng of Zhao became very anxious and asked Lord Pingyuan to write to Wei Wuji (Lord Xinling, a brother of the Wei monarch) for help, since Lord Pingyuan's wife was Lord Xinling's sister, so the two families were related.

After receiving the letter, Lord Xinling implored King Anxi of Wei to order Jin Bi into action, but the king of Wei was adamant in his refusal. Having exhausted all avenues without success, Lord Xinling said to his retainers, "The king is unwilling to send in the troops, so I have decided to go to Zhao myself to die with the people there."

Many of his retainers decided to follow Lord Xinling to Zhao.

Before his departure, Lord Xinling called on Hou Ying, a friend for whom he had the highest regard, to bid him farewell. "Pitching your troops against the Qin army in Zhao is like throwing a chunk of meat to a hungry tiger. You will be needlessly courting your own death," Hou Ying said.

"I am well aware of the futility of it all. But what else can I do?" Lord Xinling replied with a sigh.

Hou Ying cleared the room, leaving the two of them alone. "Our king has a favorite concubine called Ru Ji, correct?" he said.

Lord Xinling nodded affirmatively. "Correct."

"I understand that the tally that authorizes troop movements is hidden in the King's bedroom and only Ru Ji is able to get her hands on it. Back when Ru Ji's father was murdered, she asked the king to find the murderer, but after three years of investigation no suspect was apprehended. It was you who got your retainers to find the killer and avenged Ru Ji, and she therefore owes you a debt of gratitude for this assistance. If you ask Ru Ji to steal the tally, she will surely agree. Once you have the tally in hand, you can take it to Jin Bi and take over his command. You can then engage the Qin troops in battle. Surely this would be better than going to your death alone?" Hou Ying said.

Impressed by Hou Ying's reasoning, Lord Xinling immediately sent someone to raise the matter with Ru Ji, who quickly gave her assent. Late that night, when the king of Wei was fast asleep, Ru Ji succeeded in getting the tally out quietly and had it brought to Lord Xinling.

After receiving the commander's tally, Lord Xinling called on Hou Ying to bid him farewell a second time."When a general is on the battlefield, he may sometimes ignore the King's orders. What are you going to do if Jin Bi refuses to pass the command to you when presented with the tally? " Hou Ying said.

Lord Xinling was unprepared for the question and was rendered speechless.

"I've already anticipated this eventuality. My friend Zhu Hai is one of the strongest men in Wei. You can take him with you. If Jin Bi presents any difficulty, let Zhu Hai take care of him," Hou Ying said.

When Lord Xinling arrived in Yecheng with his retinue of retainers and Zhu Hai, he went to Jin Bi and conveyed the false order for Jin Bi to hand over his command to him. When Jin Bi examined the tally, he was a little suspicious. "This is a military matter of the highest importance. I have to confirm it with the king before carrying it out," he said.

Jin Bi had scarcely finished speaking when Zhu Hai thundered from behind Lord Xinling, "Are you defying the King's orders? Are you rebelling against him?"

Before Jin Bi could protest, Zhu Hai took out a metal rod hidden in his sleeve and hit Jin Bi on the head, killing him instantly.

Holding the commander's tally, Lord Xinling issued an order to the troops. "If both father and son serve in this army, the father can go home now; if brothers serve together, the older brother can go home. Only sons can also go home to care for their parents, since they have no brothers to do it. All the rest will follow me to relieve the siege of Zhao."

Lord Xinling assembled an elite force of 80,000 men and set out to relieve Handan, where he personally let the charges against the Qin troops. Unprepared for this unexpected attack, the Qin general Wang He soon began to lose ground.

When he learned that Wei reinforcements had arrived, Lord Pingyuan led the Zhao troops out of Handan to join the fray. Attacked from two sides, the Qin troops were routed and quickly collapsed.

This was the first time in many years that the Qin forces had suffered such a humiliating defeat. General Wang He beat a retreat with his troops, while 20,000 Qin troops encircled by the Zhao army were forced to surrender.

Lord Xinling had relieved the siege of Handan and saved Zhao. Deeply grateful, King Xiaocheng of Zhao and Lord Pingyuan came out of the city to greet him.

Meanwhile, Lord Chunshen of the state of Chu was still waiting with his reinforcements in Wuguan. When news of the rout of the Qin forces and the lifting of the siege of Handan reached him, he took his troops home to Chu.

28. Li Si Advised against the Expulsion of Foreign-born Officeholders

ALTHOUGH QIN WAS dealt a heavy blow at Handan, it did not make any significant dent in its power and strength. The next year (256 BC) it was victorious in its military campaigns against Han and Zhao. It went on to deliver the coup de grâce to the Eastern Zhou dynasty, which for years existed only in name. Following the death of King Zhaoxiang of Qin, his grandson (King Zhuangxiang) died barely three years after his accession to the throne. His crown prince Yingzheng then ascended the throne at the age of 13. In that period, real power was vested in the Prime Minister, Lü Buwei.

Lü Buwei was a wealthy merchant in Yangzhai (today's Yuzhou in Henan Province) before becoming prime minister after helping King Zhuangxiang win the throne. After being named prime minister, Lü Buwei followed the example of Meng Changjun and took in large numbers of retainers, many of whom had come from other states.

In the Warring States Period, many schools of thought vied with each other in publishing books and spreading their ideas. Historians call this the "competition of a hundred schools of thought." As he was no good at writing books, Lü Buwei enlisted the help of his retainers in compiling a book titled *Lü's Spring and Autumn Annals*. After the completion of the tome, Lü had it exhibited at the main gate of Xianyang with a bulletin saying that whoever offered suggestions on the text, even if only for the addition or deletion of a few words, would be awarded 1,000 *liang* of gold. This made his fame grow.

When King Zheng of Qin reached the age of 22, there was a palace coup involving Lü Buwei. Finding Lü a liability, the king of Qin stripped him of his office. When the king realized that Lü still possessed considerable influence, he ordered him to kill himself.

In the wake of Lü's fall from grace, members of the nobility and ministers started to make the case that people who came to Qin from other states mainly had the interests of those states in mind, and might even be spies. They urged King Zheng of Qin to expel all foreign-born officials from the country.

Taking their advice, the king of Qin issued an order that all government officials, regardless of rank, who were not born in Qin must leave the country.

An official from Chu, by the name of Li Si, was a student of a famous Confucian scholar named Xun Kuang. He had been taken in by Lü Buwei when he arrived in Qin. Li Si did not take his expulsion well. When he left Xianyang, he sent a message to the king of Qin.

"By bringing Bai Li Xi and Jian Shu into his government, Duke Mu of Qin became a powerful leader. Duke Xiao of Qin entrusted to Shang Yang the responsibility of making Qin a powerful state. King Huiwen dismantled the six-state alliance with the help of Zhang Yi. Under King Zhaoxiang, the prestige of the Qin court grew further because he placed his trust in Fan Sui. All four monarchs achieved greatness as a result of enlisting the services of foreign-born men. When Your Majesty expels foreign-born officials, you are helping enemy states build up their strength," Li Si wrote in his message.

Persuaded of the validity of the case made by Li Si, the King of Qin immediately sent people to bring him back and reinstated him. The expulsion order was then revoked.

With Li Si advising him, King Zheng of Qin stepped up attacks against other states and sent envoys to lobby the leaders of various ducal states. He supplemented military operations with covert activities to sow discord and buy support in enemy camps. Unsettled by what was going on, King An of Han sent prince Han Fei to Qin to sue for peace and offer to become Qin's vassal state.

Han Fei, like Li Si, was a student of Xun Kuang. Witnessing the steady decline of Han, he often volunteered advice to the King of Han, but was always ignored. Although he was an erudite scholar, he remained in the political wilderness; therefore, he devoted himself to the writing of a book called *Hanfeizi*, in which he advocated concentration of power in the monarch and the rule of law. When the book was brought to Qin, King Zheng of Qin read it and was impressed. "It would be wonderful if I could meet the author," he said.

When Han Fei arrived in Qin at the behest of the king of Han and saw with his own eyes how strong Qin was, he instantly offered his services to help Qin unite all the states into one country. Li Si, however, soon became anxious, even though the king of Qin had not given any thought to bringing Han Fei into his government. Li Si was afraid that Han Fei might upstage him. He said to the king of Qin, "Han Fei is a prince of Han. While Your Majesty is committed to annexing the ducal states, Han Fei is bound to defend Han's interests. If you allow him to go back to Han, he will pose a future threat. It would be more prudent to have him killed."

King Zheng of Qin was unsure about Li Si's advice. He ordered the detention of Han Fei with the intention of questioning him. Before he could protest his innocence, Fan Fei was thrown in jail. Li Si sent someone with poison to his cell, and Han Fei had no choice but to drink it.

By the time King Zheng of Qin began to have second thoughts and ordered the release of Han Fei, it was already too late. King Zheng of Qin was very upset about this incident.

Meanwhile, a man called Liao from Wei happened to be in Qin at the time. King Zheng of Qin found him to possess unusual talents and named him *Wei* (Commandant, an ancient military title) of Qin. He thus became popularly known as Wei Liao (Commandant Liao).

29. Jing Ke's Attempt on the Life of the King of Qin

KING ZHENG OF Qin placed great trust in Wei Liao and continued his military campaigns against other states in his relentless quest for a grand unified state on the Central Plain. He achieved the dismantlement of the Yan-Zhao Alliance and took several cities from Yan.

Dan, the crown prince of Yan, was retained in Qin as hostage. When he saw King Zheng's determination to annex the ducal states and the Yan land taken by Qin, he snuck back to Yan, bent on revenge. However, he chose not to achieve his purpose by building up the military or making alliances against Qin, but instead placed the fate of Yan in the hands of assassins. He offered all his fortune to anyone who would assassinate King Zheng of Qin.

Prince Dan finally recruited a formidable warrior by the name of Jing Ke, whom he invited into his household as a valued guest, giving him the privilege of the use of his own carriage. He even shared his food and clothing with Jing Ke, who naturally felt deeply indebted to Prince Dan.

In 230 BC, Qin eliminated Han from the political map. Two years later, General Wang Jian of Qin occupied Handan, the capital of Zhao, and led his troops on a northward drive toward Yan.

In a panic, Crown Prince Dan of Yan sent for Jing Ke and said to him, "Pitching our forces against Qin is tantamount to throwing eggs against rocks. Seeking an alliance with other states to oppose Qin also does not seem a viable option now. My idea is to send a warrior disguised as an envoy to see the king of Qin, get close to him and force him to return the land he annexed from various states. If he agrees, perfect. If not, he will be killed. What do you think?"

"It is feasible. But if we want to get close to the king of Qin, he must first be convinced of our desire for peace. I understand that the king of Qin has long coveted Dukang (in the vicinity of today's Zhuozhou, Gaobeidian and Gu'an in Hebei Province), which has some of the most fertile land in Yan. Also, I have heard that the king of Qin has put a big reward on the head of General Fan Yuqi of Qin, who is now in exile in Yan. If I can take General Fan's head and the map of Dukang to the king of Qin, I am sure he will see me. I will then be able to deal with him," Jing Ke replied.

The crown prince faced a dilemma. "The map of Dukang is easy. However, General Fan has come to us to seek asylum from the persecution of Qin. I cannot bring myself to hurt him."

Jing Ke therefore went to see Fan Yuqi in private. "I have an idea which can help Yan out of its dire plight and accomplish your revenge, but I do not know how to put it to you," he said.

"What is your idea? Tell me!" Fan Yuqi said eagerly.

"I have decided to assassinate the king of Qin, but it is difficult to get close to him. Since he has put a price on your head, I am sure he will see me if I offer your head to him," Jing Ke said.

"Fine! Take it with you!" Fan Yuqi said. Without hesitation he then unsheathed his sword and slit his own throat.

Prince Dan had a sharp dagger boiled in poison by a craftsman. Whoever was stabbed by the dagger would die on the spot. He therefore gave the dagger to Jing Ke to be used for the assassination. He also assigned a 13-year-old warrior called Qin Wuyang to be Jing Ke's helper.

In 227 BC, Jing Ke set off from Yan for Xianyang. Prince Dan and a few others, dressed in white clothing, saw them off by the Yi River (near today's Yi County in Hebei Province). Before his departure, Jing Ke sang a song to those present:

Hard does the wind blow,
Cold does the Yi flow.
My back I now turn
Never to return.

The song brought tears to the eyes of all those who were present. Jing Ke heaved Qin Wuyang onto the the carriage and departed without once looking back.

When King Zheng of Qin was told that Jing Ke, the envoy of Yan, had arrived with both Fan Yuqi's head and the map of Dukang, he was elated and consented to receive him in Xianyang Palace.

Jing Ke took the box that contained Fan Yuqi's head and Qin Wuyang took the map of Dukang, and together they walked up the steps leading to the royal council hall.

Awed by the imposing surroundings, Qin Wuyang started to shake with fright.

When the guards flanking the king saw this change, they asked, "Why has the envoy gone pale?"

When Jing Ke turned his head and saw Qin Wuyang had indeed turned pale, he said to the king of Qin with a laugh, "He is a country boy who has never seen such royal splendour before. It is only natural that he is a little nervous. Please forgive him."

His suspicions having been aroused, King Zheng said to Jing Ke, "Take the map from Qin Wuyang and come forward alone."

Taking the map from Qin Wuyang, Jing Ke went up to the king of Qin and presented both the map and the box to him. The king opened the wooden box and saw that the head was indeed that of Fan Yuqi. The king then asked to see the map. Jing Ke slowly unfurled the map; when it was completely laid open, the dagger hidden inside came into view.

When King Zheng of Qin saw the dagger, he jumped back in fright.

Grasping the dagger with his right hand and grabbing the King's sleeve with his left, Jing Ke raised his arm to strike the king.

King Zheng of Qin jumped up so quickly that his sleeve was torn off. He ran toward the exit, but Jing Ke, dagger in hand, soon caught up with him. Sensing his assassin closing in on him fast, the king ran in circles around a massive bronze pillar, with Jing Ke in hot pursuit.

Not one of the many officials present was armed, and the guards outside were forbidden by the regulations of the Qin court to enter without the order of the king. In the panic, no one had the presence of mind to summon the guards.

In the heat of the moment, one of the king's doctors had a sudden inspiration; he hurled his medicine bag at Jing Ke, who parried it and sent it flying in another direction.

However, in that moment of confusion King Zheng of Qin had an opportunity to take a step toward Jing Ke, pull out his sword and cut off Jing Ke's left leg.

Jing Ke fell to the ground, but managed to throw his dagger at the king. The king dodged to the dagger and it instead struck a bronze pillar.

When the king of Qin saw that Jing Ke no longer had a weapon in his hands, he attacked him with his sword. With eight stab wounds, Jing Ke knew he had failed. "I did not act earlier because I wanted to force you to return the land you took from Yan," he said with a wry laugh.

By that time the royal guards had been summoned, and they delivered the coup de grâce to Jing Ke. Qin Wuyang meanwhile, had been already killed by the guards.

30. The King of Qin Conquered the Six States

AFTER KILLING JING Ke, King Zheng of Qin immediately ordered his general Wang Jian to step up attacks against Yan. The crown prince of Yan led his troops to fight off the invaders but his troops were soon routed. King Xi of Yan and Prince Dan both fled to Liaodong. King Zheng of Qin, however, determined to capture Prince Dan, sent troops after them. Left with no choice, King Xi of Yan had Prince Dan killed and formally apologized to Qin before suing for peace.

When asked by King Zheng for advice, Wei Liao said, "Han has been annexed by us. Zhao has been reduced to only one city: the city of Daicheng (today's Wei County in Hebei Province), and the king of Yan has fled to Liaodong. They are all on their last legs. With the weather turning colder, we should turn our attention to the taking of Wei and Chu in the south."

Following the advice of Wei Liao, King Zheng sent Wang Ben (son of Wang Jian) with 100,000 men to attack Wei. When Wei solicited Qi's help, King Jian of Qi rebuffed him.

In 225 BC, Wang Ben conquered Wei and took the captured king and ministers to Xianyang.

King Zheng planned to attack Chu next. He summoned his generals for consultation. When the young general Li Xin was asked how many troops it would take to attack Chu, he replied, "No more than 200,000."

The king then asked the veteran general Wang Jian the same

question. "Chu is a large state. It will take more than 200,000 men to attack it. I estimate that the minimum number of troops needed is 600,000," he replied.

King Zheng was very unhappy with this answer. "General Wang is getting on in age. I think General Li is right," he said. He therefore dispatched Li Xin with 200,000 men on the southern expedition.

Seeing that his advice was no longer valued by the king of Qin, Wang Jian excused himself on account of sickness and returned to his home town.

However, when Li Xin arrived in Chu with his 200,000 men, he was dealt a disastrous defeat and his army was decimated. Countless soldiers died in the battle and he lost 7 generals. He escaped with his remaining troops back to Qin.

In a fury, King Zheng fired Li Xin and went to Wang Jian's home town to personally invite him back to command his troops. "I was wrong not to have listened to you. Li Xin bungled the job. I must ask you to take the command this time," he said.

"If Your Majesty insists that I command the troops, I must insist that I take 600,000 men. Chu is a large populous country and could easily mobilize a million men. 600,000 is the absolute minimum, and I may need even more," Wang Jian replied.

"Whatever you say, my general," King Zheng said. He then gave Wang Jian 600,000 men. On the day of the troops' departure, he personally attended a send-off banquet at Bashang in honor of Wang Jian.

Wang Jian led his huge army in a large-scale attack against Chu, and Chu mobilized all its fighting forces in resistance.

After Wang Jian inspected the frontline, he ordered the troops to build defensive works and refrain from engaging enemy forces. He ignored the repeated challenges of Chu's General Xiang Yan for a battle.

As this went on, Xiang Yan began to think that Wang Jian was only there to set up defenses. He therefore gradually lowered his guard against the Qin troops. Yet when Xiang Yan least expected it, the 600,000 Qin troops unleashed a sudden attack. The Chu troops put up a desultory fight in a disoriented state for a short while before dispersing in defeat. Chu was now losing men as well as territory. The Qin army then pressed on to Shouchun (west of today's Shou County in Anhui Province) and captured King Fuchu of Chu.

After learning of his King's capture, Xiang Yan crossed the Yangtze River with his troops, ready to continue the resistance. Wang Jian, who had built many battleships and personally trained his navy, led his troops in pursuit across the river. Realizing that the situation could no longer be salvaged, Xiang Yan took his sword and killed himself.

After Wang Jian conquered Chu, he returned to Xianyang. His son Wang Ben then took over his command and led an expedition to deal with Yan. Already very weak, Yan could not head off the Qin army's advance. In 222 BC, Wang Ben conquered Yan and took the last remaining Zhao city of Daicheng.

By this time, the only other ducal state left was Qi. The ministers of Qi had been paid off by Qin and King Jian of Qi had been keen to never antagonize Qin, rebuffing all requests by other states for help against Qin. He had assumed that since it was a great distance from Qin, Qi did not need to worry about an attack as long as Qi humored Qin's every whim. Only after the annexation of the other five states by Qin did he begin to feel nervous and order his western defenses to be improved. However, it was already too late.

In 221 BC, Wang Ben led hundreds of thousands of Qin troops in a march through the south of Yan. They swooped down toward Linzi with overwhelming force. It was then that King Jian of Qi realized his vulnerability. However, with the other states gone, who was he going to turn to for help? In a matter of days, the Qin army had entered Linzi and King Jian of Qi surrendered without a protest.

The six ducal states, each intent on maintaining their respective position, had fought one another in order to grab land to make up for their own losses. Their attempt to maintain the status quo of small spheres of influence afforded Qin an opportunity to destroy them one by one. Qin not only possessed political, economic and military advantages, but more importantly conformed to the historical pattern of consolidation and unification. That is why it was able to conquer the six states in less than ten years.

More than 250 years of strife among the ducal states, beginning in 475 BC when the Warring States Period commenced, finally put an end to the division of China into ducal fiefdoms and led to the founding of a unified, muti-ethnic feudal state—the Qin dynasty.

QIN DYNASTY
(221 BC–206 BC)

31. Qin Shihuang—the First Emperor of Unified China

AFTER CONQUERING the six major sovereign states, thereby ending the divisions of the Warring States Period and unifying China, King Zheng of Qin viewed his own accomplishments as dwarfing those of the legendary Three *Huang* (Three August Ones) and Five *Di* (Five Sovereigns). Believing that the title of *wang* (king) no longer did justice to his unprecedented achievements, he decided to create a new title, *huangdi*. *Huangdi* combined the word *huang* from the Three *Huang* and the word *di* from the Five *Di*. Being the first *huangdi*, King Zheng adopted the name, *Shihuangdi* (the First Emperor). He then decreed that his successor would be referred to as *Er Shihuangdi* (the Second Emperor), the successor of his successor as *San Shihuangdi* (the Third Emperor), and so on, for "ten thousand generations."

After the unification of China, questions arose as how to govern a country of such immense size.

At an imperial audience, Chief Counselor Wang Wan said to Qin

Shihuang, "Now that the conquest of these sovereign states has been so recently accomplished, it is essential that fiefs be created and princes be named to them, especially for states geographically distant from the imperial capital, Xianyang, such as the states of Yan, Chu and Qi. I urge Your Majesty to appoint your sons to rule those fiefs."

Qin Shihuang then asked his other ministers for comments on this suggestion, and many agreed. Li Si was the lone voice of dissent. He argued, "When King Wu of Zhou founded his dynasty, he created feudal lords, who soon became bitter enemies vowing each other's destruction. Not even the king of Zhou could dissuade them from this path of mutual ruin. Clearly creating fiefs is a bad idea. A better approach would be to create a nation-wide system of prefectures and counties."

This idea was music to Qin Shihuang's ears. He abolished the old feudal system in favor of this new administrative structure, dividing the empire into 36 prefectures, each subdivided into a number of counties. The governors of the prefectures were directly appointed by the imperial court. All decisions, big and small, pertaining to the administration of the state, were made by the emperor. In those days, petitions and reports were written on long pieces of bamboo. It is said that Qin Shihuang read through 120 *jin* (1 *jin* equals 1/2 kilogram) worth of these a day, and would not rest until he had finished reading all of them. This is an indication to the degree authority was concentrated in his hands.

Before Qin Shihuang unified China, each sovereign state had its own distinct system of standardization, without any thought to harmonizing its standards with another state. Thus, local vehicles varied in size depending upon the state, and the roads in each state were built to suit the width of their vehicles. With the country unified, the disparate widths of roads became a hindrance to vehicular traffic. It was henceforth decreed that for vehicles the distance between the wheels on an axle had to be uniformly exactly six *chi* (1 *chi* equals 1/3 meter). This new institution of vehicular-gauge standardization proved to be a great boon to transportation across the country.

Before unification, linguistic chaos prevailed, often with a confusing array of variations of written forms for the same word. Qin Shihuang's government adopted a standardized form of written language, and an easy-to-use system of handwriting. This new institution of written-language standardization was instrumental in promoting cultural exchange throughout the nation.

The boom in business that came with improved communication and transportation was held back by a lack of common weights and measures. Therefore, to facilitate trade and commercial exchanges, the Qin government standardized these.

As Qin Shihuang busied himself in domestic reforms, an invasion of the Xiongnu (known as the Huns in the West) surprised the country. The Xiongnu was a nomadic tribe that traditionally lived in the north. In the waning years of the Warring States Period, the Xiongnu nobility had taken advantage of the decline of the states of Yan and Zhao. They steadily pushed southward and finally grabbed vast areas in the Hetao Region (the Great Bend of the Yellow River). After unifying China, Qin Shihuang dispatched General Meng Tian at the head of a 300,000-strong army to fight off the invading Xiongnu. This army recovered the lost territory in Hetao, and Qin subsequently established 44 counties there.

In order to ward off future invasions by the Xiongnu, Qin Shihuang conscripted civilians to begin a construction project linking the walls previously built by each of the states of Yan, Zhao and Qin as part of their northern defenses. As part of the project, long segments of new walls were constructed, constituting a defensive Great Wall that extended 10,000 *li*. The Wall stretched from Lintao in the west (modern-day Min County, Gansu Province) to Liaodong in the east (northwest of modern-day Liaoyang, Liaoning Province). This world-renowned structure from antiquity has since become the symbol of the ancient civilization of China.

Qin Shihuang then went on to pacify the south of China by sending an expeditionary force of 500,000 men. He established three prefectures there. The following year, after the Xiongnu had been finally defeated by General Meng Tian, another prefecture was added to the map of Qin, which now comprised a total of 40 prefectures.

In 213 BC, a banquet was held in the imperial palace in Xianyang in celebration of Qin Shihuang's brilliant accomplishment of expanding Qin's territory. As minister after minister lavished praise on Qin Shihuang for his feat of unifying China, the erudite Chun Yuyue sounded a discordant note when he reiterated his opposition to the abolition of the giving of fiefs, arguing that any departure from the rules handed down from antiquity would be doomed to failure.

Qin Shihuang wanted to hear the view of Li Si, who had by now been appointed Chief Counselor.

Li Si said, "Now that stability has returned to the country, laws and decrees need to have a unified source. There are some intellectuals who would like to imitate antiquity instead of grappling with the present. They make ill-considered, irresponsible comments about the affairs of state, causing confusion among the public. Such a state of affairs, if allowed to go on unchecked, would undercut the authority of the imperial court."

Acting on Li Si's recommendations, Qin Shihuang immediately decreed, "With the exception of books on medicine and tree planting, all privately-held books of song and verse, ancient texts, classics, and writings representing the views of various schools of thought must be surrendered to be burned. The discussion of these books by anyone is punishable by death. Anyone who criticizes present policies by invoking the practices of antiquity will see his entire clan exterminated."

The following year, Qin Shihuang learned that two men, Lu Sheng and Hou Sheng, had been privately criticizing him. These men were alchemists who defrauded people by selling elixirs and invoking spirits. When Qin Shihuang sent agents to arrest these men, they slipped away.

This mightily annoyed Qin Shihuang. He ordered investigations which revealed that some Confucian scholars in Xianyang had also been making unflattering remarks about him. These scholars were then rounded up. Under interrogation and torture, they implicated many more people. Qin Shihuang then ordered that the more than 460 Confucian scholars accused of the most serious transgressions be buried alive. The rest were exiled to remote locations on the frontiers. This is the historically famous or infamous *fen shu keng ru* (burning-of-books-and-burying-of-Confucian-scholars) incident.

No high official dared try calming Qin Shihuang down in the heat of his anger. Finding the treatment of the Confucian scholars too harsh, Qin Shihuang's eldest son Fu Su tried to dissuade him from following it through. This advice incurred the wrath of Qin Shihuang, who ordered Fu Su off to the northern frontiers to share garrison duties with General Meng Tian.

32. Intrigues at Shaqiu

QIN SHIHUANG WAS well aware that following his conquest of the six sovereign states, an ever-present threat was that the former nobility of those states might rebel. To keep better watch over them, he ordered the relocation of the empire's 120,000 wealthiest families to Xianyang. He had all civilian weapons collected up. Those weapons not redistributed to his troops were melted down to make 12 giant bronze statues each weighing 240,000 *jin*. A number of grand bells were also made from them. After all the weapons were gathered up, Qin Shihuang believed that no one would make new weapons.

He undertook frequent inspection tours to different parts of the empire. These tours were intended to offer sacrifices to the spirits of the famous mountains and rivers, and to commission the carving of glowing tributes to himself on mountain boulders in order to remind posterity of his accomplishments. Additionally, these tours were intended as a show of force, a muscle-flexing to instill fear in the hearts of the deposed nobility of the six conquered states.

In 210 BC, Qin Shihuang's tours took him to southeast China. He was accompanied by Chief Counselor Li Si and Zhao Gao, a eunuch from his court. Hu Hai, a favored younger son, asked to tag along, and Qin Shihuang readily agreed.

The trip took him across the Qiantang River into Guiji Prefecture and then north to Langya (modern-day Jiaonan County, Shandong Province). Starting the trip in the winter, by summer he began his return to the capital. On his journey home, he fell ill at Pingyuan Ferry (south of modern-day Pingyuan County, Shandong

Province). Despite his accompanying physician's treatment and care, there was no sign of improvement.

By the time the party reached Shaqiu (west of modern-day Guangzong County, Hebei Province), his health had deteriorated. Sensing the approach of death, Qin Shihuang instructed Zhao Gao, "Write Fu Su without delay and tell him to immediately return to Xianyang. In case I do not recover, put him in charge of the funeral arrangements."

Before there was time to send the letter, Qin Shihuang passed away.

Zhao Gao was Hu Hai's confidant and had a running feud with the Meng Tian clan. He secretly consulted Hu Hai on the idea of falsifying Qin Shihuang's last will to have Fu Su put to death, thus assuring Hu Hai's ascension to the throne. As Hu Hai had been waiting all of his life just for such an opportunity, he immediately agreed.

Knowing that such an undertaking must have the approval of Li Si, Zhao Gao went to him and said, "The emperor's last will and the imperial seal are in Hu Hai's possession. Succession to the throne now hinges on the two of us. What's your thought on the matter? "

"What treasonous words! It does not behoove us servants to discuss such matters," Li Si replied in shocked disapproval.

Zhao Gao answered, "Hold on! Let me ask you this: Do you think you are more capable or have more accomplishments under your belt than Meng Tian? Do you enjoy closer ties with Fu Su than Meng Tian does? "

Li Si thought for a moment. "No, I can't compete," he replied.

Zhao Gao responded, "If Fu Su became emperor, he will definitely appoint Meng Tian as Chief Counselor. You would then have no choice but to retire to your hometown. Nothing can be more obvious. Prince Hu Hai is kind-hearted and good-natured. If he becomes emperor, you and I will be taken care of for the rest of our lives. Think about it!"

Frightened by the prospect of losing his position as Chief Counselor, with Zhao Gao's cajoling Li Si conspired with Hu Hai to forge an imperial edict under Qin Shihuang's seal. The edict accused Fu Su of giving a poor performance on his frontier duty, and of nursing a grudge against his father, the emperor. The edict went on to charge General Meng Tian and Fu Su with conspiracy. It demanded that they should cede command to the Vice-General Wang Li and commit suicide.

After he read the forged edict, Fu Su wept. He was ready to obey the order and commit suicide. However, Meng Tian suspected that the edict was forged, and urged Fu Su to appeal before Qin Shihuang. Fu Su, a simple, honest person, replied, "How can I appeal, given the fact that it is my father the emperor who desires my death?" With that remark he killed himself.

Hu Hai then ascended the throne by virtue of the "last will of Qin Shihuang," a forgery made by Zhao Gao and Li Si. He assumed the title of Qin Er Shi (literally, the Second Emperor of Qin).

After the burial of Qin Shihuang, Qin Er Shi and Zhao Gao, like all criminals, were haunted by a perpetual fear that their crime might be discovered. To keep the circumstances surrounding their usurpation of the throne secret, at Zhao Gao's urging Hu Hai ordered the death of his siblings, twelve princes and ten princesses in all, and a large number of government ministers. A year later, Zhao Gao tricked Er Shi into arresting and killing their co-conspirator, Li Si. With Li Si out of the way, Zhao Gao took his place as Chief Counselor and wielded undisputed power.

33. The Rebellion of Chen Sheng and Wu Guang

IN ORDER TO check the advances of the Xiongnu, Qin Shihuang had built the Great Wall, fielded a 300,000-strong army, and conscripted hundreds of thousands of laborers. During the reign of Qin Er Shi, an additional 300,000 troops and civilian laborers were mobilized to develop south China, 700,000 prisoners were employed in the construction of the huge, sumptuous Grand Palace at Epang, and hundreds of thousands of convict and civilian laborers were conscripted for the construction of the grand Mausoleum for Qin Shihuang.

The Mausoleum was impressively large both above and below ground. Its foundation, poured of molten copper, was surmounted by stone sepulchers, chambers, passageways and crypts. In the main burial chamber, Qin Er Shi had his craftsmen create a life-like landscape with rivers, lakes and oceans that used mercury to simulate water.

After Qin Shihuang was laid to rest in his tomb, booby-traps were installed to kill and deter would-be grave robbers. Finally, all the craftsmen involved in the construction of the tomb were ruthlessly buried alive in the underground passages. Not one was spared.

The construction of the Grand Palace at Epang was already embarked upon by Qin Er Shi and Zhao Gao even before the completion of the Mausoleum. In a country with a population of only 20 million, a total of 2 to 3 million people had at one time or another been conscripted to work on construction projects such as the Great Wall, the Grand Palace at Epang, and the Mausoleum, to garrison the southern border regions, and to engage in other projects of forced labor. Such an extravagant expenditure of human and financial resources led to universal discontent.

In 209 BC, local officials in Yangcheng (southeast of modern-day Dengfeng, Henan Province) sent two military officers supervising 900 civilian conscripts to garrison duty in Yuyang (southwest of modern-day Miyun in Beijing). The two officers picked two strong, capable men from the group as overseers. One of them was Chen Sheng, who had been a hired farmhand in Yangcheng. The other was Wu Guang, a poor peasant from Yangxia (modern-day Taikang County, Henan Province).

Chen Sheng had shown himself to be ambitious even at a young age. As he labored alongside other farmhands for their landlord, he often bemoaned the squandering of his youthful energy in this perennial slavish toil, and vowed to accomplish great things one day.

On one occasion, he exclaimed to his co-workers as they took a break by the field, "If any of us prospers in the future, he must not forget the rest of the gang!"

The others ridiculed the idea by saying, "What prosperity could a hired hand expect?"

Heaving a sigh, Chen Sheng muttered to himself, "How can a sparrow be expected to understand the aspirations of a swan?"

Chen Sheng and Wu Guang were strangers before they joined the gang of conscripts, but their common fate soon made them fast friends. Since the gang of conscripts was under a tight deadline to get to Yuyang, the group rushed north for days on end, frightened by the dire consequences of failure.

As the group reached the village of Daze (southeast of modern-day Suzhou, Anhui Province), its advance was blocked by flooding due to days of pouring rain. The conscripts had no choice but to pitch tents and wait for the weather to clear up enough for them to resume their march.

Under draconian Qin laws, the failure of the conscripts to reach their destination on time meant certain death. When the rain showed no sign of letting up, the conscripts became agitated like so many ants on a hot frying pan, not knowing what to do.

Chen Sheng pulled Wu Guang aside and said to him, "We are still thousands of *li* from Yuyang. Are we going to let ourselves be killed?"

"No way!" Wu Guang replied. "Let's escape!"

Chen Sheng answered him, "It is death for us if we are caught deserting. We will also die if we rebel and fail. Since we are going to die in either case, I find rebellion more appealing than handing ourselves over to the executioner. People have suffered enough under Qin. Qin Er Shi is a younger son and had no claim to the throne in the first place. There is a lot of sympathy for Fu Su. By all rights, he should have become emperor. Now, the valor and military exploits of General Xiang Yan of the state of Chu are widely recognized. It's not clear whether or not he's still alive, but if we revolt in the name of Fu Su and Xiang Yan, I'm sure the people of Chu will rally to our cause."

Chen Sheng's idea met with the enthusiastic approval of Wu Guang. In order to lend added credence to their cause, they came up with several ploys to fully capitalize on the superstitious beliefs prevalent at the time. They wrote "Chen Sheng is King" in vermilion on a white piece of silk, and stuffed it into the belly of a fish being sold by a fishmonger. The fish was bought by some soldiers in their unit. These soldiers were flabbergasted when they were cleaning the fish for cooking and found this handwritten message inside it.

Late one night, Wu Guang snuck into a dilapidated temple near their campsite and lit a bonfire. Mimicking the barking of a fox, he started shouting, "Great Chu is rising, and Chen Sheng is King!" All of the soldiers in the camp were filled with wonder and terror when they heard the cries.

The next day, because of these eerie happenings, the sight of Chen Sheng inspired much pointing and whispering among the soldiers. Aided by his kindly nature, Chen Sheng rose in esteem among his comrades.

One day, finding the two officers in an inebriated state, Wu Guang said in a taunting voice, "We are going to miss the deadline anyway. Why don't you just dismiss us and let us go home?" The officers were predictably provoked. One of them hit Wu Guang with his officer's staff, and then threatened him with his sword. Wu Guang wrested the sword from the officer and killed him with it. At that moment, Chen Sheng rushed up and killed the other officer.

Chen Sheng then called the soldiers together and said to them, "We men must not die in vain. We must die for a cause. Are kings and noblemen preordained?"

The men cried out in unison, "Well said! We are at your command!"

Chen Sheng had the soldiers build a command platform and make a battle flag displaying the word "Chu." The men vowed before the gods to fight together and overthrow the Qin dynasty, pledging allegiance to Chen Sheng and Wu Guang. The 900 men handily took over the village of Daze. When peasants in neighboring villages heard of the uprising, they came bearing food for the insurgents. Many young men with hoes and pickaxes on their shoulders came to the camp to enlist. Since the growing army of insurgents had insufficient weapons and flags to go around, they jury-rigged weapons using sharpened wooden rods, and made flagpoles by splitting bamboo stems. Thus was born the first contingent of peasant rebels in Chinese history. This event is historically known as *jie gan er qi* (literally, "uprising with raised sticks").

Following the fall of Chen County (modern-day Huaiyang, Henan Province) to the insurgents, Chen Sheng had a meeting with the residents, who said to him, "You are rising up against the tyrannical Qin in order to redress the grievances of the people across the nation. For a great undertaking like this, you deserve to be king."

Chen Sheng was thus declared King of Chu, and the name of his kingdom was called Zhang Chu.

34. Liu Bang and Xiang Yu

THE PEASANT REBELLION started by Chen Sheng and Wu Guang inspired the killings of officials elsewhere. Soon the tide of peasant uprisings engulfed nearly half of China.

With the help of reinforcements sent by Chen Sheng and Wu Guang, insurgents in various localities began to win victory after victory and to expand the areas under rebel control. However, with the rebel forces spread too thin and the line of command ill-defined and fragmented, the control over some areas reverted to the deposed nobility of the six conquered states. Within barely three months of the start of the rebellion, the states of Zhao, Qi, Yan and Wei all had self-proclaimed kings setting out to restore the old kingdoms.

A rebel army dispatched by Chen Sheng went on a westward offensive under the command of Zhou Wen. It moved into Guanzhong (west of Hangu Pass) like a hot knife through butter, posing a direct threat to Xianyang, the imperial capital of Qin. Thrown into a panic, Qin Er Shi posthaste sent his general Zhang Han to Lishan, where the convicts and slaves on hard labor were relieved from their work and conscripted into a fighting force to be pitched against the insurgents. However, the deposed nobility of the six conquered states refused to venture beyond the borders of their states to lend a hand to Zhou Wen. Zhou Wen's army, left to fend for itself, finally crumbled. Wu Guang was then killed by his own subordinates in Xingyang. Six months into the uprising, Chen Sheng died at the hands of traitors as his troops were in retreat.

Despite the deaths of Chen Sheng and Wu Guang, the fire sparked by their uprising against the Qin dynasty continued to spread to all parts of the empire. Guiji Prefecture (in modern-day Suzhou, Jiangsu Province) saw one of the more intense manifestations of this anti-Qin passion.

In Guiji, the armed rebellion was led by Xiang Liang and his nephew Xiang Yu. Xiang Liang was none other than the son of Xiang Yan, the famous general of the former state of Chu. Xiang Yan had committed suicide in the aftermath of an attack by the Qin General Wang Jian because he could not countenance the shame of Chu's destruction as a state. Afterwards, Xiang Liang had always harbored the thought of one day restoring the state of Chu. His nephew Xiang Yu was well-endowed both mentally and physically. However, when Xiang Liang had tried to teach Xiang Yu how to read, Xiang Yu's reading lessons lasted only a few days because of his lack of enthusiasm. Then, when Xiang Liang tried to teach him the art of the sword, Xiang Yu soon gave up on that, too.

Reacting to Xiang Liang's anger, Xiang Yu said dismissively, "What's the use of learning to read? It helps you remember how to write your own name. That's it. And so what if you master the art of the sword! It enables you to thrust and parry with a few opponents. No big deal! What I want to learn is how to fight a grand war."

Impressed by his nephew's lofty ambition, Xiang Liang brought out heirloom books that had been handed down from generation to generation about the art of war. Xiang Yu was quick on the uptake when his uncle explained the books to him, but refused to delve any deeper as soon as he had had a general grasp of the ideas in the books.

Xiang Liang had originally been from Xiaxiang (southwest of modern-day Suqian, Jiangsu Province) before he got into trouble with somebody there and was forced to flee to Guiji. Many young people in his adopted city were much impressed by his scholarly and martial accomplishments and treated him with deference, looking to him as a teacher.

Soon after learning of Chen Sheng's rebellion, Xiang Liang and Xiang Yu realized their opportunity had come, so they killed the governor of Guiji and took over the prefecture. In a few days, they had rallied 8,000 men to their cause. Since most of the members of the rebel force were local youths, it got the name of Zi Di Bing, or "the Young Folk's Army."

They led this 8,000-strong army across the Huai River and soon took over the Guangling Prefecture (in modern-day Yangzhou, Jiangsu Province). As the troops led by Xiang Liang crossed the river and continued their march, more people joined in.

The following year, a man named Liu Bang at the head of a group of more than a hundred combatants attached himself to Xiang Liang's army.

Liu Bang was originally from Pei County (in Jiangsu Province), and had previously been the head of a *ting* (a *ting* was an administrative division about ten *li*, or about five kilometers, in length). He was ordered one day by his superior to take a group of conscripted laborers to Lishan to do hard labor. Each day on their forced march, several laborers would run away, and there was nothing Liu Bang could do to stanch the loss. He realized that he would have a hard time accounting for the reduced size of his work force once he arrived in Lishan.

One day during a rest break, he said to the laborers sitting around him on the ground, "When you reach Lishan, what awaits you is either death by exhaustion or death by beating. Even if you escape death, there's no telling when you'll be allowed to go home. I'm going to free you now to find a living for yourselves."

The grateful laborers were moved to tears by this act of generosity. They asked him, "What's going to happen to you, sir?"

"I can't go back now, so I'll be on the run," Liu Bang replied.

A dozen laborers then decided to stick with him and somehow find a way to survive by pooling their wits.

Liu Bang and his followers fled into the Mangdang Mountains. Within just a few days over a hundred men joined them there.

Xiao He, a secretary in the Pei County government, and Cao Shen, a prison warden, knew Liu Bang to be a trustworthy person. Because of their sympathy for him, they maintained secret contact with him and his group.

When Chen Sheng's insurgents captured Chen County, Xiao He

and the residents of Pei County killed their own county magistrate and invited Liu Bang to come out of the Mangdang Mountains to be their new chief. Liu Bang thus came to be known as the Duke of Pei.

After Liu Bang launched his uprising in Pei County, he mustered a couple of thousands of men and had them capture his home village, Fengxiang. However, as he led a contingent of soldiers in a campaign to seize other county towns, the subordinates who had stayed behind in Fengxiang surprised him with their own little rebellion. When Liu Bang got wind of the betrayal, he wanted to turn back and march on Fengxiang but, finding himself in need of more soldiers for the attack, had to turn to other sources for support.

When he reached Liucheng (southeast of Pei County, Jiangsu Province), he encountered Zhang Liang, a very capable soldier well-versed in the art of war. Zhang had intended to join other insurgents with his hundred followers. When he met Liu Bang, the two immediately hit it off. They both reckoned that Xiang Liang's army was the largest of all the nearby insurgent groups, so they decided to cast in their lot with him.

Xiang Liang saw much promise in Liu Bang and willingly lent him the requisite troops to take back Fengxiang. Liu Bang and Zhang Liang thus came to serve under Xiang Liang.

Following the deaths of Chen Sheng and Wu Guang, the main protagonists of the rebellion, the control over the insurgencies across the country fell into the hands of the deposed nobility of the six former states. Their turf wars eventually led to a splintering of the movement. This gave the Qin generals Zhang Han and Li You an opening to divide and conquer the insurgent groups.

At this crucial juncture, Xiang Liang convoked a meeting at Xuecheng in an effort to reunite and reinvigorate the insurgency. Realizing that he needed to broaden the appeal of the rebellion, Xiang Liang followed a suggestion of his adviser Fan Zeng and got hold of Xin, a grandson of King Huai of Chu. Xin was now a mere commoner, but Xiang Liang proclaimed him King of Chu. As the heir to the throne of King Huai, Xin took the same name.

35. Xiang Yu Orders His Army to Smash All its Stoves and Sink All its Boats

AFTER REFORMING HIS army, Xiang Liang won a string of victories against the Qin general Zhang Han. An army under Xiang Yu and Liu Bang also killed the Qin general Li You. These successes caused Xiang Liang to become arrogant and to lower his guard against the Qin army, which he dismissed as of no account. In the meantime General Zhang Han regrouped and replenished his troops. He launched a fierce counterattack that caught Xiang Liang off guard, killing him in battle. Xiang Yu and Liu Bang had to beat a retreat to Pengcheng.

After defeating Xiang Liang, General Zhang Han reckoned that he had dealt a heavy blow to the Chu forces, seriously sapping its strength. He therefore decided to shift his attention away from the south bank of the Yellow River, and lead his army northward to attack the state of Zhao. This was not the same state of Zhao of the Warring States Period, but a recently established regime. He quickly captured the Zhao capital, Handan, and forced its leader, King Xie, to flee to Julu (southwest of modern-day Pingxiang, Hebei Province).

Zhang Han ordered General Wang Li to lay siege to Julu. He himself bivouacked with the main force in Jiyuan, situated to the south of Julu. He had a road built between Jiyuan and Julu expressly for the purpose of transporting food and supplies to the troops led by Wang Li.

King Xie of Zhao made repeated appeals to King Huai of Chu for relief and rescue. At the time, King Huai of Chu had already been contemplating a march to the west to attack the Qin capital of Xianyang. Eager to avenge his uncle's death, Xiang Yu volunteered to lead an invading force against Xianyang.

Some veteran ministers close to King Huai of Chu said to him in private, "Xiang Yu has a foul temper and has killed too many people. Liu Bang on the other hand is a decent man. It would be better to send him on the mission." Zhao's appeal for help gave King Huai an added reason to act on his plans. He decided to send Liu Bang on the expedition against Xianyang, and to dispatch Song Yi as Commander and Xiang Yu as Vice-Commander, at the head of an army of 200,000 soldiers, to lift the siege of Zhao at Julu.

When Song Yi arrived with his troops at Anyang (southeast of modern-day Anyang, Henan Province), he received intelligence that the Qin forces were quite large and powerful. He ordered pause in his army's advance. He hoped that the Qin army would face attrition in their battle with the Zhao army before he had to weigh in with his own troops.

The pause ordered by Song Yi lasted 46 days. Already chomping at the bit, Xiang Yu went to Song Yi and said, "Julu is under siege; the situation is untenable. Let's ford the river and attack the Qin forces! Sandwiched between the Zhao army in the city and our troops, the Qin forces will surely be defeated."

Song Yi replied, "Let's wait until a decisive battle has been fought between the Qin and the Zhao forces!" He then added, "I'm no match for you in battle, but you are no match for me when it comes to devising strategies and tactics."

Song Yi then pointedly issued a decree that any soldier or officer disobeying his orders would be decapitated according to military law.

Xiang Yu was deeply angered by this decree plainly directed against him. It was November, and the weather was already very cold in the northern country. Pouring rains did not help matters. With food and supplies dwindling, the cold and hungry soldiers started to grumble.

Xiang Yu said, "The soldiers do not have enough to eat, but the General chooses to wait. He gets to drink and make merry. What does he care about the country or the soldiers! What kind of a general is he?"

The next day during morning muster, Xiang Yu drew his sword and killed Commander Song Yi. With Song Yi's head dangling from his hand, Xiang Yu said to the troops, "Song Yi betrayed the king (meaning King Huai of Chu). I executed him on orders of the king."

Most of the soldiers and officers had previously served under Xiang Liang, and Song Yi had never enjoyed much authority in the military anyways. Now with Song Yi dead, the troops pledged their allegiance to Xiang Yu.

Xiang Yu sent a messenger to King Huai of Chu reporting the execution of Song Yi. Despite his unhappiness with this turn of events, the king had no choice but to name Xiang Yu Commander.

After killing Song Yi, Xiang Yu sent a vanguard unit of 20,000 men led by Generals Ying Bu and Pu across the Zhang River. In doing so, the Qin supply route was cut and the troops of Zhang Han were isolated from those led by Wang Li. With that accomplished, Xiang Yu forded the river with the main force.

Once on the other bank of the river, Xiang Yu gave the order that each combatant was to carry only three days' worth of rations. He had all army cooking stoves smashed, and all of their boats sunk. This is the origin of the famous Chinese saying, *po fu chen zhou* (literally, "smash the stoves and sink the boats"), meaning "cross the Rubicon." He said to the troops, "With this action, there's no turning back. The only way is forward. We have to defeat the Qin army in three days."

The courage and determination of Xiang Yu proved a great inspiration for the troops, and the morale of the Chu troops surrounding the forces of Wang Li soared. With each battle, the Chu army improved, until finally each Chu soldier became as good as ten Qin soldiers. After nine rounds of fierce fighting, Wang Li was captured alive. The other Qin officers all either died in combat or fled. The Qin army that laid siege to Julu was thus routed.

There were at the time a dozen contingents of soldiers supposedly on a mission to rescue Zhao. However, intimidated by the powerful Qin army, most of these contingents of soldiers decided to pitch tent and avoid engagement. When these soldiers heard the deafening battle cries of the Chu forces, they climbed to high vantage points to have a look. The sight of the Chu soldiers bravely storming into the Qin camp left them gaping and breathless. Afterwards, when they were invited by the nemesis of the Qin army Xiang Yu to see him in his camp, these soldiers crawled in on their knees, not daring even to raise their eyes to look at him. There was universal praise for Xiang Yu: "The generalissimo's might is unprecedented. We are at your command."

From that moment on, Xiang Yu became the supreme leader of all the anti-Qin forces.

HAN DYNASTY (206 BC–220 AD)

WESTERN HAN DYNASTY (206 BC–25 AD)

36. Liu Bang's Contract with the People

ALTHOUGH THE QIN army laying siege to Julu was routed, a large force of some 20,000 men under the command of the Qin general Zhang Han was stationed not far away in Jiyuan. He appealed to the imperial court for reinforcements. However, instead of sending relief, Qin Er Shi and Zhao Gao decided to discredit Zhang Han. Fearing that Zhao Gao was out to get him, General Zhang Han had no alternative but to surrender to Xiang Yu with his troops. When news of Zhang Han's surrender reached Xianyang, chaos broke out within the Qin regime.

At the time, all power was concentrated in the hands of Zhao Gao. After causing the death of Li Si, Zhao knew that there was animosity toward him among the ministers.

One day, Zhao Gao had brought a deer to the imperial court and declared publicly to Qin Er Shi, "I've acquired a rare, purebred horse, and I am now presenting it to Your Majesty."

Notwithstanding his muddle-headedness, Qin Er Shi was capable of distinguishing a deer from a horse. He said with a laugh, "My Chief Counselor, stop pulling my leg! This is patently a deer. How can you claim it's a horse?"

Zhao Gao gave this deadpan reply, "How can you say it's not a horse? What do your ministers think?"

Er Shi turned to his ministers for their opinion. Many were on to Zhao Gao's trick and humored him by saying, "It is indeed an excellent horse!"

Some were afraid of Zhao Gao and kept their silence. Only a handful answered that it was a deer. After a few days, the few high officials who said it was a deer were arrested on various charges trumped up by Zhao Gao.

Since then, the senior and junior officials inside and outside the imperial court were even more terrified of Zhao Gao. No one dared again voice any criticism of Zhao Gao in front of the emperor.

In 206 BC, Wuguan Pass (southeast of modern-day Danfeng County, Shaanxi Province) fell to Liu Bang's troops, which were now threatening Xianyang, the capital of Qin. This struck terror into the heart of the emperor of Qin, who immediately ordered Zhao Gao to dispatch troops to head off the attack. Knowing that he would not survive such a battle, Zhao Gao sent a trusted henchman to get rid of Qin Er Shi.

After having the emperor killed, Zhao Gao said to the ministers, "Now that the six states have been restored, Qin can no longer rightfully claim the spurious title of emperor, but should revert to the previous title of king. In my estimation, Ziying, the nephew of Er Shi is fit to be proclaimed king." Not daring to contradict Zhao Gao, the ministers nodded their heads in consent.

Ziying knew that Zhao Gao had killed Qin Er Shi with a view to becoming king himself. Only the fear of opposition from the Qin ministers and the lords of other states had checked Zhao's ambitions, reluctantly leading him to make Ziying king. Ziying feigned illness on the day of his enthronement, and stayed away from the ceremony. This was in accordance with plans he had made beforehand with his two sons. When Zhao Gao personally went to Ziying to urge him to attend the ceremony, Ziying had Zhao Gao killed.

After Zhao Gao was dead, Ziying dispatched 50,000 troops to defend Yaoguan Pass (northwest of modern-day Shang County, Shaanxi Province). When the Qin army approached, Liu Bang used a ruse suggested by Zhang Liang. They planted innumerable flags and standards on the peaks surrounding Yaoguan Pass to simulate the presence of large numbers of troops. He then sent his general Zhou Bo with all his troops on a circuitous route around the front entrance of the Pass, and attacked the Qin army's southeastern flank. The defending commander was killed in action, and the Qin troops were decimated.

As Liu Bang's troops passed through Yaoguan Pass and reached Bashang (east of modern-day Xi'an, Shaanxi Province), King Ziying of Qin greeted him and surrendered with all his high officials. He stood in a bowed posture by the wayside, with a ribbon wrapped about his neck in token of shame. The imperial seal of jade, the scepter, and the Commander-in-Chief's tally were in his outstretched hands.

Liu Bang's generals urged him to kill Ziying, but Liu Bang said, "King Huai of Chu entrusted me with this mission of taking Xianyang precisely in the belief that I have a generous disposition. Moreover it is bad form to kill someone who has surrendered."

He accepted the imperial seal from Ziying's hands and remanded him to the custody of his troops.

The mighty dynasty founded by Qin Shihuang was thus extinguished after a mere fifteen years of existence in a groundswell of a peasant rebellion.

After Liu Bang entered Xianyang, his troops went on a wild, noisy rampage through the palace storehouses, stripping them of valuables. Xiao He alone was uninterested in the treasures. He went instead to the official residence of the Chief Counselor and collected all the public records, maps and other archives, which he ordered to be put in secure storage.

Escorted by his troops, Liu Bang came to the luxurious Grand Palace of Epang, where he was struck by the sight of its sumptuous appointments, draperies, hangings, canopies and other dazzling furnishings, as well as the bevies of beautiful court ladies. He was so bewitched by all that beauty and posh that he was loath to leave the palace.

His reverie was interrupted when his subordinate Fan Kuai burst into the room and exclaimed, "My esteemed Duke of Pei! Are you interested in taking power or amassing wealth? All this luxury proved to be the undoing of the Qin dynasty. How can you still be attracted to it? Please come back quickly to the camp!"

Liu Bang ignored his pleadings, saying "Let me have some rest!"

When Zhang Liang came into the room and overheard Fan Kuai's pleas, he said to Liu Bang, "Remember the popular saying: 'Good advice offends one's ears but helps guide one's action; Effective medicine tastes bitter but helps cure the disease.' Fan Kuai has made a valid point. Hopefully you'll heed his advice."

Liu Bang, who had always had full trust in Zhang Liang, was sobered by these words. After ordering his troops to seal the storehouses, he led them back to their camp in Bashang.

Liu Bang subsequently called together the peasants from nearby counties and said to them, "You've suffered enough under draconian Qin rule. I am going to lay down only three laws: First, he who kills pays with his life; second, he who commits assault and battery causing injury to others will be prosecuted and punished; third, he who steals will be prosecuted and punished. All other laws, regulations and prohibitions of Qin, with these three exceptions, are abolished forthwith. The public can go home and go about their daily life and business without fear."

Liu Bang asked the people and Qin officials from other counties to publicize these three laws.

When the people learned of the three laws of Liu Bang, there was widespread rejoicing. Spontaneously, the public offered beef, mutton, wine and food to Liu Bang's troops. However, Liu Bang patiently explained to them that they should take the offerings back, because, he said, "We have enough food in storage. Don't worry about us anymore."

Liu Bang's troops thus created a favorable impression upon the people in the Guanzhong region, and there was a growing demand for Liu Bang to stay and rule as king.

37. The Banquet at Hongmen

SOON AFTER ACCEPTING the surrender of General Zhang Han, Xiang Yu decided to capitalize on the chaos in Qin to attack its capital Xianyang.

When the army reached Xin'an (in Henan Province), the Qin soldiers that had surrendered began to whisper to each other, "When the attacking Chu army goes into Guanzhong, where our homes are, we will be the ones that suffer. If the Chu attack fails, we will be taken east and our folks back home will be killed by the Qin troops as punishment. What are we to do?"

These private discussions eventually reached the ears of the Chu officers and were reported to Xiang Yu. He began to have doubts about his ability to keep these Qin soldiers under his thumb, and murderous thoughts started to creep into his mind. Overnight, he had all 200,000 Qin soldiers who had surrendered to him, with the exception of Zhang Han and two other generals, buried alive in a mass grave. The ruthlessness of Xiang Yu attained instant notoriety.

When Xiang Yu's army reached Hangu Pass, the troops guarding the pass would not let it through, declaring that "On orders of the Duke of Pei, no armed groups, of whatever provenance, shall be allowed in."

Xiang Yu was so incensed at this affront he ordered his troops to storm the pass. With the disadvantage of having inferior troop strength, Liu Bang's force was unable to stop the advance of Xiang Yu's army. It marched straight to Xinfeng and Hongmen (northeast of modern-day Lintong, Shaanxi Province), where it bivouacked.

One of Liu Bang's generals by the name of Cao Wushang, wanting to switch his loyalty to Xiang Yu, sent a message to the latter via a secret emissary. His message said, "The Duke of Pei has plans to set himself up as king in Guanzhong with his capture of Xianyang."

This information predictably provoked a violent reaction in Xiang Yu. With his eyes glaring fiercely, he launched into a long tirade against this outrage from Liu Bang.

Xiang Yu's adviser Fan Zeng said to him, "Liu Bang has shown himself to be immune to the lure of lucre and beautiful women after occupying Xianyang. This means he has grander designs in mind. If he is not neutralized now, he will spell no end of trouble for us in the future."

This strengthened Xiang Yu's determination to destroy Liu Bang's fighting capability. Xiang Yu's 400,000-strong force was then camped in Hongmen, only forty *li* from Bashang, where Liu Bang had stationed his 100,000 troops. This huge disproportion in troop strength put Liu Bang at a perilous disadvantage.

Xiang Yu's uncle Xiang Bo was an old friend of Zhang Liang's, and owed the latter his life. Troubled by the thought that Zhang Liang would become a collateral casualty once Xiang Yu launched his attack against Liu Bang, at nightfall Xiang Bo jumped on a fast horse and rode posthaste to Bashang to warn Zhang Liang and urge him to run for his life.

Not only did Zhang Liang refuse to abandon Liu Bang, but he conveyed Xiang Bo's information to the latter. Liu Bang then asked Zhang Liang to take him to see Xiang Bo. At the meeting, he took pains to deny any intention of doing Xiang Yu any harm, and asked Xiang Bo to intercede for him with Xiang Yu.

Xiang Bo agreed to this request, and impressed upon Liu Bang the importance of his apologizing in person to Xiang Yu.

Early the next morning, Liu Bang, accompanied by Zhang Liang, Fan Kuai and an entourage of over a hundred people, went to Hongmen to pay a call on Xiang Yu.

Liu Bang said to Xiang Yu, "My esteemed general! You and I are united in our desire to overthrow Qin rule, with you, Sir, fighting north of the river and I south of the river. It was by accident and not by design that I was the first to enter the city of Xianyang. It is indeed a pleasure and an honor to be able to meet my esteemed general here today. I can only regret that there was an unworthy attempt to drive a wedge between us, thus incurring your wrath. How unfortunate, isn't it?"

Liu Bang's deferential tone effectively placated Xiang Yu, who admitted in an unguarded moment, "All this originated with your subordinate, Cao Wushang. If not for him, I would not have acted the way I did."

The same day, Xiang Yu invited Liu Bang to stay and drink with him in his camp. Fan Zeng, Xiang Bo, and Zhang Liang were also asked to be present.

At the banquet, Fan Zeng repeatedly signaled Xiang Yu with his eyes and even raised the jade ring he was wearing to prompt Xiang Yu to kill Liu Bang when the opportunity presented itself. However, Xiang Yu turned a blind eye to his signals.

Realizing that Xiang Yu did not have the heart to kill Liu Bang, Fan Zeng used a pretext to leave the banquet, and sought out Xiang Yu's brother Xiang Zhuang. He said to Xiang Zhuang, "Our lord is too much of a bleeding heart. Why don't you go in and propose toasts, and at the right moment take out Liu Bang?"

Xiang Zhuang went into the banquet. As he proposed a toast, he said, "We need some entertainment to liven up this boring place. Why don't I amuse you with a sword dance?" Thereupon, he drew his sword and started to go through the motions of a sword play. His choreographed steps took him closer and closer to Liu Bang.

Realizing Xiang Zhuang's real intent, Xiang Bo got to his feet, drew his sword and said, "Let me join your dance!" In the thrust-and-parry *pas de deux*, he shielded Liu Bang from the murderous thrusts of Xiang Zhuang.

Sensing the mounting tension, Zhang Liang excused himself and left the banquet to look for Fan Kuai outside. Fan Kuai asked anxiously, "How is it in there?"

Zhang Liang told him, "It's tense and fraught with danger. Xiang Zhuang is performing a sword dance, apparently wanting to kill the Duke of Pei."

Fan Kuai leapt up and declared, "Then we will die together!"

He rushed toward the encampment with his sword in his right hand and his shield in his left. When the guards at the gate tried to stop him, he shoved them to the ground. Flinging open the curtains at the entrance of the main tent, he burst in. His chest heaving, his hair standing on end, and his eyeballs seemingly ready to burst out of their sockets, he glared at Xiang Yu.

Xiang Yu, startled by this intrusion, put his hand on his sword and demanded, "Who's this? What's he doing here?"

Zhang Liang, entering close on Fan Kuai's heels, replied for him, "He is Fan Kuai, the carriage driver of the Duke of Pei."

"What a brave man!" Xiang Yu remarked. He told his guards to offer a cup of wine and a pig's leg to Fan Kuai.

As he downed the drink, Fan Kuai said, his anger still simmering, "It was agreed between King Huai of Chu and his generals that whoever entered Guanzhong first with his troops would be named king there. The Duke of Pei has entered Guanzhong but has not proclaimed himself king. Instead, he ordered the storehouses and official premises sealed, and his troops billeted in Bashang to await the arrival of your troops, my esteemed general! Instead of rewarding his meritorious performance, my general now wants him dead. This smacks of the king of Qin's way of doing things. I am worried for you, my esteemed general."

Rendered speechless, Xiang Yu could only say, "Sit down please!"

Fan Kuai sat down next to Zhang Liang.

After a while Liu Bang got up to relieve himself. Zhang Liang and Fan Kuai followed him out of the tent. Leaving some gifts with Zhang Liang to be given to Xiang Yu in token of farewell, Liu Bang took Fan Kuai with him and hurriedly returned to Bashang by a back way.

After sufficient time had elapsed to aid Liu Bang's departure, Zhang Liang went back in and said to Xiang Yu, "The Duke of Pei isn't one to hold much alcohol. He got drunk and has already gone back. He instructed me to present you these two pieces of white jade. And this pair of jade wine goblets is for Ya Fu (literally, 'second father'; Xiang Yu's reverential term of address for Fan Zeng)."

Xiang Yu accepted the two pieces of white jade and placed them on a chair. Fan Zeng, on the other hand, was furious and flung the jade wine goblets on the ground. He hacked the gift to pieces with his sword, saying with a sigh, "Good ideas are wasted on this hopeless fool! The prize of reigning over China is certain to be taken by Liu Bang. We have nothing to look forward to but to be taken prisoner one day."

The tense banquet with daggers drawn and sabers rattling finally gave way to a temporary lull.

38. Xiao He Chases after Han Xin

AFTER XIANG YU entered Xianyang, he ordered the execution of Ziying, the king of Qin, and some 800 of the Qin nobility. He also ordered the Grand Palace of Epang torched. He renamed King Huai of Chu, titling him Emperor Yi, and divided the former Qin empire into 18 principalities, which he doled out to the deposed nobility of the six former states and to army commanders who had made outstanding contributions in the war. He gave himself the title of *Xi Chu Ba Wang* (Overlord of Western Chu). This is a throwback to the Spring and Autumn Period, when princes served under an overlord. By calling himself overlord, Xiang Yu effectively proclaimed himself as above all other lords and princes. The following year, Xiang Yu decided he had no more use for the nominal Emperor Yi and had him executed.

After being awarded their respective principalities, the new princes set off with their troops for their fiefs. Xiang Yu also returned to Pengcheng (modern-day Xuzhou City, Jiangsu Province), the capital of his fief Western Chu.

Of the eighteen princes, Liu Bang was the one that aroused the deepest misgivings in Xiang Yu. Xiang Yu sent him off to faraway regions of Bashu and Hanzhong with the title of Prince of Han. To contain Liu Bang, Xiang Yu gave territories in the Guanzhong region to Zhang Han and two other Qin generals who had surrendered, with the task of preventing Liu from ever breaking out of his marginalized status.

Although very unhappy with his new fief, given the small size of his army the Prince of Han Liu Bang had no bargaining power with Xiang Yu. He resigned himself to his new post in the capital of his principality, Nanzheng (east of modern-day Hanzhong, Shaanxi Province). Once settled in Nanzheng, the Prince of Han appointed Xiao He his Chief Counselor, and Cao Shen, Fan Kuai, and Zhou Bo as his generals. They were tasked with regrouping and recouping strength in active anticipation of another contest with Xiang Yu for the authority to rule the empire. Liu Bang's soldiers, however, had different priorities: They pined for home. His army suffered a daily hemorrhage of deserters. Liu Bang was so alarmed by the crisis he lost all appetite for food.

Then one day came the bombshell news that his Chief Counselor Xiao He had also deserted. The Prince of Han was thrown into a panic—sickened as though his right or left hand had been severed from him.

Three days later, Xiao He reemerged. The Prince of Han greeted his return with a combination of anger and relief. "Why did you of all people run away?" he demanded.

"Why should I run away?" Xiao He replied. "I was chasing after someone else who had deserted."

The Prince of Han inquired, "Who were you chasing after?"

"Han Xin," Xiao He replied.

Han Xin was a native of Huaiyin. When Xiang Liang's insurgent troops passed through Huaiyin, Han Xin joined up and became a foot soldier in the Chu camp. At Xiang Liang's death, he pledged his allegiance to Xiang Yu. Xiang Yu judged that Han Xin was more than a mere foot soldier in ability, and made him a junior officer.

Han Xin had become disappointed because the numerous ideas he presented to Xiang Yu were all rejected. Therefore, when the Prince of Han Liu Bang arrived in Nanzheng, Han Xin went there to offer his services.

Once in Nanzheng, Han Xin only succeeded in obtaining a minor post from the Prince of Han. On one occasion, Han Xin was arrested for breaking the law. He was on the point of being beheaded when a general under the Prince of Han by the name of Xia Houying passed by and overheard this cry for help, "If the Prince of Han desires the imperial throne, why is he killing off good men?"

Xia Houying sized him up, and found him to be indeed a good man. He ordered Han Xin released and commended him to the Prince of Han, who then assigned Han Xin to an office dealing with food and grain.

In a chance conversation with Han Xin, the Chief Counselor Xiao He found him to be a capable man and came to admire his qualities. However, his repeated recommendations that Han Xin be elevated to a position of trust fell on deaf ears.

Realizing the Prince of Han's reluctance to give him any important responsibilities, Han Xin joined the exodus of army deserters.

Xiao He was desperate when he learned of Han Xin's departure. He immediately jumped on a fast horse to pursue him. It took two days to get Han Xin to come back with him.

When the Prince of Han learned that it was Han Xin that Xiao He had ridden after, he angrily reproached him, "A dozen generals have run away and you haven't gone after any of them. Why did you chase after Han Xin?"

Xiao He replied, "You can always find generals, but a man of Han Xin's qualities is a rare gem. If you are content with spending the rest of your life in Hanzhong, then you don't need Han Xin. But, if you're interested in ruling the empire, he is indispensable. What is it to be, my Prince?"

The Prince of Han answered, "Of course I want to go back east. How can I fritter away my life here?"

"If Your Highness has made up your mind about ruling over China, then you should entrust Han Xin with major responsibilities. Otherwise, he will leave sooner or later," Xiao He declared.

"All right, I'll do as you say and make him a general," the Prince replied.

"That will not stop him from leaving," Xiao He answered.

"Then I'll appoint him Commander-in-Chief," the Prince responded.

Xiao He exclaimed with satisfaction, "A very wise decision, Your Highness!"

The Prince of Han told Xiao He to bring Han Xin before him so that he could make the appointment then and there. Xiao He replied bluntly, "Niceties of etiquette have never been a forte of Your Highness. The appointment of a Commander-in-Chief is a serious matter, not a children's game. You just can't call him in like that. If Your Highness has decided to name him Commander-in-Chief, then a propitious day should be selected, and a solemn ceremony should be scheduled to confer the title."

"All right, whatever you say," the Prince replied.

Word soon began to spread among the rank and file that the Prince of Han was going to appoint a Commander-in-Chief on a certain auspicious day. Generals who had served many years under the Prince of Han were having sleepless nights in joyous anticipation of being named to this position.

When that day finally came, everyone was stunned to learn that the new Commander-in-Chief was to be Han Xin, who had long been held in contempt by them.

Following the conclusion of the ceremony, the Prince of Han received Han Xin and said to him, "The Chief Counselor has repeatedly commended you to me. I'm sure you have excellent ideas in your head, and I am ready to hear them."

Han Xin expressed gratitude to the Prince, and then presented a detailed comparative analysis of the respective strengths and weaknesses of Chu under Xiang Yu, and of Han. He concluded that the Prince of Han would be assured of victory when he launched an attack on Xiang Yu in the east. As the briefing continued, the mood of the Prince of Han became increasingly buoyant. Liu Bang regretted not having discovered this talented man sooner.

With Han Xin in command and in charge of training the troops, conditions ripened for a military campaign against Xiang Yu to the east.

39. Rivalry between the States of Chu and Han

WITH HIS COMMANDER-IN-CHIEF Han Xin and his Chief Counselor Xiao He, the Prince of Han Liu Bang embarked in earnest on a program of internal reform and military training. In August 206 BC, the Prince of Han led his army with Han Xin as Commander-in-Chief on a campaign against Guanzhong. The people of Guanzhong still had fond memories of the Prince of Han, author of the "Contract with the People", and did not put up much of a fight as the Han army marched in. In less than three months, the Prince of Han neutralized the forces of Zhang Han and other former Qin generals, and took control of the Guanzhong region.

The Overlord of Western Chu Xiang Yu was furious at this turn of events. He wanted to move against Liu Bang to the west, but another crisis was coming to a head in the east. In the principality of Qi, Tian Rong deposed the prince installed by Xiang Yu, and declared himself prince. As the imbroglio in Qi seemed more threatening than Liu Bang's advance in the west, Xiang Yu had no choice but to deal with Tian Rong first.

Capitalizing on the deadlock between Xiang Yu and the principality of Qi, the Prince of Han Liu Bang pressed his attack further east and took Pengcheng, the capital of the Overlord of Western Chu. This compelled Xiang Yu to break off his engagement against Qi and race back towards his capital. He met the Han forces led by Liu Bang in battle at the Sui River.

The battle turned into a debacle for the Han army, as countless of their soldiers drowned in the River. Many others were taken prisoner. The Chu forces even succeeded in capturing the Prince of Han's father Tai Gong, and Liu Bang's wife Queen Lü.

The Prince of Han fell back to the vicinity of Xingyang and Chenggao (in Henan Province) to regroup. Han morale was then lifted by the arrival of two contingents of reinforcements deployed from the capital by Xiao He, and of troops led by Han Xin.

In the belief that the best defense is a good offense, the Prince of Han sent troops under Han Xin's command northward to conquer the principalities of Wei, Yan and Zhao. Meanwhile, he kept behind only a small garrison to defend Xingyang and pin down Xiang Yu's forces.

Xiang Yu's adviser Fan Zeng advocated taking Xingyang in a lightning strike. The possibility of such a strike had the Prince of Han greatly worried. Liu Bang's adviser Chen Ping, a defector from Xiang Yu's camp, came up with the idea of driving a wedge between Xiang Yu and Fan Zeng.

Paranoid by nature, Xiang Yu believed the lies and started to have suspicions about Fan Zeng. In indignation, Fan Zeng said to Xiang Yu, "The situation in the country has stabilized. I'll leave you to finish the good work, my King! I am too old and too frail. It's time to retire and go home."

On his way home from the Xingyang area, Fan Zeng fell ill, possibly because of indignation and a deep sense of having been wronged. Before reaching Pengcheng, he died from a festering sore on his spine.

With the death of Fan Zeng, there was no one left in the Chu camp able to give wise counsel to the Overlord of Western Chu, and the Han forces had lost a formidable opponent. While the Prince of Han used his small force in the Xingyang and Chenggao area to pin down Xiang Yu's army, Han Xin was able to continue his campaigns to the north and east. Working in concert with them, General Peng Yue went behind Chu lines and worked to cut off the supply routes to the Chu troops. Xiang Yu's forces shuttling between multiple fronts were thus harassed and overstretched, leading to a standoff between Chu and Han that lasted for more than two years.

In 203 BC, Xiang Yu decided to take on General Peng Yue. He instructed General Cao Jiu to stay behind and defend Chenggao. Cao Jiu had strict instructions not to engage the Han forces under any circumstances.

After Xiang Yu's departure, the Prince of Han immediately challenged Cao Jiu to a fight. At first, Cao Jiu adamantly refused to be provoked. The Prince of Han then had his soldiers hurl non-stop insults at the Chu camp from their side of the Si River, which flowed west of Xingyang.

After being bombarded by volleys of name-calling for days on end, Cao Jiu finally lost his cool. He decided to cross the Si River for a fight to the death with the Han forces.

His Chu army did not have enough boats for its soldiers, and had to ferry them across the River in batches. When half of the army was across the river, the Han army attacked, dealing this advance contingent a decisive blow. The Chu troops that were following retreated in disarray. Many were trampled to death by their own comrades. Too ashamed to face Xiang Yu again, Cao Jiu committed suicide by the Si River.

Meanwhile, Xiang Yu achieved victory on the eastern front, but then was informed of the fall of Chenggao and had to race back westward to take on the Prince of Han. At Guangwu (northeast of modern-day Xingyang County, Henan Province) the two armies met and became locked in another standoff.

As the confrontation dragged on, the Chu forces began to run out of rations. As a last resort, Xiang Yu had Liu Bang's father bound and placed on a butcher's table. He then sent someone to shout at the Han camp, "Liu Bang, surrender now, or your father will be butchered!"

Calling Xiang Yu's bluff, the Prince of Han shouted back, "We were once sworn brothers, so my father is your father, too. If you kill Father, please make a meat soup out of him and offer me a bowl of it."

Xiang Yu gnashed his teeth in anger. He seriously contemplated killing Liu Bang's father Tai Gong, but was dissuaded by Xiang Bo.

Xiang Yu then sent an envoy to the Prince of Han with the message: "The present chaos in the realm boils down to a stalemate between you and me. I dare you to a man-to-man duel."

The Prince of Han sent the envoy back with this reply: "I can agree to a duel of wits, but not of physical strength."

Xiang Yu then met Prince of Han face-to-face. The Prince of Han read out a ten-point indictment of Xiang Yu, accusing him of duplicity, the murder of Emperor Yi, and the slaughter of civilians. Deeply angered by these accusations, Xiang Yu signaled with his halberd, and the archers behind him unleashed a volley of arrows at the Prince of Han. The Prince of Han quickly maneuvered his horse to dodge the arrows, but it was too late. He was shot in the chest and seriously wounded.

Braving the pain, as a ruse he reached down and touched a foot, cursing, "The bastards shot my toe!"

His guards helped the Prince of Han into his tent. Word quickly spread that the Prince of Han had been injured, throwing the Han troops into a panic. Fearing a collapse of morale, Zhang Liang advised the Prince of Han to go on an inspection tour of the camp pretending not to be seriously injured. This inspection tour had the effect of calming the troops.

Xiang Yu was sorely disappointed when he learned that the Prince of Han had survived. Later, Han Xin routed the Chu troops in Qi territory. General Peng Yue then succeeded in cutting the Chu supply routes. The Chu army now faced a worsening logistical crisis.

Seeing that Xiang Yu was in dire straits, the Prince of Han made peace overtures. He asked for the release of Tai Gong and Queen Lü, and proposed dividing the empire along the waterway called Honggou (southeast of modern-day Xingyang, Henan Province). The territory east of Honggou would be given to Chu, and territory west of it given to Han. Thinking this proposed partition a fair bargain, Xiang Yu gave his consent. He released Tai Gong and Queen Lü, and took his troops back to Pengcheng.

However, this peace treaty was actually a tactic by the Prince of Han to buy time. Following the advice of Zhang Liang and Chen Ping, in less than two months the Prince of Han was able to merge the three armies of Han Xin, Peng Yue and Ying Bu into a single fighting force. He placed this under Han Xin's command and sent him in pursuit of Xiang Yu. Thus the stage was set for a final showdown between Chu and Han.

40. Xiang Yu Haunted by Chu Chants

IN 202 BC, Xiang Yu was trapped in an ambush by Han Xin at Gaixia (southeast of modern-day Lingbi County, Anhui Province). In the end, Xiang Yu had very few soldiers left, and was running out of food. He wanted to make a break for it, but the Chu army was encircled on all sides by ring upon ring of troops not just from Han, but from other principalities, as well. As soon as Xiang Yu would beat back one wave of attackers, a new wave would be unleashed upon him. Whenever he thought he had broken through enemy lines, he always found another army closing in on him.

After he was unable to break through the encirclement, Xiang Yu would always return to his encampment at Gaixia. He would instruct his troops to be on high alert, and then bide his time as he prepared for another round of combat.

One night, a gloomy Xiang Yu walked into his tent with his brows knit into a deep frown. The beautiful Lady Yu, Xiang Yu's favorite companion, tried to cheer him up by having a few drinks with him.

As the first watch was sounded, he heard snatches of song wafted in by the gusts of the westerly wind. As Xiang Yu listened more intently, he realized that the singing originated in the Han camp, but that all the tunes were from Chu. He could tell that a remarkable number of people had joined in the singing.

Xiang Yu was taken aback by the Chu music coming at him from all sides. Dispirited he said, "All is lost! Has Liu Bang taken control of Western Chu? How else can one explain so many Chu voices in the Han camp?"

Overwhelmed by sadness, Xiang Yu began to sing in a forlorn voice:

I was invincible with strength to move mountains.
Now my piebald steed even balks at my misfortune.
What am I to do when my piebald shirks its duty?
How do I do thee justice, Lady Yu, my beauty?

After several refrains, Lady Yu joined Xiang Yu in the singing. As the Overlord of Western Chu sang, tears began to streak down his cheeks. Even the attendants around him stood with their heads bowed in sadness.

That night, Xiang Yu mounted his piebald horse and led his 800 men in a daring dash through the Han encampment, galloping on without stopping to rest. It was only when day broke that the Han troops found out Xiang Yu had breached the encirclement. A cavalry detachment of 5,000 was immediately sent after him. By the time his flight took him across the Huai River, Xiang Yu found he had only 100 men left. As the party rode on, they lost their way.

Coming to a fork in the road, Xiang Yu saw a peasant and asked him which way led to Pengcheng. The peasant recognized him. Not wishing to help him, he pointed in the wrong direction and said, "Bear left at the fork!"

As Xiang Yu and his 100 men rode down the path to the left, they began to suspect something was awry. After a while, the path ended in a marsh. Xiang Yu turned his steed around in the realization that they had been duped, and tried to find a way out of the wetland. However, by that time, the Han detachment in pursuit had already caught up with them.

Xiang Yu's remnant troops ran toward the southeast, suffering heavy casualties as they did so. When they reached Dongcheng (southeast of modern-day Dingyuan County, Anhui Province), they counted only 28 cavalrymen left. By this time, thousands of Han soldiers had formed a tight noose around them.

Although Xiang Yu did not expect to extricate himself from this mess, he did not concede defeat. He said to his soldiers, "In more than 70 battles in the eight years since I started this rebellion, I've never once been defeated. That's how I have earned my position as Overlord. I've been trapped here not because I am unable to triumph over my foes, but because it's the will of Heaven."

Dividing his remaining 28 combatants into four groups, he instructed them, "When I get off my horse and kill one of their generals, you disperse in four different directions. We will regroup later at the foot of East Hills."

He then let out a terrible cry and charged into the Han troops. The Han defenses immediately crumbled and one of the Han generals was killed on the spot.

When Xiang Yu arrived at East Hills, he was rejoined by the four groups of remaining troops. Xiang Yu organized them into three squads to man defenses on three fronts. The pursuing Han troops launched a three-pronged attack, enveloping the Chu troops. Wading fearlessly into the enemy forces coming from all directions, Xiang Yu killed a Han commander and several hundred soldiers. Finally, he mustered his three squads together and tallied his forces. He had suffered only two casualties out of the 28 soldiers.

Xiang Yu asked his men, "What do you think of our performance?"

His men replied, "Your Highness was a hundred-percent right."

Having breached the encirclement of Han troops, Xiang Yu escaped with his remaining 26 men southward to the banks of the Wujiang River (northeast of modern-day He County, Anhui Province). The chief of the local *ting* happened to have a small boat moored at the waterside.

The chief of the *ting* urged Xiang Yu to ferry across immediately, saying "The territory east of the river may not be that vast, but it still extends a thousand *li* and boasts a population of hundreds of thousands. Once there, Your Highness will still be a king."

With a wry smile, Xiang Yu said, "When I started the rebellion in Guiji, I took 8,000 folk with me across the river. I will not be able to bring a single one of them home now. Even if the folks east of the river have sympathy for me and put me on the throne, I am ashamed to see them again."

After making a gift of his piebald steed to the chief of the *ting* and ordering his soldiers to dismount, he and the 26 braves wielded daggers and engaged the pursuing Han troops in hand-to-hand combat. They fell one by one as they killed several hundred Han soldiers. Having received a dozen wounds, Xiang Yu ended his own life with his sword on the banks of the Wujiang River.

41. Song of the Rising Wind

IN THE AFTERMATH of the decisive battle at Gaixia, the Prince of Han Liu Bang achieved final victory, and founded the Han dynasty, which proved more powerful than Qin. In 202 BC, Liu Bang ascended the imperial throne with the title of Emperor Gaozu of Han. (The start of the Western Han dynasty is sometimes predated to 206 BC, the year Liu Bang assumed the title of the Prince of Han).

Gaozu of Han made Luoyang the capital of the new dynasty. Eventually, the capital was moved to Chang'an (modern-day Xi'an, Shaanxi Province). Chang'an would remain the capital of the Han dynasty for 210 years. This period is historically called the Western Han dynasty, also known as the Former Han.

At a celebration held in the South Palace in Luoyang shortly after Gaozu's ascension to the throne, he said to his ministers, "We are gathered here today to celebrate. You can speak freely, without any inhibition. What in your opinion enabled me to win imperial power? What caused Xiang Yu to lose the contest?"

Wang Ling and other ministers said, "By always properly rewarded those who helped Your Majesty conquer cities and towns, You have secured loyalty. Xiang Yu lost because the talents and exploits of others aroused jealousy and mistrust in him, instead of earning them any credit."

Gaozu said with a smile, "There's something else you've missed. It is important to understand that success often depends on the ability to use the right people for the right job. In directing a battle to victory from thousands of miles away, I am no match for Zhang Liang. In day-to-day administration of the country, anticipating popular sentiments, and providing supplies and support for the front, I can't do any better than Xiao He. When it comes to commanding a large army to victory after victory and taking city after city, I can't hold a candle to Han Xin. These three people are the best talents of our time. I have succeeded because I have tapped their talents, while Xiang Yu couldn't even keep Fan Zeng. That was why he was defeated by me."

All those present were convinced of the truth of Gaozu's analysis. The trio of Xiao He, Zhang Liang and Han Xin was later known as the "Magnificent Three of Early Han."

As for the generals who had made major contributions to his cause in the contest for power between Chu and Han, Emperor Gaozu felt obligated to make them princes. Although these new princes were not of the deposed nobility of the old six states, they were not immune either to the ambition of carving out a turf beyond the reach of central control. The Prince of Chu Han Xin, the Prince of Liang Peng Yue and the Prince of Huainan Ying Bu were the most decorated of the princes and commanded the strongest fighting forces. Han Gaozu understandably had questions about their loyalty.

Gaozu had put out an arrest warrant for a former general under Xiang Yu called Zhong Limei. For some reason, Han Xin decided to take Zhong Limei under his wing.

The following year, Gaozu received a denunciation of Han Xin because of his alleged seditious intentions. When Gaozu consulted his ministers on the matter, many recommended a military expedition to take out Han Xin. In a lone dissenting voice, Chen Ping argued, "Han Xin has better-trained soldiers and more competent generals than we do. It would be risky to use force against him."

Adopting a ruse devised by Chen Ping, Gaozu traveled to Lake Yunmengze, which was under Chen Ping's control, ostensibly on an inspection tour. When he arrived, he ordered the princes of his fiefs to come there for a meeting. This was an order Han Xin could not have disobeyed. Upon Han Xin's arrival, Gaozu ordered warriors to bind him up for prosecution.

Some thought that leniency should be shown by Gaozu in the light of Han Xin's past contributions. This prompted Gaozu to spare him further punishment after stripping him of the title of Prince of Chu and demoting him to Marquis of Huaiyin. After his demotion, Han Xin became dispirited and often absented himself from the daily imperial audiences by feigning illness.

A few years later, a general called Chen Xi started an insurrection and proclaimed himself Acting King. In a short period, he was able to capture twenty cities.

Gaozu had intended for Han Xin and Peng Yue to lead a joint expedition against Chen Xi, but both men declined on grounds of illness. This left Gaozu no choice but to lead the expedition himself.

After Gaozu departed Chang'an at the head of his troops, Queen Lü received a denunciation of Han Xin. It alleged that Han Xin and Chen Xi were co-conspirators in the insurrection and that an orchestrated attack had been planned. After consulting Chief Counselor Xiao He, Queen Lü put out the disinformation that Chen Xi had been captured by Gaozu and that all high officials were invited to celebrate this in the palace. As soon as Han Xin stepped inside the palace, he was waylaid by armed guards and killed.

Barely three months after Han Xin's death, Gaozu put down Chen Xi's rebellion and returned to Luoyang. When he arrived, Peng Yue's own people denounced him, saying that Peng Yue was plotting sedition. Gaozu had Peng Yue arrested and put in prison. Unable to substantiate Peng Yue's seditious intent, Gaozu stripped him of all official duties and exiled him to faraway Shuzhong.

While en route to Shuzhong, Peng Yue ran into Queen Lü. In tears, he protested his innocence before the Queen and pleaded for her to intercede with Gaozu so that he would be allowed to go back to his home town. Queen Lü readily agreed and took Peng Yue back to Luoyang.

Upon her return to the capital, Queen Lü said to Gaozu, "Peng Yue is a good fighter. Banishing him to Shuzhong would be tantamount to returning a tiger to the wild. You would be courting trouble."

Acting on Queen Lü's advice, Gaozu then had Peng Yue executed.

After learning of Han Xin and Peng Yue's killings, the Prince of Huainan Ying Bu decided to rebel. He said to his staff, "The emperor is ageing and will not be able to come out here to fight us. The only generals to be worried about were Han Xin and Peng Yue, but they are now dead. The others are no match for me. We have nothing to fear from them."

Ying Bu did indeed win a string of early victories, and was able to control large areas of Jing and Chu. Gaozu had to lead his army into battle himself.

On the battlefield, Gaozu called out to Ying Bu, "I made you Prince! Why have you turned against me?"

Ying Bu said unabashedly, "I want to be emperor!"

Gaozu then unleashed his superior force against Ying Bu in a merciless attack. Gaozu was shot in the chest in a volley of arrows released by Ying Bu's archers. The injury was fortunately not very serious, and he continued the relentless assault despite the pain. Finally, Ying Bu was killed in a chaotic retreat.

After putting down Ying Bu's rebellion, on his way back to the capital Gaozu stayed a few days in Pei County, his home town. He invited town folk and old acquaintances to a feast where he wined and dined them. He was able to enjoy a few carefree days.

Even as he savored his new-found happiness, his mind began to fill with memories of how he had outmaneuvered Xiang Yu in the past, and thoughts about how he must run the country in the future. He marveled at the complexity of government: On the one hand, there were subordinates always up to some mischief and, on the other hand, troubles always abounded on the frontiers. Where could he find a few good men to help him defend the empire? As emotions churned in his chest, a song came unbidden to his lips:

Clouds billow, roiled by the rising wind's fury.
The native son returns in imperial glory-
Eager for a few good men to defend the country.

42. The Oath of the White Horse

IN HIS OLD age, Gaozu heaped favors on Lady Qi, who had a child by him named Ruyi. This son was given the title of Prince of Zhao. Gaozu had always found Crown Prince Liu Ying, son of Queen Lü, a weak character and doubted his ability to accomplish great things in the future. On the other hand, Ruyi reminded him of himself in his manner and problem-solving sills. Gaozu started thinking about making Ruyi crown prince instead of Liu Ying.

He consulted his ministers on this idea, but received little support. Even Zhang Liang, whose opinion he had always highly valued, threw his support behind Queen Lü. Zhang Liang then enlisted the "Venerable Four of Shangshan" (four renowned hermits of the time) to mentor Crown Prince Liu Ying.

Seeing his effort to replace the Crown Prince frustrated, Gaozu said to Lady Qi, "The Crown Prince now has received support and is no longer the fledgling that he was. It's too late to change the situation." Lady Qi was saddened beyond words by this development.

Gaozu had been shot in the chest by an arrow during his expedition against Ying Bu. The wound later festered. One day someone whispered to him, "Fan Kuai (Queen Lü's brother-in-law) has been conspiring with the Queen to kill Lady Qi and the Prince of Zhao Ruyi once Your Majesty departs this world."

In a fit of rage, Gaozu summoned Chen Ping and General Zhou Bo and said to them, "Go this moment to Fan Kuai's barracks and decapitate him. Then come back to me with his head."

Fan Kuai was then in the Principality of Yan with his troops. After receiving their orders, Chen Ping and Zhou Bo huddled together and concluded, "Fan Kuai has rendered the country great services and is moreover the brother-in-law of the Queen. We can't just kill him like that. The emperor ordered him killed in a fit of rage. What if he later regrets that decision?"

After some discussion, the two put Fan Kuai in a pillory cart and escorted him to Chang'an, where Queen Lü ordered him freed.

As Gaozu's health worsened, he summoned his ministers before him and ordered a white horse butchered. He then had the ministers swear this oath while smearing the blood of the white horse on their mouths: "From now on the title of prince can only be given to members of the Liu clan and to men who have rendered outstanding service to the country. Whoever violates this pact will be subject to collective sanctions."

After the ministers swore this oath, Gaozu had peace of mind.

When Gaozu's condition deteriorated, he summoned Queen Lü to hear his last wishes.

Queen Lü asked Gaozu, "After Your Majesty's ascension to Heaven, who should take the place of Chief Counselor Xiao He when he dies?"

"Cao Shen will do," Gaozu replied.

"And after Cao Shen dies?" Queen Lü asked.

Gaozu responded, "Wang Ling can take his place. But Wang Ling is sometimes a little too blunt and tactless, so he can use some help from Chen Ping. Chen Ping is astute and resourceful, but can't make independent decisions. Zhou Bo has a generous disposition, and is prudent and meticulous, but not cultured enough. Still, Zhou Bo will be the key to ensuring the continuation of the Liu lineage."

Queen Lü had more questions, but Gaozu shook his head and said, "There's no telling what may come."

In 195 BC, Gaozu of Han died. Keeping the death under a tight lid, Queen Lü summoned Shen Yiji, a minister and close confidant, and said to him, "The generals were the late Emperor's comrades in arms right from the beginning of the rebellion. However, they were already grumbling when the emperor was alive. Their loyalty is now even more questionable. We should kill them all."

Sensing he would not be able to handle the tough assignment all by himself, Shen Yiji sought the help of Queen Lü's brother Lü Shizhi. Lü Shizhi's son Lü Lu leaked the secret to his good friend Li Ji, who in turn informed his father Li Shang.

Upon learning of the secret goings-on, Li Shang paid an urgent call on Shen Yiji and said to him, "I've learned that the emperor died four days ago, and that the Queen has put a hold on funeral arrangements while hatching a plan to kill ministers and high officials. This would surely provoke a rebellion by these ministers and generals. The country would be in chaos and, more importantly, your own life would be in jeopardy."

Alarmed at this prospect, Shen Yiji sought urgent consultations with Queen Lü. The Queen, no longer so sure her plan to purge the old guard would work, gave the go-ahead for the funeral to take place.

In the wake of Gaozu of Han's funeral, Crown Prince Liu Ying ascended the throne and became Emperor Hui of Han. Queen Lü became the Empress Dowager.

Emperor Hui turned out indeed to be a gentle soul lacking the qualities required for the job. He left all decisions to the Empress Dowager. Empress Dowager Lü, with real power now concentrated in her hands, had no qualms about exercising that power as she saw fit.

The time had come for settling accounts with Lady Qi and the Prince of Zhao Ruyi, for whom she had always had a visceral hatred. First, Lady Qi was made a slave. Then, Ruyi was recalled to Chang'an from his fief.

Well aware of the Empress Dowager's intention to engineer the death of his brother Ruyi, Emperor Hui decided to frustrate the Empress Dowager's scheme by giving him a room in his palace and keeping him at his side during mealtime and bedtime.

One morning, Emperor Hui was going to his morning archery practice after getting out of bed. He had intended for Ruyi to accompany him, but did not have the heart to wake up his younger brother, who was still in a deep sleep. He left by himself. On his return, he found Ruyi dead in his bed and immediately knew his brother had been poisoned. He took the corpse in his arms and wept bitterly.

After having Ruyi killed, the Empress Dowager cold-bloodedly ordered the hands and feet of Lady Qi hacked off and her eyes gouged out. Lady Qi was forcibly fed a substance that made her mute. Subsequently, she was thrown into a pig sty.

Emperor Hui cried inconsolably when he saw the cruel torture of Lady Qi by the Empress Dowager. The experience was so traumatic that he fell ill. He then sent word to the Empress Dowager, "The things that you've done are inhuman. As your son, I no longer feel I have the ability to rule."

From then on, Emperor Hui studiously tried to refrain from intervening in affairs of the state.

43. Cao Adopts the Ways of Xiao

IN THE SECOND year of Emperor Hui's reign, the ageing Chief Counselor Xiao He fell seriously ill. The emperor visited him and asked him who would be a good candidate to take his place.

Noncommittal, Xiao He merely said, "No one understands me better than Your Majesty."

Emperor Hui then asked, "What do you think of Cao Shen?"

Cao Shen and Xiao He had been officials in the Pei County government before joining the rebellion of Gaozu of Han. Their earlier cordial relations became strained after Cao Shen realized that he would always remain in Xiao He's shadow, despite his own brilliant war exploits. That did not stop Xiao He from recognizing Cao's leadership qualities. At Emperor Hui's mention of Cao Shen, Xiao He immediately expressed agreement, saying "Your Majesty has made a good choice. With Cao Shen to take my place, I can leave with peace of mind."

Cao Shen was a general by profession. When Gaozu made his eldest son Liu Fei Prince of Qi, Cao was drafted to be the Prime Minister of Qi. Cao Shen arrived in the Principality of Qi at a time when China had only recently emerged from civil strife. He called a meeting with more than a hundred local residents and intellectuals to hear their ideas about good government. No consensus emerged out of the meeting because of the diverse range of views.

A renowned local hermit called Gai Gong came to the attention of Cao Shen, who invited the recluse for consultation. Gai Gong was a believer in the laissez-faire philosophy of the

Huangdi and Laozi (Lao Tzu) school of thought, which advocated less government so that the people could be left in peace. Cao Shen took Gai Gong's advice and was careful not to bother the people with too much red tape. In his nine years as Qi's Prime Minister, relative peace reigned in all the seventy-odd cities of the Principality.

Upon Xiao He's death, Emperor Hui immediately summoned Cao Shen to Chang'an to succeed Xiao He as Chief Counselor. Following Gai Gong's advice to have minimal governmental intervention, Cao Shen kept Xiao He's system and policy in place without making the slightest change.

Some ministers became alarmed at Cao Shen's philosophy of government by inaction. They were eager to offer him advice, but every time they called on him he would invite them to drink with him. Whenever the conversation at the table turned to politics, he would steer it towards other topics, effectively forestalling any serious discussion. The guests would go home in an inebriated state without having said their piece.

Emperor Hui himself was unsettled by what he perceived as a paternalistic, patronizing attitude towards him by Cao Shen. On one occasion, Emperor Hui said to Cao Shen's son Cao Zhu, who was an attendant in the emperor's court, "When you go home, ask your father this question: 'With Gaozu departed, and the emperor still very young, you are the Prime Minister entrusted with the weighty responsibility of government. How can you ensure good government when you indulge in drinking instead of governing?' I'd like to know your father's answer to that."

When Cao Zhu went home on leave, he duly relayed the emperor's question to his father.

Cao was angered by the question, and started to scold his son, "What does a callow youth like you know about the affairs of state? You've overstepped your bounds!" Cao Shen had a servant fetch a rod, and then went on to give his son a good beating.

Cao Zhu felt deeply wronged by the unwarranted scolding and beating, and naturally recounted the incident to the emperor upon his return to the palace. The emperor was also upset about it.

The next day, Emperor Hui said to Cao Shen during the daily

imperial audience, "Cao Zhu merely relayed my question to you. Why did you beat him?"

After presenting his apologies to the emperor, Cao Shen asked, "Your Majesty! How do you rate your wisdom in comparison with that of Gaozu?"

"It goes without saying that I pale before Emperor Gaozu!" Emperor Hui replied.

Cao Shen continued, "How does my talent compare with Xiao He's?"

"Well, you probably can't compare to Xiao He," the emperor responded with a smile.

Cao Shen responded, "Your Majesty is right on both counts. Your Majesty can't compare to Gaozu and I can't compare to Prime Minister Xiao He. After winning political power, Emperor Gaozu and Prime Minister Xiao He have left us a fine legacy of institutions and rules. All we need to do is to implement their system faithfully and dutifully."

With this, Cao Shen's approach to government finally began to make sense for Emperor Hui.

In his three years as Prime Minister, Cao Shen pursued a policy underpinned by the philosophy of the Huangdi and Laozi school of thought. In that particular period, with the country just emerging from protracted conflict, what the people most needed was stability and peace. His policy met that need by ensuring that no unnecessary, extra burdens were placed on the people. Both Xiao He and Cao Shen were therefore celebrated in folk song that circulated during their own lifetimes. In Chinese history, this instance of seamless transition is known as *Xiao gui Cao sui* ("the Xiao ways are adopted by Cao").

44. Zhou Bo Wrests Control of the Army

SINCE EMPEROR HUI did not have a son, Empress Dowager Lü had a baby boy brought in to be passed off as the son of the emperor. The boy was made Crown Prince. He later ascended the throne upon the death of Emperor Hui in 188 BC, thereby guaranteeing the continued power of the Empress Dowager as Regent.

In a bid to consolidate her power further, Empress Dowager Lü planned to create principalities for the Lü clan. She consulted the ministers on the feasibility of her idea.

The Right Prime Minister Wang Ling, never one to mince words, said, "Emperor Gaozu had us swear the Oath of the White Horse, which forbids us from making princes of people outside the Liu clan."

Resentful of his reply, Empress Dowager Lü turned to the Left Prime Minister Chen Ping and Commander-in-Chief Zhou Bo for their views.

The two answered, "It was only logical that Emperor Gaozu awarded principalities to his own folk after taking political power. By the same token, there's nothing wrong with the reigning Empress Dowager making her clansmen princes."

Empress Dowager Lü, placated by this reply, nodded her approval.

After the audience was over, Wang Ling took Chen Ping and Wang Bo to task. He said to them, "You were both present when

Emperor Gaozu swore us to the Oath of the White Horse. By violating your oath, you're dishonoring Gaozu's memory!"

Chen Ping and Wang Bo retorted, "Don't be too quick to pass judgment. You may be better at confronting the Empress Dowager, but we will be better at keeping the Liu clan in power."

Emboldened by the endorsement of the ministers, Empress Dowager Lü created principalities for her nephews and grandnephews, including Lü Tai, Lü Chan, Lü Lu, Lü Jia, and Lü Tong. The Lü clan was also given control of the military. Soon, all the levers of power in the country were in Lü hands.

Although Empress Dowager Lü's maneuver to grab power from the Liu clan had provoked private grumblings among numerous ministers, they did not have the courage to openly air their anger.

Gaozu's grandson the Marquis of Zhuxu Liu Zhang was married to Lü Lu's daughter. One day the Empress Dowager put Liu Zhang in charge of a banquet she was planning to host. Liu Zhang said to the Empress Dowager, "I am descended from a general. Will you allow me to oversee the banquet in the military tradition?" The Empress Dowager Lü gave her consent to this.

In the general merriment, aided by much imbibing of alcohol, Liu Zhang proposed to further liven up the party by performing a farmer's chant for the Empress Dowager. Empress Dowager Lü said, "Go ahead! Sing it for us!"

In a booming voice Liu Zhang sang,

Plough deeply and plant well-apart!
Pull up seedlings that don't belong!

This ditty incurred the great displeasure of the Empress Dowager.

When a guest from the Lü clan got drunk and left without taking proper leave, Liu Zhang went after him and killed him on the pretext of his breach of etiquette. When Liu Zhang returned to the banquet and reported this incident to the Empress Dowager, the ministers attending her greatly feared for him. However, having given him permission to conduct the affair under military law, the Empress Dowager could not pin any blame on him.

In the eighth year of her regency, Empress Dowager Lü

became seriously ill. Before her death, she made the Prince of Zhao Lü Chan Chief Counselor and gave him command of the Southern Army. Lü Lu was promoted to general in command of the Northern Army. The Empress Dowager warned them, "The ministers are not happy with the passage of power into our hands. It is important that after my death, you stay here with your troops to protect our interests. Do not attend the funeral, because you might walk into a trap."

Thus, after the death of Empress Dowager Lü the control of the military was concentrated in the hands of Lü Chan and Lü Lu, who bided their time as they planned a dynasty change.

Through his wife, who was a Lü, Liu Zhang got wind of the plot being hatched by the Lü clan. He sent a messenger bearing the intelligence to his elder brother the Prince of Qi Liu Xiang, and invited him to march on Chang'an.

When Lü Chan received information that the Prince of Qi Liu Xiang was leading his troops on a westward march, he immediately sent a force commanded by his general Guan Ying to thwart the attack. When he reached Xingyang, Guan Ying summoned his staff for a consultation and said to them, "With the military under their control, the Lü clan now has designs on the throne of the Liu dynasty. If we attack the Prince of Qi, we will be accomplices in this seditious Lü plot."

The decision was then made to put a hold on any military action against the Prince of Qi. Secret emissaries were sent to the Prince urging him to coordinate with the chiefs of the other principalities a well-timed attack against the Lü clan. After receiving this communication, the Prince of Qi halted his advance.

When Zhou Bo and Chen Ping cast about for ways to thwart the seditious plan of the Lü clan, they had limited options because the army was in Lü hands. Then they remembered that Minister Li Shang's son Li Ji was on good terms with Lü Lu, so they sent an emissary asking Li Ji to lobby Lü Lu.

Li Ji said to Lü Lu, "With the Empress Dowager dead and the emperor so young, you, the Prince of Zhao, have chosen to stay in Chang'an with your troops. As a result, the ministers are beginning to question your loyalty. This is not in your interest. If you cede control of the army to the Commander-in-Chief and return to your own fief, the Prince of Qi will also withdraw his troops. This will set the ministers at ease."

Li Ji thus succeeded in persuading Lü Lu to cede command of the Northern Army to the Commander-in-Chief Zhou Bo.

With the General's seal in hand, Zhou Bo immediately went to the headquarters of the Northern Army and issued this order: "The Lü clan is plotting to wrest imperial power from the Liu clan. It's up to you to decide what to do. Those on the side of the Lü clan will bare their right arms, and those on the side of the Liu clan, their left arms!"

The troops of the Northern Army had always been on the side of the Liu clan, so when the order was given they instantly bared their left arms. Zhou Bo was thus able to handily wrest control of the Northern Army from Lü Lu.

Unaware that control of the Northern Army had passed from Lü Lu to Zhou Bo, Lü Chan marched his troops to Weiyang Palace with the intention of launching a coup. Zhou Bo sent 1,000 troops under the command of the Marquis of Zhuxu Liu Zhang to confront Lü Chan. In the ensuing battle Lü Chan was killed. With Zhou Bo at its command, the Northern Army went on to root out all remnants of the Lü clan.

With their courage restored, the ministers now said, "The emperor put on the throne by Empress Dowager Lü is really not Emperor Hui's son. Now that the Lü clan has been neutralized, we don't want this puppet to usurp power, because when he grows up he will become a supporter of the Lü cause. From among the Liu princes, we should pick the best of the crop to be the emperor."

After deliberating, the ministers came to the conclusion that, of all the sons of Emperor Gaozu of Han, the Prince of Dai Liu Heng was the most senior and had the highest moral caliber. A delegation was then dispatched to Dai (in modern-day Wei County, Hebei Province) to escort Liu Heng to Chang'an. There, he was enthroned and given the title Emperor Wen of Han.

45. Zhou Yafu, Martinet of Camp Xiliu

AFTER ASCENDING TO the throne, Emperor Wen of Han continued the policy of pacifying the Xiongnu by arranging marriages of convenience with the Xiongnu nobility. No major conflict erupted between the two sides until the Chanyu (i.e., King) of the Xiongnu was instigated by forces inimical to Han-Xiongnu amity to sever relations with the Han dynasty. In 158 BC, the Chanyu of the Xiongnu Junchen led a 6,000-strong invading force against Shangjun Prefecture (southeast of modern-day Yulin, Shaanxi Province) and Yunzhong (northeast of modern-day Tuoketuo, Inner Mongolia). His army carried out wanton looting and caused heavy civilian casualties. As the watchtowers on the frontier lit up bonfire after bonfire to alert of the invasion, the smoke and flames could be seen from as far away as Chang'an.

Emperor Wen immediately sent three forces, each under the command of a general, to confront the invading Xiongnu. Three other generals were deployed with their troops around the Chang'an area for the defense of the capital: General Liu Li at Bashang, General Xu Li at Jimen (northeast of modern-day Xianyang, Shaanxi Province) and General Zhou Yafu at Xiliu (southwest of modern-day Xianyang).

The emperor then undertook a tour through these three camps to boost morale and inspect the troops.

The tour took him first to Bashang, where General Liu and his troops eagerly rode out to greet the emperor. The emperor's party freely passed through the camp perimeter without being stopped or challenged at any point. After a pep rally, the emperor was ready to move on and the troops gave him a rousing sendoff.

A no less elaborate welcoming ceremony awaited him when he arrived at Jimen.

Then he arrived at Xiliu, the final stop of his tour. A sentinel at General Zhou Yafu's camp saw in the distance the advance of the emperor's party, and immediately sent back this intelligence to the General. The troops instantly snapped into battle alert, with armor on their backs, arrows on their bows, and swords out of their scabbards.

When the advance group of the emperor's party approached the camp gate, it was immediately halted and barred from entering.

The officials at the head of the advance group barked with authority, "The emperor will be arriving in no time!"

Unruffled, the guards manning the gate replied, "In the army, we go by the commanding general's orders. Without his authorization, we cannot let you in."

Before the officials had time to argue, Emperor Wen's carriage had arrived at the gate. However, it was also stopped by the guards.

The emperor was left with no choice but to order his attendants to show his imperial stave, and to send word to Zhou Yafu that the emperor was here to boost troop morale.

Zhou Yafu then gave the order to open the gate to let the imperial carriage through.

Once inside the gate, the emperor's entourage was told in no uncertain terms, "In accordance with military regulations, vehicles and horses are forbidden to travel at high speed inside the camp."

All the attendant officials were incensed by this injunction, but Emperor Wen gave the order to relax the reins and proceed at a leisurely pace.

When the party approached the commander's tent, it was greeted by the sight of a forbidding-looking, armed General Zhou Yafu in full battle dress. He stood before Emperor Wen and bowed. Raising his clasped hands in salute several times, he said to the emperor, "I am unable to kowtow because of the armor on me.

Please grant me permission to give the military salute."

Disconcerted by this request, the emperor returned the salute by slightly inclining his body as he steadied himself with one hand on his carriage. He then sent greetings to the troops through messengers.

On their return to Chang'an from Camp Xiliu at the end of the morale-boosting tour, the members of the emperor's entourage expressed their indignation at Zhou Yafu's rudeness to the emperor.

They were surprised to hear Emperor Wen's unreserved praise for the General. The emperor said, "Now we see a real general worthy of the title! The troops at Jimen and Bashang were a laid-back bunch. They acted as if they were in a make-believe sport. It will be a wonder if they can avoid being taken prisoner in a surprise attack by the enemy. But an enemy would think twice before taking on a general like Zhou Yafu, who is able to enforce iron discipline in his troops."

A month later, the Xiongnu invading force was forced to retreat before the advancing Han vanguard. Afterwards, the three units defending Chang'an returned to normal duty.

After the inspection tour, Emperor Wen was convinced that Zhou Yafu was a military talent, and so he elevated him to the post of Commander of the Capital.

A year later, a seriously ill Emperor Wen summoned the Crown Prince to his deathbed, and left him this fatherly advice: "In any future upheaval, you will do well to give the command of the army to Zhou Yafu."

Crown Prince Liu Qi succeeded Emperor Wen, and became Emperor Jing of Han.

46. Li Guang, the "Flying General"

BOTH EMPEROR WEN and Emperor Jing pursued a policy of peace and rebuilding. In the six decades of their reigns, no major conflict occurred, with the exception of the short Seven State Rebellion. This relative peace and stability fostered economic recovery and development. It is said that, by the end of Emperor Jing's reign, the coffers of the treasury were so full that the ropes used to string up the coins by their holes in the center snapped from the weight of the metal. Some of the unconsumed, surplus grain that accumulated year after year in the state's granaries had to be stored in the open air, with inevitable spoilage. In Chinese history, this is known as the Prosperous Wen-Jing Years.

The powerful and prosperous Han Dynasty was however not immune to threats from the Xiongnu in the north. Since the besiegement of Emperor Gaozu by the Xiongnu at Baideng, the Han dynasty had implemented a policy of "peace by marriage." This was in effect a compromise on the part of the Han Dynasty, which was obliged to give its daughters to the Chanyu of the Xiongnu in marriage, and to make yearly offerings of large amounts from the treasury. The conciliatory efforts of the Han dynasty did not stop the Xiongnu from making frequent forays into Han territory, killing and pillaging, looting food and rustling cattle. North China was in a perpetual unsettled state as a result.

After the death of Emperor Jing, his more ambitious successor

Liu Che, Emperor Wu of Han, was determined to remedy this humiliating situation.

In 129 BC, the Xiongnu attacked Shanggu (southeast of modern-day Huailai, Hebei Province). Emperor Wu of Han sent four generals, Wei Qing, Gongsun Ao, Gongsun He, and Li Guang, with their respective troops to confront the invaders.

Li Guang was the oldest and most senior of the four generals. He had been made a general in the time of Emperor Wen. Under Emperor Jing, he shared credit with Zhou Yafu for the suppression of the Seven State Rebellion. He was later appointed by Emperor Jing to the governorship of Shangjun Prefecture (southeast of modern-day Yulin, Shaanxi Province).

In a previous foray of the Xiongnu into Shangjun, Li Guang in command of 100 cavalrymen went in pursuit of three Xiongnu archers. He caught up with the three after dozens of *li*, shooting two of them dead and captured the third alive. As they prepared to return to camp, they saw thousands of Xiongnu warriors riding towards them.

Li Guang's soldiers were thrown into panic by the enemy's overwhelming superiority in numbers. Li Guang said to them, "We are dozens of *li* from our camp. If the Xiongnu catch up with us while we retreat, we are done for. We have a better chance if we stay put. That will give the Xiongnu the impression that we are luring them into some kind of an ambush, and will deter their attack."

Li Guang then gave the order to advances towards the Xiongnu. When they were only two *li* from the Xiongnu camp, he ordered his soldiers to dismount and unsaddle all their horses for a rest.

The soldiers cried out in anguish, "With so many Xiongnu so close, what will we do if we are attacked?"

Li Guang reassured them, "We want to dupe them into believing that we are here to lure them into a trap."

The Xiongnu generals began to feel uneasy at this maneuver by Li Guang. They decided to watch the Han troops from afar and not take any risks.

When a Xiongnu general astride his white steed was seen inspecting his troops, Li Guang and a dozen soldiers jumped on their horses and dashed in his direction, killing him with an arrow. Returning just as quickly to their camp, they jumped off their horses and resumed their rest.

This had the effect of deepening Xiongnu suspicions. At nightfall, they became increasingly convinced that a Han ambush was imminent. Fearing an attack under the cover of night, they beat a hasty retreat. At daybreak, after making sure there were no more Xiongnu soldiers in the hills, Li Guang brought his 100 cavalrymen back to the main camp without a single casualty.

After a careful assessment of the four generals sent against him, the Chanyu of the Xiongnu Junchen concluded that his toughest opponent was Li Guang. He accordingly concentrated his forces in Yanmen. He set ambushes along the way and gave orders for Li Guang's capture, wanting him to be taken alive. Since their numbers were superior, after a fierce battle the Xiongnu were able to break apart the forces of Li Guang. He was wounded and captured by Xiongnu soldiers.

The Xiongnu soldiers put the gravely wounded Li Guang in a rope hammock and slung him between two horses to transport him to the Chanyu's main camp. Li Guang lay in the hammock motionless and lifeless. After a dozen *li*, he caught a glimpse of a Xiongnu soldier riding a good horse. Mustering all his strength, he heaved himself onto that horse, grabbed the soldier's bow and arrows, and pushed the soldier off. He jerked the animal around and galloped south.

With hundreds of Xiongnu soldiers riding in pursuit, Li Guang dug his heels into the belly of horse, prodding it to run even faster as he turned in his saddle and fired off his arrows, killing several pursuers. Unable to catch up with Li Guang, the pursuing party gave up and gazed after the fast-disappearing general.

Although out of danger in this instance, Li Guang was convicted of the capital offense of losing a battle and incurring heavy casualties. Under Han law, a person convicted of a crime could redeem himself by paying a fine. Li Guang redeemed himself and went home, stripped of all his official functions.

Not long after his fall from grace, the Xiongnu began to make trouble again on the frontier. Emperor Wu of Han brought Li

Guang out of disfavor, and made him governor of Youbeiping Prefecture (southwest of modern-day Lingyuan, Liaoning Province).

In all the years which Li Guang manned the northern defenses, his agility, accuracy with the bow, and ability to confound the enemy by appearing and disappearing at unexpected moments earned him the nickname the "Flying General" among the Xiongnu. With the feared Li Guang as governor of Youbeiping, the Xiongnu left the prefecture alone.

Although Youbeiping was now free from the threat of marauding Xiongnu, there were frequent injuries and deaths caused by prowling tigers. Li Guang never missed an opportunity to hunt tigers with his deadly accurate arrows. No tiger ever survived an encounter with him.

Legend has it that on his way home one day in failing light, Li Guang and his attendants were walking. They were looking eagle-eyed for signs of a tiger when they sighted a bright-striped specimen crouched in the grass at the foot of a hill. Li Guang armed his bow with an arrow and made bull's eye with his usual accuracy.

His soldiers, armed with swords and lances, ran towards the tiger. As they came closer to the quarry, they did a double take. It was not a tiger, but a big rock that Li Guang had shot. The arrow had gone so deep into the rock that no one could pull it out. The soldiers' surprise was mixed with admiration.

When Li Guang came to have a look, he was also filled with disbelief at how far his arrow had penetrated the rock. He went back to where he was before, and fired another shot at the rock. This time the arrow glanced off the rock, causing only sparks. However, that first shot cemented his legendary reputation as the Flying General who could shoot through a rock.

Li Guang devoted the better part of his life to fighting the Xiongnu. By a display of courage and battle skills in more than 70 battles, he became a formidable nemesis to the Xiongnu nobility. However, he was no stranger to unexpected reversals of fortunes in the course of his battles. In this sense, he was unlike the newly promoted younger generals, Wei Qing and Huo Qubing, who were credited with unalloyed success in the war against Xiongnu invasion.

47. Generals Wei Qing and Huo Qubing

WEI QING HAD modest beginnings. His father was a servant in the household of the Marquis of Pingyang Cao Shou, so when he grew up he also became a servant in the employ of the Marquis of Pingyang. His position improved markedly after his sister Wei Zifu was presented to the imperial palace and found favor with Emperor Wu.

The same year Li Guang escaped after being captured by the Xiongnu in combat, three of the four armies sent against the Xiongnu invading force suffered defeat. Only Wei Qing led his army to victory. As a reward, he was made Marquis of Guannei. He went on to win an impressive string of victories against the Xiongnu marauders.

In 124 BC, Wei Qing's pursuit of the Xiongnu took his 30,000-strong cavalry force outside the Great Wall. Under the false impression that the Han troops were still some distance away, the Right Virtuous King of the Xiongnu had let down his guard and was drinking and making merry in his camp. He got stone drunk.

In the meantime, under cover of night, Wei Qing's troops endured a forced march of seven hundred *li* in order to surround the Right Virtuous King. When the Han troops charged into the Xiongnu camp from all sides, the Xiongnu troops broke up in disarray and dispersed in all directions. The sobered Right Virtuous King tried to put up a fight, but it was already too late. He got away with only a few hundred of his closest associates.

In this battle, Wei Qing's army captured 15,000 enemy soldiers, including a dozen princes.

The Right and Left Virtuous Kings of the Xiongnu were next in rank to the Chanyu. Because of this battle, the Right Virtuous King lost his entire army. This was a heavy blow to the Chanyu.

As soon as news of this victory reached Emperor Wu, he sent an emissary to Wei Qing. He was given the General in Chief's seal, officially making him the General in Chief. With all of the honors bestowed to him, even his three minor sons were to be made marquises.

Wei Qing declined these honors, saying "All credit for my victories goes to my officers and soldiers. Moreover, my three sons are still young boys who have never rendered any service to the country. If His Majesty makes them marquises, how's that going to motivate the soldiers to give their best in battle?"

Sobered by Wei Qing's remarks, Emperor Wu awarded the title of marquis to seven of Wei Qing's generals.

The next year, the Xiongnu launched another invasion. Emperor Wu sent a large expeditionary force to repel the invaders with Wei Qing in command aided by six generals.

An 18-year-old nephew of Wei Qing's called Huo Qubing, who was known for his daring and equestrian and archery skills, also participated in the campaign. He organized a detachment consisting of 800 brave men to seek out Xiongnu troops. They marched north, but did not see a single Xiongnu. They had rode hundreds of *li* before they finally saw Xiongnu tents in the distance.

Moving stealthily towards the enemy camp by a circuitous route, they found the largest tent and charged in. The sharp-eyed and fast-moving Huo Qubing killed a Xiongnu nobleman with one swing of his sword, and his soldiers captured two more.

The now leaderless Xiongnu troops dispersed in a disorderly flight. The 800 braves chased after them, and killed more than 2,000 of them before returning to camp.

The anxious Wei Qing was waiting for them when Huo Qubing went into his tent. He carried a severed head in his hand

and was followed by soldiers escorting the two captives. After an interrogation, they learned that one of the captives was the Chanyu's uncle, while the other was the Chanyu's Chief Minister. The man killed by Huo Qubing in the big tent turned out to be a Xiongnu king who was of the same generation as the Chanyu's grandfather.

Thus, the 18-year-old Huo Qubing had captured two Xiongnu generals in his very first battle. This was no mean feat, and so he was made Marquis of Guanjun when the campaign was over.

In 121 BC, Emperor Wu made Huo Qubing Cavalry General and ordered him to take 10,000 soldiers on an attack against the Xiongnu. Huo's troops marched from Longxi (western Gansu Province), and fought the Xiongnu for six days before the Xiongnu could no longer hold and started to beat a retreat. Huo Qubing with his cavalry engaged the fleeing Xiongnu across the Yanzhi Mountains (west of modern-day Yongchang County, Gansu Province) on a 1,000-*li* pursuit that took them through some vassal states loyal to the Xiongnu. These included Hunxie (in modern-day Gansu Province) and Xiutu (north of modern-day Wuwei County, Gansu). The Han troops captured the prince and the chief minister of the king of Hunxie, and carted away the Golden Statue (actually, a bronze figure) used by the king of Xiutu for his sacrifice to the gods.

For this, Emperor Wu wanted to reward Huo Qubing with a new house, but the latter declined, saying "I have no use for a house as long as the Xiongnu have not been annihilated."

In 119 BC, after painstaking preparations, Emperor Wu sent Wei Qing and Huo Qubing with 50,000 elite troops on a two-pronged attack against the Xiongnu with a view to stopping the Xiongnu invasions for good.

Wei Qing passed through the Great Wall at Dingxiang Prefecture into the Gobi Desert. His soldiers then marched more than a thousand *li*, until they ran into well-trained and well-armed troops led by Yizhixie (also known as El'chishye), the Chanyu of the Xiongnu. A fierce battle was joined. As night fell, a gale-force wind rose in the desert, kicking up a storm of sand and gravel that darkened the theater of the raging battle. Despite having a strong wind and sand blowing in his face, Wei Qing ordered his cavalry to carry out a two-pronged attack. El'chishye was overwhelmed by the assault. He made a dash toward the north with a few hundred of his horsemen, and succeeded in breaking through the encirclement. Wei Qing pressed on in pursuit until his troops reached Zhaoxin City at the foot of the Tianyan Mountains (a southern spur of modern-day Hang'ai Mountains on the Mongolian Plateau). The city had been deserted by the Xiongnu soldiers, who left behind large quantities of rations. Wei Qing's troops feasted on the food, before torching the remaining grain and embarking on a triumphant return.

Meanwhile, Huo Qubing also crossed the Gobi, marching 2,000 *li* to engage the troops of the Left Virtuous King of the Xiongnu. These were soundly defeated. Huo's troops chased them all the way to the Langjuxu Mountains (either northwest of modern-day Wuyuan, Inner Mongolia on the north bank of the Yellow River; or alternately, in modern-day People's Republic of Mongolia). A stele was planted at the location as a monument.

This was the largest-scale military campaign ever undertaken by the Han dynasty, with the deepest penetration into Xiongnu territory. In the aftermath of the campaign, the Xiongnu retreated to regions north of the Gobi Desert. South of the Gobi, all vestiges of Xiongnu presence were removed.

48. Zhang Qian's Mission to the Western Regions

WHEN DEBRIEFING XIONGNU defectors in the early years of his reign, Emperor Wu of Han was able to glean some knowledge of the situation in Xiyu, a region which includes modern-day Xinjiang and the regions west of it. According to these defectors, a kingdom called Yuezhi (also known as Indo-Scyths, or Tokharians) had migrated westward to settle in Xiyu after being defeated by the Xiongnu. The people of Yuezhi were feuding with the Xiongnu and were seeking revenge, but had failed to find an ally in their vendetta against the Xiongnu.

Emperor Wu realized that if the Han dynasty could make an ally of Yuezhi, which was situated west of the Xiongnu's dominion, the Xiongnu's links with other countries in Xiyu would be severed and the Xiongnu would lose, as it were, their right arm.

He issued an imperial edict seeking qualified people to initiate a liaison with Yuezhi. Very few people knew then where or how far away Yuezhi was. It would take great courage to volunteer for such a mission.

A young *langzhong* ("gentleman-of-the-interior"; a low-ranking official) called Zhang Qian found this a worthy cause and was the first to respond. Emboldened by his example, more than 100 brave men also signed up. A man of Xiongnu extraction called Tang Yifu volunteered to join Zhang Qian's quest for the kingdom of Yuezhi.

In 138 BC, this group led by Zhang Qian embarked on the quest ordered by Emperor Wu. To reach Yuezhi, however, they needed to pass through territory under Xiongnu control. Zhang Qian and his team took great pains to avoid detection, but still fell into the hands of Xiongnu soldiers after a few days of travel. The entire group was taken into custody.

They were not killed by the Xiongnu, but were separated into small groups for easier surveillance. Zhang Qian was paired with Tang Yifu, and spent more than a decade in Xiongnu country.

With the passage of time, the Xiongnu gradually relaxed their control. Seizing upon a moment of the guards' inattention, Zhang Qian and Tang Yifu grabbed two fast horses and escaped.

Their flight to the west took them on an odyssey that lasted dozens of days. After enduring numerous ordeals, when they finally escaped Xiongnu country they did not find Yuezhi but instead found themselves in a kingdom called Dayuan ("Great Ionian," near Ferghana in Central Asia).

Dayuan was a close neighbor of the Xiongnu. Since the people of Dayuan understood the Xiongnu language, the Xiongnu-speaking Zhang Qian and Tang Yifu could easily communicate with them. The king of Dayuan had heard about the power and prosperity of the Han dynasty, and was eager to show good will towards its envoys. He warmly received the two men and provided them with an escort that took them safely to Kangju (between Lake Balkhash and the Aral Sea), and from there to the Yuezhi.

After their defeat by the Xiongnu, the Yuezhi migrated to an area bordering Daxia (Bactria, in the north of modern-day Afghanistan). There, they founded the kingdom of Great Yuezhi. By this time the Yuezhi had lost appetite for war with the Xiongnu, and so the king of Great Yuezhi was not interested in Zhang Qian's proposals. However, he treated him with great courtesy because he was envoy of the Han Emperor.

Their stay in Great Yuezhi lasted over a year. During that time, Zhang Qian and Tang Yifu made a trip to Daxia, and were intrigued by the many wonders they saw there. Unable to persuade Great Yuezhi to join an alliance against the Xiongnu, they finally started their journey home. When they passed through Xiongnu country, they were once again captured and taken prisoner. However, thanks to internal conflict among the Xiongnu they found a chance to escape and return to Chang'an.

Upon returning from his thirteen-year-long peregrination abroad, in reward for his great accomplishments Zhang Qian was made Superior Grand Master of the Palace by Emperor Wu.

In a full account of his travels through the countries and kingdoms of Xiyu, he reported, "In the kingdom of Daxia I saw bamboo canes produced in Qiongshan (modern-day Sichuan Province), and fine fabric made in Shudi (modern-day Chengdu, Sichuan Province). The people in Daxia told me these had been imported from Tianzhu (modern-day India)." Zhang Qian went on to say that if products of Shudi were available in Tianzhu, Tianzhu could not be too far from Shudi.

Emperor Wu named Zhang Qian his envoy charged with the mission to establish friendly ties with Tianzhu. Zhang Qian's party, loaded with gifts, used Shudi as a jumping-off point. He organized his team into four groups. Each went off in different directions in search of the kingdom of Tianzhu. After traveling 2,000 *li*, none of the groups found it, and some were turned back by local tribes.

The group that went south was barred passage at Kunming. Circumventing Kunming, the Han travelers arrived in Dianyue (in the east of modern-day Yunnan Province). The king there was a descendant of the old state of Chu, but the area had not been in contact with China proper for generations. The king was willing to help Zhang Qian find his way to Tianzhu, but they still could not get past Kunming.

Zhang Qian thus returned to Chang'an without finding Tianzhu, but Emperor Wu was still quite pleased because of the re-establishment of ties with Dianyue, which had long ago lost contact with China.

After Wei Qing and Huo Qubing neutralized the main fighting forces of the Xiongnu and forced them to flee beyond the northern edge of the Gobi Desert, the countries in Xiyu lost their incentive to pay tribute to the weakened Xiongnu Empire. Emperor Wu saw these changed circumstances as an opportunity, and sent Zhang Qian on a new mission to Xiyu.

In 119 BC, Zhang Qian and his aides, carrying the imperial stave of the Han Empire before them, embarked on another goodwill mission through the Xiyu region, taking with them 300 soldiers, each of whom had in his care two horses. The gifts the delegation bore included 10,000 head of cattle and large amounts of gold, coins, silk and other fabrics.

When Zhang Qian arrived in Wusun (in modern-day Xinjiang), its king came out to greet him. Zhang Qian presented him with a handsome gift, and proposed an alliance by marriage to counter the threat of the Xiongnu. The king of Wusun only knew that the Han Empire was very far from his kingdom, but had no idea of its military might. Although he wanted to receive assistance from the Han Empire, he was afraid to antagonize the Xiongnu. Days of discussions between the king and his counselors about the proposed anti-Xiongnu alliance produced no decision. Since he did not want to lose time, Zhang Qian sent aides bearing gifts to the kingdoms of Dayuan, Great Yuezhi and Yutian (near modern-day Hetian, Xinjiang). The king of Wusun provided them with interpreters.

After the aides had been gone for a long time, the king of Wusun decided to send Zhang Qian back to Chang'an first. A visiting mission composed of dozens of Wusun nationals traveled with Zhang Qian to the Han capital. They brought dozens of strong horses as a tribute to the imperial court of the Han. Emperor Wu was pleased to receive the foreign visitors. The gift of strong horses he received from the king of Wusun added to his pleasure, and the Wusun emissaries were accorded privileged treatment.

A year later, Zhang Qian died of illness. The aides he had sent to other countries of the Xiyu region slowly began returning to Chang'an after visiting a total of 36 countries between them.

From then on, Emperor Wu sent emissaries on yearly visits to these countries, cementing friendly ties between the Han Empire and the countries of Xiyu. Emissaries and traders also flocked to China from Xiyu. Silk and silk products of China were exported to West Asia through Xiyu, and from there on to Europe. This was the beginning of the legendary Silk Road.

49. Su Wu, the Shepherd

FOR MANY YEARS after the generals Wei Qing and Huo Qubing defeated the Xiongnu, there was no war between the two sides. However, the Xiongnu's professed willingness to be at peace with the Han Empire was belied by their persistent yearnings for a push into the central plains of China. Though a steady stream of envoys were sent between the Chanyu and the Han imperial court to negotiate a peace treaty, some of the Han envoys were detained on visits to the Xiongnu court, and a number of Xiongnu emissaries were detained by the Han.

In 100 BC, Emperor Wu was in the midst of planning an attack on the Xiongnu when a Xiongnu envoy arrived with a peace proposal. As a goodwill gesture, all detained Han envoys were to be freed. To reciprocate, Emperor Wu sent Su Wu, his Leader of Court Gentlemen, on a diplomatic mission to the Xiongnu court. Su Wu embarked on his mission carrying the imperial stave, symbolizing his official status, and accompanied by his deputy Zhang Sheng and his aide Chang Hui. He brought with him freed Xiongnu emissaries and gifts for the Chanyu. As Su Wu waited for a letter from the Chanyu to be carried back to Emperor Wu, he suffered a stroke of bad luck.

Prior to Su Wu's mission to the Xiongnu, a Han emissary called Wei Lü had defected to the Xiongnu court. The Chanyu made him a prince, and particularly valued his service.

One of Wei Lü's subordinates, Yu Chang, had long been critical of him. Yu Chang was also an old friend of Su Wu's deputy, Zhang Sheng. Yu Chang confided to Zhang Sheng his plan to kill Wei

Lü, take the Chanyu's mother hostage, and then escape back to his homeland China. Zhang Sheng was sympathetic to Yu Chang's plan. However, the plot backfired and Yu Chang was arrested by the Xiongnu. The furious Chanyu put Wei Lü in charge of the trial of Yu Chang in order to ferret out of co-conspirators. Zhang Sheng was afraid of being implicated, so he told Su Wu the truth about the plot. Previously, Su Wu had been kept in the dark.

Responding to Zhang Sheng's report, Su Wu said, "Considering the way things are going, I am bound to be implicated. To be executed after being dragged through a trial would bring disgrace on the emperor!" So saying, he drew his sword to commit suicide. With their quick reflexes, Zhang Sheng and Chang Hui wrested the sword from him. They then talked him out of killing himself.

Under prolonged torture, Yu Chang only admitted to being a friend of Zhang Sheng's. He said that he had exchanged some words with him, but adamantly denied conspiring with him.

When Wei Lü reported to the Chanyu that Yu Chang had talked with Zhang Sheng, the Chanyu was furious and wanted to kill Su Wu. However, his counselors held him back. The Chanyu then ordered Wei Lü to pressure Su Wu to defect.

When Wei Lü demanded that Su Wu defect, Su Wu replied, "I am a Han envoy. If I fail my mission and lose my integrity, I've no right to continue living."

He then drew his sword and swung it towards his neck.

Wei Lü rushed to take the sword away from him. However, before he could do this, Su Wu had seriously cut himself in the neck and lost consciousness. Emergency medical care was administered to him, and he slowly recovered.

The Chanyu was deeply impressed by the integrity and courage of Su Wu. After Su Wu had recovered from his wound, the Chanyu once again tried to pressure him to defect by having Wei Lü interrogate Yu Chang in Su Wu's presence. At the end of the interrogation, Wei Lü sentenced Yu Chang to death and had him executed. Then Wei Lü raised his sword and threatening to kill Zhang Sheng. Terrified, Zhang Sheng immediately defected to the Xiongnu.

Wei Lü then exclaimed to Su Wu, "Because of your association to your deputy, you also are guilty and must be punished."

Su Wu retorted, "I didn't conspire with him and I am no relative of his. By what association must I be punished?"

Wei Lü raised his sword to threaten Su Wu, but Su Wu remained unruffled. Seeing the threat had no effect on him, Wei Lü lowered his sword and began cajoling him, "I defected because I was left with no other option. The Chanyu has been very kind to me. He made me a prince, gave me tens of thousands of soldiers, and enough sheep and cattle to fill an entire hill. My life is now sweet. If you agree to defect today, tomorrow you will be like me. Life is too precious to throw away!"

Su Wu rose to his feet in a huff and said, "Wei Lü! You are a Han and a Han public official, but you have now bitten the hand that feeds you. You've betrayed your parents and your Emperor and have become a shameless traitor. You are unworthy to talk to me! Despite all your threats and sweet talk, I will never defect."

Snubbed by Su Wu, Wei Lü reported what had happened to the Chanyu. The Chanyu threw Su Wu into a cellar and deprived him of food and water, trying to force him to yield by putting him through a long, slow ordeal.

It was winter, and big snowflakes fell heavily outside the cellar. Su Wu was racked with hunger pangs. He slaked his thirst by scooping up handfuls of snow, and assuaged his hunger by chewing on pieces of sheepskin. After some days had passed, he was still alive.

When the Chanyu saw that this slow torture did not work, he exiled Su Wu to Beihai ("Northern Lake"; modern-day Lake Baikal) as a shepherd. He separating him from his aide Chang Hui, and forbade them to communicate with each other.

The Chanyu told Su Wu, "You will be released when a ram gives birth to a kid." Since no one has ever heard of a ram giving birth, it was the Chanyu's way of telling him that he would be in prison for a long, long time.

At Beihai, Su Wu was alone in the northern landscape with only the imperial stave for company. When food ran out, he would dig into moles' burrows for grass roots to eat. With the passage of time, all of the decorative yak's hair on his stave fell off.

In 85 BC, the Chanyu died. This triggered infighting that led to the partition of the Xiongnu Empire into three kingdoms. The new Chanyu was too weak to go to war with the Han Empire, and so he sent an envoy with an olive branch. Emperor Wu had also died by that time, and was succeeded by his son, Emperor Zhao of Han. Emperor Zhao sent an envoy to the Xiongnu court to demand the release of Su Wu. However, after being given false information by the Xiongnu side that Su Wu had died, the gullible envoy did not press the matter.

On another visit by a Han envoy to the Xiongnu, Su Wu's aide Chang Hui, who was alive in Xiongnu territory, bribed a Xiongnu to obtain a private meeting with the envoy. He told the envoy that Su Wu was herding sheep at Lake Baikal.

Later, when the envoy met the Chanyu, he harshly criticized him, saying "Since the Xiongnu court is determined to be at peace with the Han Empire, it should not deceive the Han. My Emperor shot a goose in his imperial garden, and found a silk ribbon tied to its foot with a message saying that Su Wu is still alive. Why did you tell us he had died?"

The Chanyu was taken aback by the account. He actually believed that Su Wu's loyalty must have so moved the goose that it had agreed to carry the message. He apologized to the envoy, saying "Su Wu is indeed alive. We will free him and let him go home."

Su Wu was 40 when he went on the diplomatic mission to the Xiongnu. After nineteen years of ordeal, his beard and hair had turned completely white. On his return to Chang'an, the residents turned out to give him a massive welcome. They were deeply touched by the sight of Su Wu, with his white beard and hair and imperial stave now completely shorn of its decorative yak's hair.

"Here is a real man of courage and integrity!" exclaimed the crowd with admiration.

50. Sima Qian, Author of *Shi Ji*

IN THE SECOND year of Su Wu's diplomatic mission to the Xiongnu court, Emperor Wu of Han sent Li Guangli, the General of Ershi (Sutrishna) with a 30,000-strong expeditionary force against the Xiongnu. Li Guangli suffered a rout resulting in the decimation of his force and fled back to the capital.

His grandson, Li Ling, who was then Commander of Calvary, engaged the Xiongnu with 5,000 soldiers. However, Li Ling's troops were then surrounded by 30,000 cavalrymen personally commanded by the Chanyu of the Xiongnu. Li Ling had legendary skill as an archer and his soldiers were quite brave. They were able to kill five or six thousand Xiongnu horsemen, but they were seriously outnumbered by a Xiongnu army that seemed only to keep growing in size. With no reinforcement coming to their rescue, only 400 Han soldiers succeeded in slipping through the noose of the encircling Xiongnu cavalry. Li Ling surrendered and was taken prisoner by the Xiongnu.

News of Li Ling's surrender shocked the Han court. Emperor Wu put Li Ling's mother, wife, and children in jail, and then summoned his ministers for a discussion of Li Ling's crime.

The ministers denounced Li Ling's cowardice in surrendering to the Xiongnu. Emperor Wu then asked his Grand Scribe Sima Qian for his view on the matter.

Sima Qian said, "With barely 5,000 infantrymen, Li Ling penetrated deep behind enemy lines, and inflicted heavy casualties on an enemy force tens of thousands strong. He had something to show for his efforts despite being finally defeated. Li Ling must have his reasons for not choosing to die now. He must be thinking of one day vindicating himself and repaying the emperor with a valiant act."

His apology for Li Ling sounded to the emperor like a pointed put-down of Li Guangli, the brother of the emperor's favorite concubine. The emperor replied in fury, "How can you defend someone who has surrendered to the enemy? Your behavior is blatantly against the interests of the imperial court."

In a thundering voice he ordered Sima Qian incarcerated, pending a trial by the Chamberlain for Law Enforcement.

At the conclusion of the trial, Sima Qian was convicted. As a penalty, he sentenced to be castrated. Since he could not afford the sum necessary to redeem the crime, Sima Qian submitted to the punishment and remained in jail.

Overwhelmed by the stigma and shame of castration, Sima Qian was tempted to commit suicide. He banished these thoughts by remembering that he had important, unfinished business. He was then totally absorbed in the writing of a book which would later become known as the greatest work of ancient Chinese history. The book was called *Shi Ji* (*Historical Records of the Grand Scribe*).

For generations, Sima Qian's forefathers had been court historiographers. His father Sima Tan was also a Grand Scribe at the Han court. At ten years of age, Sima Qian followed his father to Chang'an. Even at this young age, he was already well-read.

In order to collect historical data and materials and to broaden his knowledge, at the age of 20 Sima Qian began traveling to various places in China. He went to Guiji in Zhejiang to visit the spot where, according to legend, Da Yu had convoked tribal chiefs for a meeting. In Changsha, he paid respects to the patriotic poet Qu Yuan on the banks of the Miluo River. He toured the ruins of what used to be Confucius's academy in Qufu. His travels took him to Pei County, the hometown of Emperor Gaozu of Han, where he was regaled with tales about Liu Bang's rebellion. His journeys combined sightseeing and study, broadening his knowledge. In the process, the rich local languages he came across helped inform Sima Qian's future writing in a major way.

After being appointed an attendant to Emperor Wu of Han, Sima Qian accompanied the emperor on imperial inspection tours to various places. He was sent on inspection tours to the Ba Shu (modern-day Sichuan) and Kunming areas on several occasions.

At his father's death, Sima Qian succeeded him as the Grand Scribe. In his new post, he had the opportunity to read and collect more historical data and materials.

Just when he readied himself to write his historical record, the emperor had him thrown into jail and castrated as punishment for defending Li Ling. Sima Qian was agonized by the thought, "I brought it on myself. I am now castrated, and my manhood is ruined. I'm finished."

On the other hand, he thought, King Wen of Zhou had finished his work *Zhou Yi* (*Changes of Zhou*) when he was jailed at Youli. Confucius completed his *Spring and Autumn Annals* after being stranded in Chencai on his wanderings through the various states. Qu Yuan wrote the poem *Li Sao* (*The Lament*) in exile. Zuoqiu Ming authored *Guoyu* (*Remarks of Monarchs*) after he lost his sight. Sun Bin wrote his treatise on *The Art of War* after being punished by having his kneecaps cut out. Most of the 300 poems of the *Book of Songs* were composed by poets filled with indignation and sadness. Behind every one of these famous works of antiquity one could find an author who was oppressed by a deep sense of frustration and disillusionment. "Why can't I also take advantage of this opportunity to finish my historical work?" thought Sima Qian.

And so he completed his great work, *Shi Ji*. It is comprised of 130 chapters and 520,000 words, and covers China's history from the Yellow Emperor of legend down to the second year (95 BC) of the Taishi Era, during the reign of Emperor Wu of Han.

In *Shi Ji*, Sima Qian gave detailed accounts of the lives and deeds of famous personalities in China's history, and translated the obscure and arcane language used in ancient texts into easier-to-understand contemporary expressions. With its vivid imagery in depicting history's protagonists, and its vibrant, captivating prose, *Shi Ji* is at once a great work of history, and a literary masterpiece.

After being released from jail, Sima Qian was made Director of the Secretariat. He remained in depression until the day of his death, but was assured of an exalted place in the history of China's literary and historical studies.

51. Wang Zhaojun Carried off in Marriage by a Xiongnu

AFTER EMPEROR WU died, Emperor Zhao of Han succeeded to his throne and reigned for 12 years. In 73 BC, he was succeeded by a great-grandson of Emperor Wu, Liu Xun, who ascended the throne as Emperor Xuan of Han. By that time, the Xiongnu had entered a period of steady decline as its noblemen jostled for power. The Xiongnu Empire eventually split up with five separate Chanyus embroiled in perpetual internecine conflict.

One of the Chanyus was Huhanye. His army had been defeated in war and suffered heavy casualties by the hand of the Chanyu Zhizhi, his brother. To forestall complete disaster, after consulting his counselors Huhanye decided to sue for peace with the Han. He personally led a delegation to pay tribute to Emperor Xuan of Han.

Being the first Chanyu to come to the central plains of China for an audience with the Han Emperor, Emperor Xuan rolled out the red carpet for Huhanye, personally greeting him at the outskirts of Chang'an, and throwing a gala in his honor.

After he had stayed in Chang'an for over a month, Huhanye asked Emperor Xuan to help him return to his country. The emperor had him escorted to the southern fringe of the Gobi Desert by two generals at the command of 10,000 cavalrymen. Since there was a food shortage besetting the lands under Xiongnu control at that time, the Han sent with him 34,000 *hu* (equivalent to about 10 decaliters) of grain.

The grateful Chanyu Huhanye was committed to peace with the Han. Hearing of the reconciliation between the Xiongnu and the Han, other countries and kingdoms in the Xiyu region eagerly scrambled to improve ties with the Han.

At his death, Emperor Xuan's son Liu Shi succeeded him as Emperor Yuan of Han. A few years later, the Xiongnu Chanyu Zhizhi invaded countries in Xiyu and killed the envoys sent there by the Han dynasty. A Han army was then sent to Kangju, where it defeated the Chanyu Zhizhi and killed him.

The death of the Chanyu Zhizhi led to the consolidation of Huhanye's power. In 33 BC, the Chanyu Huhanye made another trip to Chang'an and asked to marry a lady in the imperial family. Emperor Yuan gave his consent.

Traditionally, when a marriage was proposed between the Xiongnu and the Han, the bride had to be a princess or a daughter in the imperial clan. This time, Emperor Yuan decided to give him a palace lady-in-waiting. He had word circulated in the imperial harem, "Whoever volunteers to be married off to the Xiongnu court will be treated by His Majesty like a princess."

The ladies-in-waiting in the imperial harem had all been recruited from among the common people. Once they were brought into the palace, they were confined like birds in a cage. While their fondest wish was to leave the palace, when they learned that the bride had to leave the country for a foreign land, their interest waned. However, a beautiful and sophisticated lady-in-waiting called Wang Qiang, also known as Wang Zhaojun, wanting to make something of her life, volunteered to be married off to the land of the Xiongnu.

The minister entrusted with the task of finding a candidate was fretting over the lack of volunteers when he received Wang Zhaojun's application. He reported her name to Emperor Yuan. The emperor then instructed the official to pick an auspicious date for the wedding of Huhanye and Wang Zhaojun in Chang'an.

The Chanyu Huhanye, needless to say, was elated and grateful at the prospect of having such a beautiful, young woman for wife. However, when the Chanyu Huhanye and Wang Zhaojun went before Emperor Yuan to give their thanks, the emperor was dazzled by Wang Zhaojun's beauty and grace. He was a little reluctant to let her go and soon had thoughts of keeping her for himself, but it was too late.

Legend has it that when Emperor Yuan returned to his quarters he was increasingly annoyed by what had just happened. Emperor Yuan had Wang Zhaojun's portrait brought to him from the collection of portraits of the ladies in the harem. He found that although the portrait bore some resemblance to Wang Zhaojun, it failed miserably to do justice to her exquisite beauty.

In truth, the ladies-in-waiting were not normally interviewed by the emperor in person. Instead, their likenesses were painted by court painters, and presented to the emperor for his perusal. One court painter, Mao Yanshou, would paint more flattering portraits of the ladies in return for favors or gifts. Since Wang Zhaojun had no wish to give Mao Yanshou a present, he had chosen not to do full justice to her true beauty.

When Emperor Yuan saw the painting, in fury he had Mao Yanshou executed.

Escorted by Han and Xiongnu officials, Wang Zhaojun departed Chang'an. Braving the bitterly cold wind, she rode thousands of *li* to the land of the Xiongnu, where she was made Queen of the Chanyu Huhanye. In time, she became accustomed to Xiongnu life and got along very well with the Xiongnu, who loved and respected her.

Wang Zhaojun settled in the land of the Xiongnu, thousands of *li* away from home. She counseled the Chanyu Huhanye against making war and introduced the Han culture to the Xiongnu. Under her influence, the Xiongnu and the Han Empire coexisted in peace for six decades.

Not long after Wang Zhaojun's departure from Chang'an, Emperor Yuan died. His son Liu Ao succeeded him as Emperor Cheng of Han.

52. Wang Mang Restores the Old System

AFTER THE ASCENSION of the profligate Emperor Cheng to the Han throne, power in the Han court gradually fell into the hands of his mother, the Empress Dowager, and the Queen. Wang Zhengjun, the Empress Dowager, had eight brothers. With the exception of one who had died young, all the others were all made marquises. Wang Feng, the eldest of them, also held the titles of Commander-in-Chief and Chief General.

The concentration of power in the hands of Wang Feng fueled the arrogance, insolence and extravagance of his brothers and nephews. Only Wang Mang, a nephew who had lost his father at a young age, remained unspoiled by this power and wealth. Like the average scholar, he was prudent and frugal. He had the reputation of being the most decent young man in the Wang clan.

After Wang Feng's death, the post of Commander-in-Chief was held by a succession of his brothers. Finally, the position of Commander-in-Chief was occupied by Wang Mang. His reputation as a judge of talent attracted many a scholar who volunteered their service. Wang Mang took them all under his wing.

Within a ten-year period after the death of Emperor Cheng of Han, two emperors, Emperor Ai and Emperor Ping, followed one another in the throne. Emperor Ping was only nine years old when he ascended the throne, and so all the important decisions of the empire were left in the hands of Wang Mang. Some sycophants began beating the drum to have Wang Mang's great contribution to the stability of the Han Empire recognized. They lobbied the Grand Empress Dowager Wang Zhengjun to make him the Duke of Anhan (literally, "the stabilization of the Han"). Wang Mang steadfastly refused to accept the title or the fief that came with it. At the insistence of the other ministers, he finally accepted the title. However, he declined the fief.

In 2 AD, the central plains of China were ravaged by draught and locusts. For years, the nobility, the rich, and the powerful had been grabbing land and exploiting the peasants. The people were already on the brink of starvation, so whenever a natural disaster struck there was civil unrest.

In order to appease popular anger at the imperial court and public officials, Wang Mang proposed reducing the government's consumption of grain and fabrics. He donated 1,000,000 *qian* of his own money and 30 hectares of land to be used for disaster relief. His example was followed, albeit grudgingly, by some members of the nobility and high officialdom.

The Grand Empress Dowager's offer of 20,000 hectares of land in Xinye (modern-day Xinye, Henan Province) to Wang Mang was declined once again by him.

Wang Mang sent eight of his trusted ministers to different parts of the country for a first-hand understanding of the places and the people. They widely publicized Wang Mang's refusal to accept a fief in Xinye, making much of his modesty and his willingness to listen to the people's concerns. When the smaller landowners, who deeply resented the powerful and wealthy land-grabbers, heard about Wang Mang's refusal of the fief offered to him, they became convinced that he was a very decent man.

Wang Mang's refusal only prompted more lobbying of the Grand Empress Dowager to reward him. It is said that there were a total of over 480,000 requests from court ministers, local officials, and commoners for Wang Mang to receive a fief. The official tributes and praises for Wang Mang were compiled and totaled 30,000 words. Wang Mang's authority and popularity soared.

The rising popularity of Wang Mang only heightened Emperor Ping's fear and resentment of him. When Emperor Ping grew older, he sometimes complained about Wang Mang behind his back. To reciprocate, Wang Mang prevented the emperor's mother, the Empress Dowager, from staying with him, and then had all of her relatives killed.

Then, at a party organized by ministers to celebrate the emperor's birthday, Wang Mang offered a poisoned glass of wine to the emperor, who drank it without suspecting foul play. The next day, word spread from the palace that Emperor Ping was seriously ill. He died a few days later and Wang Mang made a show of crying disconsolately over his death. The emperor naturally died without an heir, as he was only fourteen years old. Wang Mang selected a two-year-old boy called Ruzi Ying from the Liu clan and set him up as Crown Prince. Then he granted himself the title of Acting Emperor.

Eager to become the founding fathers of a new dynasty, some civilian and military officials urged Wang Mang to proclaim himself emperor. Wang Mang also preferred to be an actual emperor instead of a mere acting one. Superstitious omens and myths were invented by sycophants to mislead the public. Thus books were "discovered" that declared Wang Mang to be a preordained "Son of Heaven," and a bronze case was "found" in the Temple to Emperor Gaozu that proved "Gaozu ceded the throne to Wang Mang."

The famously self-effacing Wang Mang was no longer so self-effacing. He went before the Grand Empress Dowager to demand the imperial seal of the Han Empire. Wang Zhengjun, belatedly shocked by the turn of events, refused to surrender it. When pressed further, she angrily threw it to the floor.

In 8 AD, Wang Mang ascended the throne and created the Xin dynasty, keeping the capital at Chang'an. The Western Han dynasty founded by Gaozu of Han thus came to an end after 210 years of rule.

After becoming Emperor, Wang Mang proclaimed a host of new laws under the guise of restoring the golden age of antiquity. First, he decreed that all the land in the Empire was now owned by the Empire. All land transactions were thus henceforth banned. Second, he banned slave trading. Third, he announced price controls and monetary reform.

These reforms looked fine on paper, but all of them failed in actual execution. Land reform and the ban on slave trading fizzled early on after meeting strong resistance from the nobility, the powerful, and the wealthy elite. The administration of price controls was given to the nobility and bureaucrats, who were only too glad to have one more opportunity to use their position to enrich themselves through speculation, corruption and extortion. Instead of helping the populace, his price-stabilizing measures only added to their misery. In successive waves of monetary reform, the size of coins got smaller while their face value kept increasing. His monetary reform in effect took more money out of the pockets of the people.

These reforms were not only opposed by the peasants, but also alienated many small landowners. Three years after the introduction of the new policies, Wang Mang reversed the ban on land transactions and slave trading.

Wang Mang tried to distract attention from domestic tensions by waging war against foreign lands, but this had the effect of antagonizing the Xiongnu, and countries and tribes in Xiyu and southwest China. Wang Mang's use of conscripted labor, his tax increases, and his acquiescence in the cruel and harsh punishments meted out by ruthless officials pushed the peasants toward rebellion.

53. Uprising of the Red Eyebrows and the Army of the Green Woods

IN 17 AD, famine struck the Jingzhou region in the south of China. The people were forced to resort to digging up wild water chestnuts in marshland for food. However, there were not enough wild water chestnuts to feed all the hungry people, and disputes broke out. Wang Kuang and Wang Feng, two respected men from Xinshi (northeast of modern-day Jingshan, Hubei Province), came forward to mediate the disputes. The appreciative peasants made them their leaders.

Wang Kuang and Wang Feng led the hungry peasants in an uprising. Soon the force grew to several hundred, and some escaped prisoners joined their ranks.

The insurgents made the Lülin (Green Woods) Mountain (modern-day Dahong Mountain, Hubei Province) their base of operations and seized nearby villages. In a few months, the ranks of insurgents had swelled to 8,000.

Wang Mang sent an army of 20,000 to smash the Army of the Green Woods, but the government forces were soundly beaten by the insurgents and fled in a rout. Riding the momentum of victory, the Army of the Green Woods captured several county towns, and freed the inmates of the local jails. They distributed a small part of the grain stored in government granaries to the local poor, and transported the rest to their mountain base. As more impoverished people joined the insurgents, the rebel army grew to 50,000.

The next year, an unfortunate epidemic decimated the rebel

camp, killing nearly half of the 50,000 combatants. The survivors were forced to leave Lülin Mountain. They eventually split into three groups: the Xinshi Regiment, the Pinglin Regiment (Pinglin was northeast of modern-day Sui County, Hubei Province) and the Xiajiang Regiment (Xiajiang was downstream the Yangtze from western Hubei). The three regiments grew stronger in their respective spheres of operations.

While the Army of the Green Woods was fighting government forces in Jingzhou, an insurgency was also gaining strength in the east. In Langya (modern-day Rizhao County, Shandong Province), an old woman by the name of Lü lost her son. Her son was a bailiff in the county government who had been killed by the county magistrate because he had defied orders to beat up a citizen who was too poor to pay his taxes. This created a public uproar. About a hundred impoverished peasants avenged Mother Lü by killing the county magistrate. The peasants followed Mother Lü and sought refugee on the Yellow Sea. They made frequent sorties against government forces on the shore.

At about that same time, another rebel leader, Fan Chong, occupied Tai Mountain with a force of several hundred. After Mother Lü died, her followers joined Fan Chong's group. Within a year the rebel force grew to 10,000. It attacked government installations and landlords in the area between Qingzhou and Xuzhou.

In the insurgent army of Fan Chong, discipline was strict. Any of his group who killed a civilian would be put to death, and any harm caused to a civilian would be punished. As a result, the army enjoyed wide popular support.

In 22 AD Wang Mang sent a nobleman, Wang Kuang (not the Wang Kuang of the Army of the Green Woods) and General Lian Dan with 100,000 soldiers to put down the rebellion of Fan Chong. Fan Chong was meanwhile primed for a pivotal battle with the government force. In order to avoid confusion, he instructed his soldiers to paint their eyebrows red to distinguish themselves from Wang Mang's soldiers. This earned them the moniker of the "Red Eyebrows Army."

In the battle with the Red Eyebrows, Wang Mang's forces were routed, and half of the soldiers melted away. Fan Chong stabbed the nobleman Wang Kuang in the leg with his lance, causing him to flee back to his camp. General Lian Dan was killed in the confusion of the battle. The Red Eyebrows grew stronger in combat, and swelled to more than 100,000 men.

As news spread of the defeats of Wang Mang's forces by the Army of the Green Woods in the south, and the Red Eyebrows in the east, peasants in other areas were galvanized into action. Dozens of insurgencies of varying scale were active on the plains on both sides of the Yellow River. Some noblemen, landlords, and erstwhile powerful and wealthy clans who had fallen on hard times also jumped on the anti-Wang Mang bandwagon.

The brothers Liu Yin and Liu Xiu, local gentry from the village of Chongling in Nanyang Prefecture (north of modern-day Ningyuan, Hunan Province) were deeply resentful of Wang Mang for stripping the Han royal clan of their titles, and for denying public office to anyone whose surname was Liu. They led a force of 8,000 clansmen and retainers in an uprising in Chongling. In alliance with the three regiments of the Army of the Green Woods, they were able to defeat forces led by several of Wang Mang's best generals, gaining in strength in the process.

The regiments of the Army of the Green Woods suffered from a lack of unified command. The troops realized that to ensure a unified line of command in their vastly expanded force they must have a leader. Some of their generals descended from nobility or land owners. They argued that, for the movement to have legitimacy, their leader should have the surname of Liu.

There were many with the surname of Liu in the Army of the Green Woods, so it was a question which one should be selected leader. The forces from Chongling wanted to nominate Liu Yin. However, fearing Liu Yin, the generals of the Xinshi and the Pingling Regiments insisted on Liu Xuan, a ruined aristocrat, as emperor. Liu Yin proposed to delay the setting up of an emperor until after eliminating Wang Mang and co-opting the Red Eyebrows, but they opposed his suggestion. Sensing that he was in the minority, Liu Yin did not insist on having his way.

In 23 AD, the Army of the Green Woods and allied forces

proclaimed Liu Xuan Emperor, seeking to reinstitute the Han dynasty. Since they gave the era the name "Gengshi", Liu Xuan was also known as Emperor Gengshi. Upon installation as Emperor, he conferred upon Wang Kuang and Wang Feng the title of Superior Duke, and named Liu Yin Grand Minister of Education and Liu Xiu Deputy General. Many other generals were also awarded titles. From then on, the Army of the Green Woods became known as the Han Army.

EASTERN HAN DYNASTY
(25 AD–220 AD)

54. Liu Xiu Restores the Han Dynasty

AFTER LIU XUAN ascended the throne as Emperor Gengshi, the Han Army led by Wang Feng, Wang Chang and Liu Xiu annihilated the bulk of Wang Mang's army in a major battle at Kunyang (north of modern-day Ye County, Henan Province).

As the fame of Liu Yin and Liu Xiu grew, Liu Xuan was advised to get rid of Liu Yin, and so he was executed on a dubious charge of insubordination. When Liu Xiu learned that his elder brother had been killed, he rushed to Yuan County (modern-day Nanyang City, Henan Province) to present his apologies to Liu Xuan, knowing very much that he was no match for Liu Xuan in military strength. When asked about the Battle of Kunyang, he declined all credit for himself and attributed the victory to his officers and soldiers. He was careful not to betray the slightest sign of mourning for his brother, and continued to show a healthy appetite for food, drink, conversation, and a good laugh.

Feeling a little guilty by Liu Xiu's apparent forgive-and-forget attitude, Emperor Gengshi named Liu Xiu as Po Lu (Barbarians' Exterminator) Chief General, but gave him no real responsibilities. It was not until after Wang Mang was killed, Chang'an fell, and the emperor Gengshi arrived in Luoyang that Liu Xiu received the command of a small force, which was entrusted with the pacification of the prefectures and counties in Hebei.

In that period, many powerful families and local gentry across China were well-provisioned in arms. They proclaimed themselves generals, princes, kings, and even emperors in their respective spheres of influence. Liu Xiu's mission of pacification to Hebei gave him a heaven-sent opportunity to broaden his power base and influence. He abolished some draconian laws and regulations dating to the Wang Mang period, and released some prisoners. Devoting equal attention to eliminating the pockets of armed local gentry and to suppressing the peasant insurgencies in Hebei, soon he extended control over the entire region.

In 25 AD, Liu Xiu and his officials considered the time ripe for him to proclaim himself emperor. He ascended the throne as Emperor Guangwu of Han at Hao (north of modern-day Boxiang County, Hebei Province).

Emperor Gengshi had made Luoyang his capital before moving it to Chang'an. Once in Chang'an, he became complacent because he believed his imperial rule was assured. Becoming corrupt, he doled out patronage without regard to merit, and indulged in a life of profligacy in the palace to the neglect of the running of state. He even condoned the looting and pillaging of his troops. His excesses were deeply resented by some of the generals who had served with him in the Army of the Green Woods.

Reckoning that the days of Emperor Gengshi were numbered, Fan Chong, the leader of the Red Eyebrows, led 200,000 troops in an assault on Chang'an. The army sent by Emperor Gengshi to repel the attack suffered a series of setbacks throwing the emperor into a panic. Generals of his army urged the emperor Gengshi to leave Chang'an, but this aroused his suspicion, and he had them killed. Some other generals went over to the Red Eyebrows. The turmoil in Emperor Gengshi's court enabled the Red Eyebrows to easily penetrate their defenses at Hangu Pass.

The Red Eyebrows wanted to overthrow Emperor Gengshi, but Fan Chong and his followers were deeply attached to the idea of legitimacy, and insisted on having an Emperor from the Liu clan. Of the more than 70 members of the Liu clan in the Red Eyebrows Army, a 15-year-old cow herder called Liu Penzi was said to be closest in blood to the royalty of the Western Han. He was made Emperor without his own consent.

When the Red Eyebrows entered Chang'an, Emperor Gengshi fled the city. Fan Chong's emissary gave Emperor Gengshi 20 days in which to surrender. Having little choice, he went with his imperial seal to the Red Eyebrows.

The huge size of the Red Eyebrows Army had the downside that there were not enough rations for the hundreds of thousands of soldiers in Chang'an. The wealthy local merchants and landowners capitalized on the chaos to hoard grain. Daily, people died from starvation in Chang'an. The chaotic situation in the capital spiraled out of control.

Fan Chong led his army on a westward trek to find food, but food was hard to come by anywhere. Near Tianshui (in modern-day Gansu Province), they were attacked and turned back by armed local gentry and landowners. Fan Chong had no choice but to take his troops east.

Emperor Guangwu of Han took control of Luoyang at the same time the Red Eyebrows captured Chang'an. When he received intelligence that the Red Eyebrows were marching east, he led a force of 200,000 to waylay them.

Emperor Guangwu sent General Feng Yi to Huayin to lure the Red Eyebrows further east. By a ruse, Feng Yi was able to surround a contingent of the Red Eyebrows at the foot of the Xiaoshan Mountain. He delivered a letter to the Red Eyebrows daring them to battle at an appointed time and place. The unsophisticated Fan Chong fell for the enemy's trick and sent 10,000 of his troops into battle. Feng Yi deployed only a small force at first. When the Red Eyebrows saw the small size of the Han army, they came out in force. Feng Yi'd had a large contingent of his army made-up and dressed like soldiers in the Red Eyebrows Army. Suddenly, in the midst of the melee, these troops surged around the Red Eyebrows.

Before the Red Eyebrows had time to recover from their initial shock and confusion, the Han soldiers in the guise of Red Eyebrows started shouting, "I surrender! I surrender!"

The Red Eyebrows panicked when so many of their "comrades" apparently surrendered, and the Han troops were able to disarm the demoralized and disoriented enemy soldiers without much difficulty.

In January of 27 AD, when Feng Yi received intelligence that Fan Chong and his remnant force of Red Eyebrows were moving towards Yiyang (modern-day Yiyang County, Henan Province), he immediately reported it to Emperor Guangwu. The emperor came out to take personal command of two armies already positioned in that vicinity. They intercepted and encircled the Red Eyebrows. With his back to the wall, Fan Chong sent a messenger to Emperor Guangwu suing for peace.

Emperor Guangwu brought Liu Penzi and his followers back to Luoyang. He gave them land and houses so that they could settle down, but within a few months had Fan Chong killed on charges of sedition.

55. The Quest for Buddhist Sutras and Statues

EMPEROR GUANGWU reunified China after suppressing the two largest insurgencies, the Army of the Green Woods and the Red Eyebrows. He subsequently toppled the separatist regimes at Longyou and Shudi, and made Luoyang his capital. To distinguish it from the Han dynasty founded by Liu Bang, historians call this new dynasty "Eastern Han" or "Later Han."

Dying of illness at the age of 63, Emperor Guangwu was succeeded by Crown Prince Liu Zhuang, who took the title Emperor Ming of Han.

One day Emperor Ming dreamed of a golden giant with a halo around his head. The golden giant flew around the palace, then abruptly soared into the sky and disappeared to the west.

When he recounted this dream to his ministers, they were unable to surmise the identity of the haloed, golden giant.

A learned man called Fu Yi said, "There is a god in Tianzhu called Buddha. The golden giant in Your Majesty's dream must have been the Buddha of Tianzhu."

The Tianzhu referred to by Fu Yi was alternatively known as Yuandu. It was reputed to be the birthplace of Sakyamuni, founder of Buddhism (Tianzhu was another name for ancient India. Sakyamuni was born in Kapililavastu in the north of ancient India, now in Nepal). Sakyamuni, or Gautama Buddha, was born circa 565 BC. According to legend, he abandoned the good life of a prince at the age of 29 to lead the life of asceticism dedicated to learning. He went on to found Buddhism.

Sakyamuni traveled about spreading his Buddhist philosophy. In his more than 40 years of teaching, he acquired a large following and was venerated as Buddha by the believers. After his death, his disciples wrote down his teachings and compiled them into sutras, or Buddhist scriptures.

Emperor Ming was intrigued by what Fu Yi told him, and sent his officials Cai Yin and Qin Jing to Tianzhu to acquire the sutras.

After an odyssey over "thousand mountains and ten thousand rivers," Cai Yin and Qin Jing finally arrived in the kingdom of Tianzhu. When the people of Tianzhu learned that China had sent a delegation on a quest for Buddhist sutras, they gave the envoys a warm welcome. Two *sramanas* of Tianzhu called Dharmaraksa (Zhufalan) and Kasyapa Matanga (Moteng) taught Cai Yin and Qin Jing about Buddhism, and were invited by them to visit China.

In 67 AD, Cai Yin and Qin Jing brought the two eminent monks, white horses carrying a statue of the Buddha, and *The Sutra of Forty-two Sections Spoken by the Buddha* through the Xiyu region back to Luoyang.

Although he had little understanding of Buddhist scriptures or philosophy, Emperor Ming treated the two monks bringing the scriptures to his court with great respect. The next year, he ordered a Buddhist temple to be built in the Indian style west of Luoyang. The temple (in the eastern outskirts of modern-day Luoyang City) came to be known as *Bai Ma Si* (White Horse Temple) because the white horses carrying the scriptures back to China were kept on the temple grounds.

Emperor Ming was unfamiliar with the Buddhist scriptures, and his ministers and nobility were not Buddhist believers. Very few people visited White Horse Temple to burn incense or pray to Buddha. Liu Ying, the Prince of Chu, was an exception. He took Buddhism seriously and sent an emissary to Luoyang for the express purpose of seeking enlightenment from the two Indian monks. They made a copy of the image of Buddha and of the Buddhist text for the emissary to take back to Liu Ying. After the emissary returned to Liu Ying's fief of Chu, the Prince of Chu put the statue of Buddha in his palace and worshipped it regularly.

Liu Ying was an ambitious man. In the name of Buddhist worship, he linked up with many alchemists and used schemes playing on people's superstitions to fool them.

In 70 AD, Emperor Ming heard accusations that the Prince of Chu was building a power base and setting up a parallel system of government in preparation for a rebellion. After an investigation, the emperor found that Liu Ying was indeed preparing to commit treason. He was stripped of his title and exiled to Danyang, where he committed suicide after realizing the serious nature of his crimes.

Emperor Ming then ordered an inquiry into people who had been in contact with Liu Ying. The Prince of Chu had entered the names of eminent persons across the country into a roster. This was discovered, leading to the systematic arrest of numerous people. Many of the implicated subsequently died during the investigation, which lasted over a year.

A minister made the case to the emperor that most of those arrested were innocent of the crime they had been charged with. After personally looking into the matter, Emperor Ming found that over a thousand people were wrongly incarcerated in the jails of Luoyang. He issued an edict that granted them amnesty.

Although Emperor Ming sent a delegation to India to bring back Buddhist scriptures and Buddha's statue, he was not a believer in Buddhism but was a proponent of the Confucian school of thought. It is said that he gave lectures on Confucian classics at the National University to a combined audience of 100,000 people.

56. Ban Chao Discovers that the Sword is Mightier than the Pen

AFTER FOUNDING THE Eastern Han dynasty, Emperor Guangwu commissioned the erudite scholar Ban Biao to write a history of the Western Han. Ban Biao had two sons, Ban Gu and Ban Chao, and a daughter, Ban Zhao. All of these were initiated by him into the study of literature and history at a tender age.

At the death of Ban Biao, Emperor Ming appointed Ban Gu as Clerk of the Orchid Pavilion (the Palace archive or library) to complete the *Book of Han*, or the history of the Western Han, which was left unfinished by his father upon his death. Ban Chao did clerical work to help out his brother. The two brothers were equally well-read, but had different temperaments. Ban Gu enjoyed studying the contemporary schools of thought and was devoted to the writing of the *Book of Han*. Ban Chao, on the other hand, was not interested in being glued to his desk doing clerical work. One day after hearing reports of how the Xiongnu were constantly violating their borders, pillaging towns and rustling cattle, he angrily threw down his writing brush and said, "A real man should serve his country on the frontier like Zhang Qian, and not waste his life in study!"

He decided to abandon his desk to enlist in the army.

In 73 AD, when Chief General Dou Gu led an expedition against the Xiongnu, Ban Chao served with distinction as Deputy Commander under him.

In order to counter the threat of the Xiongnu, Dou Gu decided to follow the approach of Emperor Wu of Han and send envoys to the countries of Xiyu (the western regions) to lobby for an anti-Xiongnu alliance. Impressed by Ban Chao's capabilities, General Dou sent him on this mission.

With an entourage of 36, Ban Chao arrived first at Shanshan. Shanshan was a kingdom that existed roughly from 200 BC to 1000 AD at the north-eastern end of the Taklamakan Desert (in modern-day Xinjiang). It included a great salt lake, known as Lop Nur. As a vassal of the Xiongnu, it was forced to pay levies and tributes, and to meet other extortionate demands. Since for decades the Han imperial court had been too busy to interest itself in the Xiyu region, although he was deeply resentful of the Xiongnu the king of Shanshan had no choice but to submit to their exactions. Consequently, the envoy sent by the Han after this long hiatus was enthusiastically received by the king of Shanshan.

After a few days in Shanshan, Ban Chao detected a sudden cooling in the King's attitude towards him. He discussed his suspicions with members of his delegation, "Have you noticed that the king of Shanshan is behaving very differently from a few days ago? I bet he has a Xiongnu visitor!"

However, this was only speculation. When the King's attendant brought in their food and drink, Ban Chao tested him by remarking in a knowing tone, "How long has the Xiongnu emissary been here? Where is he staying?"

The king of Shanshan had meant to keep Ban Chao in the dark about his talks with the Xiongnu envoy, so the servant was startled by Ban Chao's question. Thinking that Ban Chao knew about the matter, the servant saw no reason to lie, and replied, "He's been here three days, and is staying at a place 30 *li* from here."

Ban Chao detained the servant and immediately summoned the 36 members of his delegation. He said to them, "You've come with me all the way to Xiyu for no other purpose than to render a great service to your country. You can see the about-face of the king of Shanshan only days after the arrival of the Xiongnu envoy. If they bind us up and hand us over to the Xiongnu, not even our remains will get back to our country. What do you think we should do?"

His entourage replied in unison, "We're in grave danger. We put our lives in your hands."

Ban Chao then responded, "If a man does not dare to enter a tigers' lair, how can he get his hands on tiger cubs? There is only one thing we can do now: We'll sneak to the Xiongnu's tents under the cover of night, set them on fire, and attack the Xiongnu. Not knowing how many we are, they'll panic. Once we kill the Xiongnu envoy, the matter will be settled."

"Agreed!" his aides answered. "Let's give it a try!"

At midnight, Ban Chao led his 36 combatants on a stealth attack against the Xiongnu. A strong wind was blowing that night. Ban Chao placed ten soldiers with drums behind the Xiongnu tents, and twenty soldiers in ambush in front of the tents. He then started a fire with the remaining six. Fanned by the strong wind, the fire raced towards the tents. The ten men behind the tents started beating their drums and shouting at the top of their lungs, and the twenty ambushers charged into the tents with loud battle cries.

The Xiongnu soldiers, roused from their sleep, fell into disarray. With Ban Chao in the lead, the Han soldiers went in and killed the Xiongnu envoy and his 30 staff. All the tents burned to the ground.

Ban Chao returned to his camp at daybreak and invited the king of Shanshan to come to his tent. When the king found out the Xiongnu envoy had been killed by Ban Chao, he switched his allegiance to the Han.

Upon his return, Ban Chao was promoted to Division Commander by Emperor Ming and sent to Yutian. When the emperor suggested that he take more people with him on the mission, Ban Chao replied, "Yutian is a large country a great distance from here. Even if I bring a few hundred more soldiers with me, it would still be a drop in the bucket. If something untoward happens, a larger force would be more a hindrance than a help."

In the end, Ban Chao went to Yutian with his original 36 staff. With his small entourage, Ban Chao received a less than enthusiastic welcome from the king of Yutian. When Ban Chao explained to him the advantages of distancing himself from the Xiongnu and strengthening ties with the Han, the king was unable to make a decision. He asked his sorcerer to seek the gods' advice.

Long opposed to rapprochement with the Han, the sorcerer assumed the voice of a spirit said to the king of Yutian, "Why do you want to befriend the Han? By the way, I want that nice, dark horse of the Han envoy!"

The king of Yutian asked the Couselor-Designate (sort of a high commissioner appointed by the Han court) to persuade Ban Chao to part with his horse. Ban Chao agreed. "Fine!" he said. "Tell the sorcerer to pick it up himself."

When the gloating sorcerer came to Ban Chao for the horse, Ban Chao drew his sword and killed him on the spot, not bothering to exchange a word with him. He then went to see the king of Yutian with the sorcerer's head dangling from his hand.

Threatening the king, he said, "If you continue your collaboration with the Xiongnu, you'll end up like the sorcerer here."

Already in awe of the tough-guy reputation of Ban Chao, the king of Yutian now felt his knees weakening. He replied with alacrity, "Yes, I am ready to strengthen ties with the Han court."

Shanshan and Yutian were major kingdoms in Xiyu. Their rapprochement with the Han set an example for other countries such as Qiuci (near modern-day Kuche, Xinjiang) and Shule (near modern-day Kashgar, Xinjiang), which soon renewed ties with the Han.

After 65 years of estrangement since the start of Wang Mang's rule, relations between the countries of Xiyu and the Han Empire were finally normalized. They returned to where they had been at the time of Zhang Qian's diplomatic missions to Xiyu. Frequent diplomatic and commercial exchanges resumed.

Two years later, Emperor Ming died and was succeeded by his son Liu Da as Emperor Zhang of Han.

57. Zhang Heng and His Seismometer

DURING THE REIGN of Emperor Zhang of Han, the Eastern Han enjoyed relative political stability. At the death of Emperor Zhang, Empress Dowager Dou acted as regent for his successor, Emperor He, who was then only ten. She vested real power in her brother Dou Xian. This marked the beginning of the Eastern Han's decline.

This period produced a noted scientist whose name is Zhang Heng.

Zhang Heng was a native of Nanyang, which he left at the age of seventeen. His studies took him to Chang'an and then Luoyang, where he was an assiduous student at the National University. Chang'an and Luoyang were booming and bustling cities, in which the elite led dissolute lives. Disgusted by the decadence of high society, Zhang Heng penned the satirical *Xi Jing Fu* (*Western Metropolis Rhapsody)* and *Dong Jing Fu* (*Eastern Metropolis Rhapsody*), referring respectively to Chang'an and Luoyang. It is said that it took him ten years of reflection and revisions to complete these works of poetry. This attests to his serious and meticulous nature.

However, Zhang Heng's excellence was not confined to literature; he was also absorbed in mathematical and astronomical studies. Impressed by his erudition, the imperial court offered him a position in the capital. He started as a Gentleman of the Interior, but later became a Grand Scribe in charge of astronomical observations. This was a happy marriage between his job and his hobbies.

Through his observations and research, he reached the

conclusion that the Earth was round, and that the Moon's glow was only a reflection of the light emanating from the Sun. He also theorized that the sky was like an eggshell cloaking the Earth, which could be likened to the egg yolk inside the shell. Although his theory was not entirely accurate, the mere fact that such a scientific view was propounded 1,800 years ago is cause for much admiration from later astronomers.

As a hands-on scientist, for astronomical measurements Zhang Heng crafted from copper an instrument called the *hun tian yi* (armillary sphere). It had representations of constellations and other astronomical phenomena on it, and was hydraulically driven. It is said that the device enabled users to know clearly which stars would be rising in the east, and which would be setting in the west.

This was a time of frequent earthquakes. At the rate of one or two per year, each occurrence of one of these seismic events was felt in dozens of prefectures. They caused city walls and buildings to collapse, and took a heavy toll of human and animal lives.

The rulers and common people of feudal times believed earthquakes were bad omens. These natural phenomena became tools for some to spread superstitious rumors against the government.

Zhang Heng did not believe earthquakes were manifestations of the will of the gods or evil spirits. Based on his careful scrutiny, his analysis of seismic records, and his experiments, he invented an instrument called the *di dong yi*. It was a seismometer that helped measure and forecast earthquakes.

The seismometer was made from bronze and shaped like a wine vat. Eight dragons were represented on the exterior of the device, with their heads pointing in eight directions. Each of the dragons had a small copper ball in its mouth, and a copper toad squatting below it with its mouth open. When a seismic event occurred, the dragon pointing to the direction of the quake would automatically open its mouth and drop its ball, which would then fall into the toad's mouth with a loud sound that warned of an earthquake.

One February day in 138 AD, the dragon pointing due west on Zhang Heng's seismometer suddenly opened its mouth and spat out the copper ball. By Zhang Heng's design, this meant that an earthquake was occurring in the west of China.

However, no sign of an earthquake was discernable that day in the western metropolis of Luoyang, nor was any earthquake anywhere reported. People began voicing their doubts about the device, saying it was a hoax. Some even accused him of spreading rumors and making mischief.

A few days later, the imperial court received information via a messenger on a fast horse that a devastating earthquake had occurred a thousand *li* away in Jincheng and Longxi. There were reports that whole mountainsides had collapsed in the quake. This vindicated the value of Zhang Heng's seismometer.

Unfortunately, the power in the imperial court was usurped by eunuchs and maternal relatives of the emperor. This led to a tendency to suppress and isolate, instead of fully tapping, the talent of able people such as Zhang Heng. When he was a palace attendant, his proximity to the emperor caused anxiety among the eunuchs who were afraid he might denounce their misconduct to the emperor. To forestall this eventuality, the eunuchs preemptively maligned Zhang Heng before the emperor whenever they had a chance. As a result, Zhang Heng was transferred out of the capital, and dispatched to the princedom of Hejian as Counselor-Designate.

Zhang Heng died of illness at the age of 61. He left a splendid legacy of scientific development in China.

58. The Dang Gu Incidents

STARTING WITH EMPEROR He, most emperors of the Han dynasty were young children when they ascended the throne, the youngest being a baby 100 days old. During an emperor's minority, normally the queen mother exercised ruling power as regent. Not uncommonly, the queen mother would in turn give power to members of her clan. As a result, imperial power would rest entirely in the hands of the emperor's maternal relatives. When an emperor died without a male heir, the queen mother or other maternal relatives would sometimes select a young boy from the royal clan as his successor. This would facilitate their continuance in power.

When the emperor grew up and became more knowledgeable and sophisticated, he would often resist being manipulated like a puppet, and would try to find freedom from the control of his maternal relatives. However, since the imperial court was crawling with people loyal to those same relatives, the emperor had few people to turn to, and so would seek advice and counsel from his eunuchs. The eunuchs had daily access to the emperor, and the emperor found in them the levers with which to pry loose the power of the maternal relatives. As a result, the eunuchs would accrue power. In the ensuing power struggles between these two interest groups, political corruption deepened in the Eastern Han dynasty.

Some officials of gentry and landowner stock were critical of the eunuchs' rising influence. They stepped forward to propose political reform, and to demand the institution of eunuchs be abolished. Students of the National University were by and large from small-landowner families. They saw their career prospects dimmed by the ubiquitous corruption, and so clamoring for reform, as well. They lashed out at the way the country was governed, and abhorred the power-usurping eunuchs and yes-men.

In 165 AD, Chen Fan was appointed Defender in Chief and Li Ying, a man of respect, became Metropolitan Commandant. Both were resentful of the eunuchs. Since the university students saw these men as models, they also had their support.

Metropolitan Commandant Li Ying received a complaint regarding the corrupt and extortionate practices of Zhang Shuo, the brother of the eunuch Zhang Rang and the county magistrate of Yewang (modern-day Qinyang County, Henan). When Li Ying began investigative and impeachment procedures against him, Zhang Shuo fled to Luoyang, seeking refuge at his brother's residence. Li Ying took bailiffs with him, and conducted a search of Zhang Rang's residential compound. There, he found Zhang Shuo hiding in a hollow wall. After Zhang Shuo was taken away, Zhang Rang immediately got an intermediary to intercede in his brother's behalf, but it was too late: Li Ying had already executed Zhang Shuo after a quick prosecution and trial. The incensed Zhang Rang made a tearful complaint before Emperor Huan of Han. However, the emperor took no action against Li Ying because he knew Zhang Shuo was guilty as charged.

Li Ying saw his fame grow after this incident. He became much in demand as educated people considered meeting him a great honor. Being received by him was described as "ascending to the dragon gate."

The next year, an alchemist close to the eunuchs called Zhang Cheng was tipped off by the eunuch Hou Lan that a general amnesty was soon to be announced by the imperial court. Armed with this reassuring information, he told his son to go ahead and kill someone who had long been on his revenge list. Li Ying arrested the murderer, Zhang Cheng's son, and was all set to bring him to justice.

When the general amnesty was announced the next day, Zhang Cheng crowed in public, "The imperial amnesty has been announced! The Metropolitan Commandant will have to release my son now."

This brag was brought to the attention of Li Ying, annoying him to no end. He said, "Zhang Cheng had known about the amnesty before instigating his son to commit murder. Therefore, his son is not eligible for the amnesty."

With this interpretation of the edict, Li Ying had Zhang Cheng's son beheaded.

Zhang Cheng was not going to take this lying down. He asked the eunuchs Hou Lan and Zhang Rang to help him avenge his son. They hatched this malicious plot: Zhang Cheng's follower Lao Xiu was to accuse Li Ying falsely before the emperor, saying that Li Ying had formed of a clique of university students and eminent personalities with the purpose of slandering the imperial court and corrupting good morals.

After receiving Lao Xiu's complaint, Emperor Huan of Han immediately ordered the arrest of partisans of this supposed clique. Apart from Li Ying, 200 other people, including Du Mi, Chen Shi and Fan Pang, were purged as partisans. To demonstrate its resolve, the imperial court put out a reward across China for the arrest of these people.

Du Mi was, like Li Ying, also an official not afraid to tangle with the all-powerful eunuchs. Both men were equally famous for their uprightness, and were often mentioned in one breath as the "Li-Du" duo. After Li Ying was thrown in jail, Du Mi predictably suffered the same fate.

Chen Shi was an alumnus of the National University put on the blacklist because of his prominence. Some urged him to flee, but he was unafraid, saying "If I run away, what will become of the others? If I go to jail, maybe I can boost their morale." He went to the capital and surrendered. He too was incarcerated.

In the same way, Fan Pang proudly went to jail.

When the imperial decree for the arrest of the partisans arrived at the prefectures, the local officials reported all who had had any association with the clique. In each area, the list of partisans sometimes ran into the hundreds. Only Shi Bi, the governor of Pingyuan Prefecture in the Qingzhou region, did not report any partisans.

Imperial edicts came down from the capital to demand names from him. Finally, an official was sent from the regional government of Qingzhou to make an inquiry into the situation.

The regional official had Governor Shi Bi brought before him, and upbraided him for failing to provide a list of partisans. Shi Bi replied to him, "We don't have anyone belonging to the clique here. What do you want me to report?"

The official's face hardened, and he responded, "Of the six prefectures of Qingzhou, five have reported partisans, how can Pingyuan be the only exception?"

Shi Bi replied, "Each place has its own distinct customs and natural environment. Just because there are partisans in other locations, doesn't necessarily mean we must also have them."

The official, unable to come up with a counter-argument, was speechless.

Shi Bi added, "If you insist on rounding up innocent people, then everyone is a partisan here. I would rather die than give you a list of partisans, because I don't know of any."

Unable to get anything out of Shi Bi, the regional official summarily put all the Pingyuan officials in jail, and reported the matter to the central government.

The jailed partisans were subjected to cruel torture by the hands of the eunuchs' supporters. They were beaten while wearing neck shackles, handcuffs and leg irons, and hoods over their heads. The ordeal lasted for over a year.

The next year, a man called Jia Biao, a native of Yingchuan, went to Luoyang to try to get the suspects exonerated. Dou Wu, the father of Queen Dou, also petitioned Emperor Huan for the partisans' release.

Inspired by the dictum, "The best defense is a good offense", Li Ying fingered many of the eunuchs' young relatives as partisans. This tactic scared the eunuchs, who said to the emperor, "This abnormal climate is an omen that a general amnesty is in order."

Since Emperor Huan was under the eunuchs' thumb, he obliged them by announcing a general amnesty. As a result, all 200 partisans in the capital were freed.

However, on order of the eunuchs, these freed partisans were forbidden to stay in the capital, and all had to go back to their hometowns. Their names were given to the local authorities to ensure that they could never again hold public office. This is known as the Dang Gu Incident (Disaster of Partisan Prohibitions).

Before long, Emperor Huan died. Queen Dou and her father Dou Wu arranged the selection of 12-year-old Liu Hong of the royal clan to succeed Emperor Huan. He would go on to become the notoriously corrupt Emperor Ling of Han.

59. Fearless Fan Pang Goes to Jail

IN THE PERIOD immediately after the ascension of Emperor Ling to the Han throne, Empress Dowager Dou acted as Regent. She made her father Dou Wu Chief General and Chen Fan Defender in Chief. Dou Wu and Chen Fan had been on the side of the partisans and eminent intellectuals. They brought Li Ying and Du Mi, who had been permanently stripped of their civil liberties, back to the capital to serve in the government.

Chen Fan said to Dou Wu, "As long as the eunuchs are not neutralized, there will be no peace in our country. I am going on 80 years old. Not much in life tempts me now. The only reason I'm still here is that I want to rid the court of this cancer, and to help you accomplish this worthy cause."

Dou Wu, in fact, had the same thoughts. The two agreed that Dou Wu would present a proposal to eliminate the eunuchs to Empress Dowager Dou. However, the Empress Dowager shared with Emperor Huan the same total trust in the eunuchs, and was unable to make up her mind to act on the proposal. Chen Fan followed with a petition enumerating the crimes and misdeeds of the eunuchs Hou Lan, Cao Jie and Wang Fu. The Empress Dowager simply put the petition aside.

These actions had the unintended effect of alerting the eunuchs. Cao Jie and Wang Fu mounted a preemptive strike against their accusers. First, they grabbed the imperial seal from Empress Dowager Dou. They then put her under house arrest. Finally, in the name of Emperor Ling, they charged Dou Wu and Chen Fan with treason and had them killed.

Imperial power thus swung back to the eunuchs. All officials owing their offices to the support and patronage of Dou Wu and Chen Fan were purged.

After Li Ying and Du Mi were once again ousted and sent home, their prestige rose even higher among intellectuals and university students, and their abhorrence of the eunuchs intensified. The eunuchs reciprocated this hatred, seeing them as sworn enemies. The eunuchs did not pass up any opportunity to do them harm.

Zhang Jian was an intellectual. He had once denounced the eunuch Hou Lan, and now Hou Lan was waiting for an opportunity to get even with him. The chance finally came in the shape of a servant recently expelled from Zhang Jian's household. Hou Lan had the servant falsely accuse Zhang Jian of forming a clique with 24 partisans from his village to slander the imperial court and plan sedition.

The eunuch Cao Jie also seized the opportunity to have a trusted supporter present a petition to the emperor, asking him to issue an edict rounding up the partisans once again.

The emperor, who was barely fourteen, had no idea what the partisans were or did. He asked Cao Jie, "Why do you want them killed? What crime have they committed?"

Cao Jie made up a juicy story of how the truculent partisans were working feverishly for the overthrow of his imperial rule, and Emperor Ling fell for the story hook, line and sinker. An imperial edict went out immediately for the arrest of the partisans.

The new arrest order immediately caused a stir in all the regions and prefectures. When the news was broken to Li Ying, he said with equanimity, "If I run, others will suffer. Besides, I am already 60. Life or death is no longer much of a concern for me. So I am not running from this."

After voluntarily surrendering, he was thrown in jail, and was beaten and tortured to death. Du Mi killed himself in anticipation of a similar fate.

A local inspector in Runan Prefecture was sent to Zhengqiang (modern-day Yancheng, Henan Province) to arrest Fan Pang. When he arrived at the post house in Zhengqiang, he went to his room and cried inconsolably on his bed. The arrest warrant was clutched in his hand. The staff and guests in the post house were mystified by his wailing.

When Fan Pang heard about this, he said, "I am sure he cried because he didn't want to arrest me."

Therefore, Fan Pang went of his own accord to the county office to give himself up. The County Magistrate Guo Yi, himself a man of integrity, was startled to see Fan Pang. He asked him, "Of all the places in the wide world you are free to travel to, why have you chosen to come here?"

Guo Yi even considered aloud the idea of resigning from office by surrendering his official seal so that he could go on the run with Fan Pang.

Fan Pang said in gratitude to Guo Yi, "There's no need for that. After my death, the central government may suspend this witch hunt against the partisans. There is no way I am going to implicate you. Besides, if I become a fugitive, my ageing mother will suffer."

Unable to shake Fan Pang's determination, the County Magistrate had no alternative but to jail Fan Pang. He then sent for Fan Pang's elderly mother and his son to visit him in jail.

Fan Pang's mother was escorted by a bailiff to the county jail to visit him. She was accompanied by her grandson. Fan Pang consoled her by saying, "After my death, you still have your younger son to take care of you. Try not to grieve too much."

His mother replied, "I am content that you will leave a name comparable in goodness to that of the Li-Du duo (Li Ying and Du Mi). Don't feel too bad yourself."

After receiving his mother's encouraging words, Fan Pang knelt and turned his head toward his son. He said to him, "I won't tell you to do evil, because one shouldn't do evil. I want you to grow up to be a decent man. But look at me: This is what happens to a man who has been decent all his life."

All those present were moved to tears by that observation.

All in all, over a hundred people were executed as was Fan Pang. Additionally, about 700 people were falsely accused of being partisans. Some were arrested; others, killed; others, assigned to hardship military duty in faraway places. All, at a minimum, were stripped of their civil liberties for life by the eunuchs, who either envied their high national standing, or had private accounts to settle with them.

Only Zhang Jian, nemesis of the eunuch Hou Lan, slipped through the government's dragnet. At peril of death, many were willing to provide succor and refuge to him as he eluded capture. This assistance enabled him to stay always one step ahead of the government agents hot on his trail and armed with the latest information. However, it also meant that those who provided him with refuge ended up being jailed or even killed after he escaped. Sometimes, entire prefectures or counties were penalized.

In the aftermath of the two "Disasters of Partisan Prohibitions," the more decent among the court officials were dealt a heavy blow. The eunuchs and their followers were able to monopolize all offices, high and low.

60. The Yellow Turban Uprising

THE HOPELESSLY FATUOUS Emperor Ling put all his trust in the eunuchs. Neglecting the running of state, he led a life of debauchery. When the coffers were depleted by his and the eunuchs' extravagant living, they invented new ways of raising money. They opened up a special shop in West Garden, a sort of patronage mill, where wealthy people could openly buy offices, commissions and titles. A bulletin posted outside Hongdu Gate listed the prices of public offices. A prefecture governorship cost 20 million. One could become a county magistrate by paying 4 million. Those who were temporarily cash-shy could buy on credit, and pay back at double the purchase price. Those who bought their commissions would naturally doubly bleed the public once in office to recoup their investment. Thus, the corruption permeating the Eastern Han dynasty plummeted to abysmal depths.

Corruption in the central government, oppression by the landowning class and powerful gentry, and a spate of natural disasters forced people, now on the brink of starvation, to rise up in revolt.

Peasants in the area of Wu Prefecture fired the opening salvo by attacking the county seat and killing county officials. Xu Sheng, originally from Guiji, started an insurgency in Gouzhang (modern-day Cixi, Zhejiang Province) that attracted more than 10,000 followers in a few days. The troops sent by Emperor Ling to suppress the insurrection, commanded by the Regional Inspector of Yangzhou and the Governor of Danyang Prefecture, were defeated by the peasants. As Xu Sheng's forces gained momentum, he proclaimed himself Emperor Yangming.

In 174 AD, the government sent out a combined force of regional and the prefectural armies, reinforced by soldiers newly recruited from Wu Prefecture. This force defeated Xu Sheng. However, while the insurgency in Wu Prefecture was put down, even bigger armed insurgencies were in the making.

There were three brothers in Julu Prefecture noted for their skills, and willingness to help the people. They were, listed by age, Zhang Jiao, Zhang Bao, and Zhang Liang. Zhang Jiao, being versed in medicine, was well-loved by the poor because he always treated them free of charge. He knew that the people were caught between the oppression of the landowners and gentry, and the ravages of natural disasters, but were thirsting for a *tai ping* (peaceful) society and a normal, secure life. Deciding to use religion as a unifying force, he founded a sect called Way of Supreme Peace (Tai Ping Dao) and started proselytizing with his disciples.

Soon gathering a large following, Zhang Jiao sent his brothers Zhang Bao and Zhang Liang with their disciples across the country on an evangelical mission that provided people medical care. In ten years' time, the Way of Supreme Peace spread to all corners of the country and had a following of hundreds of thousands. Everyone in the country, believer or non-believer, knew about the Tai Ping Dao.

In those days, prefecture and county officials did not at first pay much attention to the phenomenon, thinking that the Tai Ping Dao was merely a sect that advocated good deeds and offered medical treatment. A couple of ministers in the imperial court did believe that there was more than met the eye regarding the sect. In a petition to the emperor, they called for a ban on the Way of Supreme Peace. However, Emperor Ling was busy with the construction of his imperial hunting grounds, so he dismissed the Tai Ping Dao from his mind.

Zhang Jiao organized the hundreds of thousands of peasants from eight regions into 36 branches. The bigger branches each consisting of 10,000 men, and the smaller ones were formed of six to seven thousand. The branch leaders were all directly accountable to Zhang Jiao. With his leaders, he created a secret plot that called for a simultaneous uprising by the insurgents in the imperial capital and across China on March 5 of the year of Jia Zi (184 AD). Their battle cry would be: "The blue sky is dead and the yellow sky begins, in this auspicious year of Jia Zi." The "blue sky" was a reference to the Eastern Han dynasty, and the "yellow sky" meant the Tai Ping Dao. The characters *jia zi* were furtively written in chalk on temple doors in Luoyang, and on the doors of regional and prefectural government offices across the country, as a secret signal to start the insurrection.

In the crucial one-month period leading up to the insurrection, a traitor from among the insurgents' ranks informed the Eastern Han government of the planned attack. The imperial government immediately searched for and arrested rebels in Luoyang. Ma Yuanyi, the group's liaison in the city, was executed after his arrest, as were 1,000 people associated with the sect.

Faced with this unexpected turn of events, Zhang Jiao decided to move the schedule for the planned attack ahead by one month. He gave himself the title General of the Sky, Zhang Bao the title General of the Earth, and Zhang Liang the title General of Humanity. At the command of Zhang Jiao, all 36 branches of the sect started attacking simultaneously. As an identifying mark, all the peasants in the insurgency wore yellow head scarves or turbans. This was the origin of the name "Yellow Turban Uprising."

The various contingents of the uprising attacked and torched prefectural and county government offices, freed prison inmates, seized government property, opened up granaries to the public, and punished officials, landowners and members of the gentry. Within ten days, other insurgencies sprang up across the country. These converged on the imperial capital. The imperial court in Luoyang was bombarded by requests for help from prefectures and counties across the country.

Emperor Ling summoned his ministers for an emergency session to discuss ways to put down the rebellion. He appointed his maternal relative He Jin as Chief General, and sent Huangfu Song, Zhu Jun and Lu Zhi with their troops to attack the Yellow Turbans from two sides. However, government forces were unable to stop the insurgent armies, and the uprising surged forward like flood water that had broken through a dike. Stymied, Chief General He Jin asked the emperor to issue an edict telling local governments to raise their own armies to fight the Yellow Turbans. The nobility, local government leaders, powerful landowners and gentry capitalized on this opportunity to grab turf and expand their influence, all in the name of fighting the Yellow Turbans. Consequently, the country was grievously fragmented.

In the face of this bloody suppression by the imperial government, the local landowners, and the gentry, the Yellow Turbans put up stiff resistance for nine difficult months. At a critical stage of fighting, the Yellow Turbans' leader Zhang Jiao died from illness, and Zhang Liang and Zhang Bao were killed in fierce, fight-to-the-death combat.

Even after the defeat of the main force of insurgents, pockets of Yellow Turbans managed to keep up their fight for twenty years. This large-scale insurgency dealt a fatal blow to the corrupt and decadent Eastern Han dynasty. From that point on, the dynasty went into a rapid decline.

61. Yuan Shao Kills the Eunuchs

IN 189 AD, Emperor Ling of the Han dynasty died. He was succeeded by his 14-year-old son Liu Bian, who became Emperor Shao. In accordance with practice, Empress Dowager He acted as regent, with the reins of power entrusted to General-In-Chief He Jin, who was a maternal relative of the emperor. One of the newly empowered He Jin's first acts was to arrest and execute Jian Shuo, a eunuch who had been captain of the Palace Guard, who had recently attempted to assassinate him.

Under He Jin's command was a subcommander of the Middle Army by the name of Yuan Shao, who was descended from a family of mandarins. For four generations the family had provided officials of exalted rank, including Defenders-In-Chief, Ministers of Education or Ministers of Works (the so-called *san gong*, or Three Dukes), to the state. The fact that many officials of the imperial court had also been students or subordinates of members of this renowned family further added to its power and influence.

After the execution of Jian Shuo, Yuan Shao advised He Jin to eradicate the influence of the eunuchs once and for all, arguing "Dou Wu once tried to eliminate the eunuchs, but ended up instead being killed by them when news of the plan was leaked. Now that you have control of the army, you mustn't pass up this opportunity to remove them for good."

Afraid to take sole responsibility for such a decision, He Jin consulted the empress dowager on the matter. She adamantly rejected the idea.

Yuan Shao then suggested another approach. He urged He Jin

to secretly order troops to converge on the capital with a view to forcing the empress dowager to go along with the plan to eliminate the eunuchs. He Jin agreed and began to muster troops stationed in various parts of the country. Of all the regions, Bingzhou (covering the bulk of today's Shanxi Province and parts of Inner Mongolia and Hebei) possessed in his estimation the strongest military force, which was under the command of governor Dong Zhuo. A messenger was dispatched with a letter for Dong Zhuo, instructing him to march on Luoyang without delay.

The eunuchs soon got wind of the plan. A number of them came to the same conclusion. "If we don't act now, it will be the end for us all." They set dozens of armed men in ambush inside the palace, then summoned He Jin for an audience with the empress dowager.

Once inside the palace, He Jin walked into the trap set by the eunuchs and was killed by the armed men waiting for him.

When news of He Jin's murder reached Yuan Shao, he immediately instructed his brother Yuan Shu to launch an assault on the imperial palace. Yuan Shu started a fire and burned down the palace gate before large numbers of his troops surged into the palace grounds and began attacking every eunuch in sight. A number of hapless unbearded officials were even mistaken for eunuchs and killed in the massacre. While this battle raged inside the palace, the Dong Zhuo's troops marched into Luoyang.

Dong Zhuo, originally from a powerful clan in Liangzhou (made up of today's Gansu, Ningxia, Qinghai and Inner Mongolia), became a force to reckon with by allying with powerful members of the Qiang ethnic minority. During the Yellow Turbans Uprising he rose to the position of governor of Bingzhou by helping to suppress the insurgencies. He had always had designs on China's central plains, and He Jin's invitation came none too soon. Dong Zhuo had quickly obliged with three thousand troops.

Once in Luoyang, Dong Zhuo was eager to take power. However, he was worried that his troops might not be strong enough to face down the government forces. So he employed a ruse: in the dead of night, he surreptitiously marched his troops out of the city, only for these same troops to march back into the capital in full fanfare the next day. After he had done this a few times, the residents of Luoyang were no longer sure of the size of Dong Zhuo's army. Some of He Jin's troops, impressed by the apparent strength of Dong Zhuo's military force, went over to his side. Dong Zhuo thus easily managed to seize control of the military.

In order to concentrate all power in his hands, Dong Zhuo formed a plan to depose Emperor Shao and install in his place his brother Liu Xie, Prince of Chenliu. Well aware that the Yuan family wielded an influence unmatched by the other mandarins in Luoyang, Dong Zhuo consulted Yuan Shao about the matter.

Dong Zhuo said, "In my view the Prince of Chenliu is more capable than the present emperor. I plan to install him as emperor. What do you think?"

Yuan Shao replied, "The emperor is still young and has only recently ascended the throne. Besides, he is not known to have made any mistake. If you depose him, the country will probably not view it with favor."

Dong Zhuo was enraged by the snub—he put his hand on the handle of his sword and spoke threateningly, his eyeballs almost bursting from their sockets. "I have the power and I will do what I want. I dare anyone to oppose my will. Do you doubt the sharpness of my sword?"

Yuan Shao, his face red with anger, retorted, "Do you think you are the only hero in the world?" With that parting shot, he drew his sword and walked out. Fearing that Dong Zhuo would hunt him down, he fled to Jizhou (a combination of the central and southern parts of today's Hebei, the northwestern part of Shandong and the northern part of Henan). When his brother Yuan Shu heard of what had happened, he too fled Luoyang to seek safety in Nanyang (in today's Henan).

Following the departure of Yuan Shao and his brother, Dong Zhuo summoned select officials to hear his decision to depose the emperor. Liu Xie soon ascended the throne as Emperor Xian of the Han dynasty, while Dong Zhuo himself took the position of Counselor-in-chief.

Dong Zhuo was a cruel and ruthless man. On his watch as

Counselor-in-chief he condoned the killing of innocent civilians by his soldiers. The barbarities and excesses committed under his rule wreaked havoc in Luoyang and prompted an exodus of officials, including a Commandant of the Control Army of Luoyang by the name of Cao Cao.

62. Cao Cao Launches Military Action

CAO CAO WAS from Qiao County, in the state of Pei. His father, Cao Song, was the foster son of a eunuch. There was at the time a famous writer named Xu Shao who was noted for his keen eye for judging character. The young Cao Cao once went to him for an evaluation. Xu Shao told him, "A character like you would make a capable minister in peace time, but troubled times may make a scheming scoundrel of you."

When the 20-year-old Cao Cao became Defender of Northern Luoyang, overseeing public security in the northern part of the capital, he immediately had twenty big, multi-colored wooden sticks made by workers to be hung on the left and right walls of his office. He then issued a list of prohibitions. Whoever violated the prohibitions would be punished with a beating with those sticks, even if the transgressor happened to come from a prominent family.

Jian Shuo's uncle was a notorious villain who terrorized Luoyang neighborhoods. No one dared to stand up to his lawless behavior because of his powerful nephew. One night he was seen creating havoc wielding a knife in a public place, thus breaking one of Cao Cao's prohibitions. Despite his powerful connections, he was arrested and given a thorough beating with one of the multi-colored sticks. The humiliation proved more than the local tyrant could take and he died on the spot. This created a sensation that rippled across Luoyang, where the citizens praised Cao Cao's strict, impartial enforcement of the law even when the perpetrators had powerful connections. However, he inspired a mixture of loathing and fear in the eunuchs, who eventually transferred him out of Luoyang to become a county magistrate.

During the Yellow Turbans Rebellion, Emperor Ling made Cao Cao a Commandant of Calvary and sent him to the Yingchuan area (in today's Yu County in Henan) to quash the rebellion. Cao Cao soon defeated the Yellow Turbans. To show the emperor's gratitude, the imperial court promoted Cao Cao to the position of Administrator of Jinan. Several years elapsed before he returned to Luoyang.

When Dong Zhuo entered Luoyang with his troops, as part of his plan to increase his popularity he bought the loyalty of some officials by offering favors and patronage. Aware of Cao Cao's fame, he promoted him to Subcommander of Courageous Guards. However, as he was not willing to serve under someone he did not respect, Cao Cao fled Luoyang at great risk to stay with his father in Chenliu (today's Chenliu County in Henan).

Once back in Chenliu, Cao Cao got his father's backing in financing an expeditionary army against Dong Zhuo. A wealthy man, Wei Zi, also contributed a great deal of money and food to help. Cao Cao's cousin Cao Hong also arrived with a thousand men to reinforce Cao Cao's army, which eventually soon grew to number around five thousand men. Cao Cao placed his troops under intensive combat training and sent out scouts to gather information about the situations in various places.

In response to the Yellow Turbans Rebellion, every region and every commandery had raised their own armies. Governors of many regions had long harbored ambitions to carve out their own individual kingdoms, and the anarchy in Luoyang gave them the opportunity to raise arms under the pretense of ousting Dong Zhuo. Yuan Shao commanded the largest expeditionary force of all.

After having fallen out with Dong Zhuo, Yuan Shao had left Luoyang to go to Jizhou, where he became governor of Bohai. Helped by the fact that he came from a prominent family of mandarins, as well as the fact that Han Fu, the governor of Jizhou, had served in the troops loyal to the Yuan family in the past, Yuan Shao had no trouble raising an army in a short space of time in Bohai.

In 190 AD, the various expeditionary forces (including the one led by Cao Cao) totaling more than a hundred thousand men converged in Suanzao (southwest of today's Yanjin in Henan), not far from Chenliu. They were then organized into an allied force under the command of Yuan Shao, who had been chosen as leader of the alliance.

When news of the creation of these expeditionary forces reached Luoyang, fear grew in Dong Zhuo's heart. Over the objections of the ministers, he decided to move Emperor Xian and a million people to Chang'an, while he staying behind in the Luoyang area to face the allied force himself. As Emperor Xian reluctantly left Luoyang, Dong Zhuo set fire to all the palaces, government buildings and civilian dwellings in the city. Within a radius of two hundred *li* of Luoyang, everything was burned to the ground. Many of the civilians forcibly displaced from Luoyang died on the road, either from starvation, from being trampled in the panic or from fighting. Roads leading from the capital were strewn with countless corpses.

Meanwhile, the allied forces were waiting in Suanzao. At a meeting of commanding officers in Yuan Shao's tent, Cao Cao said to those present, "We are here to oust Dong Zhuo. Now that he has abducted the emperor and burned down the palaces, there is widespread anxiety in the country. This is our best opportunity to eliminate the traitor. Why are we still hesitating?"

Cao Cao's impassioned plea failed to elicit an enthusiastic response. Even Yuan Shao, the leader of the alliance, showed apathy. No one was willing to be the first to launch an offensive.

Cao Cao realized that they were more interested in preserving their fighting strength than in battling Dong Zhuo. He decided to go it alone and marched with his five thousand troops toward Chenggao (today's town of Sishui in Xingyang, Henan).

Alerted of Cao Cao's advance on Chenggao, Dong Zhuo arrayed his troops on the banks of the Bian River (southwest of today's Xingyang in Henan), in order to intercept him. No sooner had Cao Cao's army reached the Bian River than Dong Zhuo's general Xu Rong cut it off.

Outnumbered by Xu Rong's troops, Cao Cao's army was routed

in the very first encounter. Cao Cao was shot in the shoulder by an arrow as he rode away in retreat. Another arrow then hit his horse, which startled it so much that it panicked and threw Cao Cao to the ground.

Xu Rong's soldiers were closing in on Cao Cao, who could hear their battle cries with increasing clarity. Fortunately, Cao Hong arrived in the nick of time. He jumped off his horse and helped Cao Cao to his feet; they were able to ride off together on Cao Hong's horse to safety.

When Cao Cao returned to Suanzao after suffering heavy losses, he found the other allied forces still holding back their troops, while their generals were drinking and carousing without giving any thought to fighting Dong Zhuo.

Filled with indignation he went to where Yuan Shao and others were having a feast and reproached them. "You have come here with your troops ostensibly to oust a usurper, but you are wavering and taking a wait-and-see attitude. You've let the country down and I feel ashamed for you!"

Very soon the hundreds of thousands of troops camping in Suanzao had depleted all their food rations and dispersed.

This experience convinced Cao Cao that he would not be able to accomplish much if he continued to associate with these men. He went alone to Yangzhou (south of the Huai River and the Yangtze in Jiangsu) to raise an army with a view to returning in the future.

63. Wang Yun Snares Dong Zhuo

DONG ZHUO HAD already presided over the execution of a large number of officials in Luoyang, but after the move to Chang'an he became even more of a tyrant. Officials and military officers had to choose their words very carefully in Dong Zhuo's presence because if they offended him they risked their necks. Some ministers entertained a secret desire to get rid of this scoundrel, if only to ensure their own survival.

Dong Zhuo had a trusted subaltern called Lü Bu, a renowned warrior with amazing physical strength and outstanding archery and equestrian skills. He had at an earlier time served under Ding Yuan, governor of Bingzhou. When Dong Zhuo marched into Luoyang, Ding Yuan was in command of the troops defending the capital. Dong Zhuo began to ply Lü Bu with precious gifts in order to encourage him to kill Ding Yuan. Lü Bu succumbed to Dong Zhuo's offers and betrayed Ding Yuan.

Dong Zhuo adopted Lü Bu as his godson and even entrusted his personal safety to him, and from that time onward Lü Bu would follow Dong Zhuo around like a shadow in his capacity as bodyguard. His brawn and bravery served to act as a deterrent to attempts on Dong Zhuo's life.

Meanwhile, the minister of education Wang Yun was determined to eliminate Dong Zhuo. He knew that to get at Dong Zhuo, he must first of all get past Lü Bu. He therefore invited Lü Bu to his home for frequent get-togethers to chat over a glass of wine. As time went on, Wang Yun's friendship won over Lü Bu, who began to reveal the truth about his relationship with Dong Zhuo.

It turned out that notwithstanding their father-son relationship, the irascible Dong Zhuo would often vent his fury on Lü Bu when he felt even the slightest frustration. In one instance Dong Zhuo hurled a halberd at Lü Bu for a defiant comment. Had it not been for Lü Bu's agility and quick reflexes, he would have been seriously injured.

Lü Bu apologized to Dong Zhuo after the incident and received absolution but the incident rankled in his heart. After hearing this, Wang Yun then told Lü Bu about his plan to assassinate Dong Zhuo. "Dong Zhuo is an enemy of the state and needs to be removed from power. Can you help by offering support from the inside?"

However, Lü Bu became hesitant at the idea of harming Dong Zhuo. "I am his adopted son. How can a son kill his father?"

Shaking his head, Wang Yun said, "My general, don't be ridiculous! Your surname is Lü and his is Dong. You are not related by blood. Besides, where was his fatherly affection when he hurled the halberd at you?"

Lü Bu found Wang Yun's analysis to make sense and agreed to be a party to the plot.

One day in 192 AD, Emperor Xian, who had recently recovered from an illness, called a meeting of his ministers in Weiyang Palace. As a precaution against assassination attempts, Dong Zhuo wore armor under his official robe and deployed two solid walls of armed guards to form a secure corridor around him, leading all the way to the palace. With Lü Bu protecting him with a lance just a step behind, Dong Zhuo felt he was fully protected and secure.

How was he to know that Wang Yun and Lü Bu had already agreed on a plan? Lü Bu planted a number of trusted warriors among the guards manning the secure corridor at the gate of the palace. As soon as Dong Zhuo's carriage went through the gate, someone thrust a halberd at his chest. However, it did not pierce the armor he wore beneath his robe.

Dong Zhuo's arm was wounded as he raised it to parry the thrust. Braving the pain, he jumped from his carriage and cried, "Where is Lü Bu?"

Lü Bu stepped out from behind the carriage and announced in

a booming voice, "By imperial edict, I am here to take the traitor Dong Zhuo!"

When he saw that he had been betrayed by his son, Dong Zhuo railed at Lü Bu, "You dog of a slave! I dare you to..."

Yet before he had time to finish the sentence, Lü Bu's raised lance had already pierced Dong Zhuo's throat. The soldiers swarmed toward Dong Zhuo and cut off his head.

64. Cao Cao Discusses Heroes over Wine

SINCE DONG ZHUO'S death, the Eastern Han dynasty had been on its last legs. With the loss of central control over many of the regions, local bureaucrats and gentry took advantage of the power vacuum to grab spheres of influence and establish semi-independent kingdom of varying sizes. The more powerful local rulers included Yuan Shao of Jizhou, Yuan Shu of Nanyang, Liu Biao of Jingzhou (straddling today's Hubei and Hunan Provinces and parts of Henan, Guizhou, Guangdong and Guangxi), Tao Qian of Xuzhou (the part of Jiangsu north of the Yangtze and southeastern Shandong) and Lü Bu. They were in perpetual turf wars with one another, engulfing the country in turmoil and claiming the lives of hundreds of thousands of civilians. Many towns and villages were left deserted and in ruins.

Cao Cao's force started out small. After defeating the Yellow Turbans that captured Yanzhou (the southwestern part of today's Shandong and the eastern part of Henan), he established a foothold there. From among the Yellow Turbans that had surrendered to him, he selected the best soldiers to augment his armed force. He went on to defeat Tao Qian and Lü Bu and establish a powerful regime of his own.

In 196 AD, Cao Cao installed Emperor Xian of the Han dynasty in Xucheng, which thus became the interim capital of the Eastern Han dynasty and was named Xudu ("du" means capital).

Cao Cao built a palace for Emperor Xian in Xudu so that the

emperor could hold court there. Cao Cao named himself General-in-chief and was the real power behind the throne. He assured the supply of rations for his troops by creating a system combining garrison duty with land cultivation, and by surrounding himself with capable advisers he further enlarged his power base.

In the year of Emperor Xian's arrival in Xudu, Liu Bei, the governor of Xuzhou, came to Cao Cao to offer his services following his defeat by Yuan Shu and Lü Bu, who had mounted a coordinated attack against him.

Liu Bei was from the Zhuo Commandery of Hebei (today's Zhuo County in Hebei) and was descended from the royalty of the Western Han dynasty. His father had died when he was a child and had left behind an impoverished household subsisting on meager earnings brought in by Liu Bei and his mother from selling shoes and weaving mats. With help from his clansmen, he was later able to acquire a basic education from a local tutor. However, his real interest did not lie in learning but in fighting for great causes. Two prosperous horse traders passing through the Zhuo Commandery got to know Liu Bei and developed a high regard for him. They provided funding for his effort to raise an army.

The effort attracted two men eager to take up Liu Bei's cause: Guan Yu and Zhang Fei. Liu Bei was deeply impressed by their combat skills and their commitment to the same cause, and soon developed a special affection for them. As time went by, the three became closer than brothers.

After Liu Bei joined forces with Cao Cao, they launched an attack against Lü Bu, as a result of which Lü Bu's kingdom was annihilated. Upon their triumphant return to Xudu, Cao Cao recommended to Emperor Xian that Liu Bei be made Left Leader of Court Gentlemen. He showed great respect for Liu Bei and insisted on his new friend's company wherever he went.

Liu Bei was uneasy about the respect Cao Cao showed him, since he was worried that his own ambitions might arouse Cao Cao's suspicions.

Behind his publicly-avowed high regard for Liu Bei, Cao Cao was privately keeping a close eye on him. He often sent his soldiers to covertly spy on Liu Bei. They would invariably find him planting and watering vegetables in his garden, and failed to detect any sign of suspicious goings-on. In this way, Cao Cao's fears were gradually allayed.

One evening, Cao Cao invited Liu Bei to join him for a drink. The two of them had a pleasant chat over wine. Their conversation segued from one thing to another until they eventually turned to the political situation of the country.

"So many are fighting for control of the country. In your opinion, how many of them can accurately be called heroes?" Cao Cao asked.

"I am not sure," Liu Bei replied.

Cao Cao flashed a smile. "As I see it, there are only two heroes in this country: you, honorable general, and myself. Yuan Shao and the like don't count."

Liu Bei had already been nervous about his secret dealings with Dong Cheng; this pronouncement from Cao Cao sent a chill down his spine, causing him to drop his chopsticks.

A bolt of lightning flashed across the sky just at this moment, followed by a burst of thunder. Liu Bei bent down to pick up the chopsticks, saying "That crash of thunder really scared the wits out of me!"

He was thus able to dissimulate the disconcertment caused by Cao Cao's remark and Cao Cao did not seem to detect any unusual reaction in Liu Bei.

Afterwards, Liu Bei gave much thought to Cao Cao's remark about heroes. He came to the conclusion that Cao Cao was treating him as his sole rival and would surely not make life easy for him. Though he kept up his meetings with Dong Cheng to form a plan to eliminate Cao Cao, he also began looking for an opportunity to leave Xudu.

At this time Yuan Shao happened to send his son to Qingzhou to reinforce Yuan Shu's army; he would have to pass through Xuzhou on his way. Knowing that Liu Bei was familiar with that area, Cao Cao sent him to intercept Yuan Shu. This was the opportunity he had been looking for. Liu Bei therefore lost no time in following Cao Cao's orders and taking Guan Yu, Zhang Fei and their troops on the road.

When Cao Cao's adviser Guo Jia learned that Cao Cao had allowed Liu Bei to leave, he rushed over to Cao Cao and said, "Liu Bei has grand ambitions. You shouldn't have let him leave."

Sobered by Guo Jia's warning, Cao Cao began to regret his decision and immediately sent his men after Liu Bei's party. However, by this time Liu Bei was out of reach.

After defeating Yuan Shu and capturing Xuzhou, Liu Bei decided not to return to Xudu. Since Liu Bei had been a good governor of the region of Xuzhou in the past, the nearby commanderies and counties switched their allegiance from Cao Cao to him.

Cao Cao was furious at Liu Bei's betrayal and decided to personally lead an expedition against him.

In the following spring, Cao Cao launched a large-scale attack against Xuzhou. Liu Bei's troops were too few in number to put up a large scale defense and soon buckled under Cao Cao's offensive. Liu Bei had no alternative but to abandon Xuzhou and take his troops to Jizhou to join Yuan Shao.

65. The Battle of Guandu

LIU BEI'S FLIGHT to Jizhou (southwest of today's Linzhang in Hebei) finally convinced Yuan Shao that Cao Cao was a formidable foe and so he steeled his resolve to capture Xudu.

In 200 AD, Yuan Shao created a 100,000-strong elite force with Ju Shou as Army Supervisor to march to Liyang (today's Jun County in Henan). He first ordered General Yan Liang to cross the Yellow River to attack Baima (today's Hua County in Henan).

At this time, Cao Cao had already returned to Guandu with his troops. When he learned of the siege of Baima, he wanted to head straight to the scene of the battle to lift the siege. His adviser Xun You warned him against it, "We are outnumbered by the enemy. Instead of confronting them we could divert part of our troops to go west and pretend to cross the river at Yanjin. This would draw Yuan Shao's main force away to the west. We would then send a light cavalry to attack Baima when they least expect it."

Cao Cao decided to adopt the diversionary tactic suggested by Xun You. When Yuan Shao heard that Cao Cao planned to cross the river at Yanjin, he sent a large force to head Cao Cao off, little knowing that the latter had led a light cavalry to attack Baima. The Yuan army under the command of General Yan Liang that was laying siege to Baima was caught off guard and routed by the Cao army. General Yan was killed and the siege of Baima was lifted.

Yuan Shao was furious when he learned that Cao Cao had lifted the siege of Baima. Ju Shou, the Army Supervisor, advised Yuan Shao to send only part of his troops to fight Cao Cao, while keeping his main force south of Yanjin. However, the distraught

Yuan Shao dismissed Ju Shou's idea and ordered all of his troops to cross the river in pursuit of Cao Cao's army. He then put General Wen Chou in charge of of six thousand cavalrymen. As Cao Cao withdrew his forces from Baima to march toward Guandu, he received intelligence that Yuan Shao was hot on his trail. He set up an ambush of six hundred cavalrymen near the south hills of Yanjin, with instructions to unsaddle the horses and let them loose to roam the hills. The soldiers were also to leave their weapons and suits of armor strewn about on the ground.

When Wen Chou's cavalrymen reached the south hills and saw the abandoned horses and weapons, they were led to believe that the fleeing Cao force was far in the distance. When Wen Chou ordered his soldiers to retrieve the weapons strewn about on the ground, six hundred ambushers leapt out of hiding to attack them. The Yuan troops were taken by surprise and suffered heavy casualties, while Wen Chou was killed before he had time to figure out what was happening.

Yuan Shao had lost two generals, Yan Liang and Wen Chou, in two battles—morale therefore sank very low among the Yuan troops. Yet Yuan Shao refused to take it lying down and insisted on pursuing Cao Cao. Ju Shou, the Army Supervisor, said, "We may have a greater number of troops, but they lack the fierce fighting spirit of the Cao army. Cao Cao's troops are fierce fighters on the battleground. However, we have a larger supply of rations than they do. We should wait here until the Cao force runs out of supplies. They will move out of here of their own accord when that happens."

Ignoring Ju Shou's advice once again, Yuan Shao ordered his troops to continue their march until they came to Guandu, where they pitched their tents. By that time, Cao Cao had returned to Guandu and finished deploying his troops behind stockades and other defenses.

Seeing that the Cao troops had barricaded themselves, Yuan Shao ordered his soldiers to construct earth mounds and high structures outside the Cao camp so that they could shoot arrows into it from a high vantage point. This meant that the soldiers inside the Cao camp were forced to constantly move around behind shields.

In response, Cao Cao and his advisers devised a catapult that could hurl large stones weighing a dozen *jin* when a mechanism on it was released. The stones smashed the high structures built by the Yuan troops, many of whom were injured by the flying projectiles.

Yuan Shao then countered with another stratagem. Under cover of night, he had his soldiers dig a tunnel, with the intention of using it for a stealth attack. However, the secret undertaking did not escape the notice of the Cao camp and Cao Cao instructed his soldiers to dig a long, deep trench at the front edge of his camp to cut off the enemy tunnel, thus thwarting the surprise attack planned by Yuan Shao.

When the stand-off at Guandu entered its second month, supplies were beginning to become depleted in the Cao camp, and the soldiers seemed increasingly weary and worn out. Even Cao Cao showed signs of nearing breaking point. He wrote to Xun Yu in Xudu about his intention to stand down and withdraw his force. Xun Yu wrote back urging him to hold his ground at all costs.

In the meantime, Yuan Shao was receiving a steady supply of rations for his troops from Yecheng. Yuan Shao entrusted his general Chun Yuqiong with the task of escorting the rations with ten thousand troops, and large amounts of them were stored in Wuchao, 40 *li* from Guandu.

Having confirmed the intelligence that the Cao camp was running out of supplies, Yuan Shao's adviser Xu You proposed that a small force be sent to launch a surprise attack on Xudu, bypassing Guandu. The idea met a cold reception from Yuan Shao. "No! I want to defeat Cao Cao first!" he said.

Just as Xu You got ready to make a further effort to persuade Yuan Shao of the soundness of his idea, Yuan Shao received a letter from Yecheng. It informed him that someone from Xu You's household had broken the law and had been arrested by the local authorities. After reading the letter, Yuan Shao began to shout at his adviser.

Filled with hurt and rancor, Xu You remembered his old friend Cao Cao and that very night he abandoned the Yuan camp to go over to Cao Cao.

Cao Cao had taken off his boots and was getting ready for bed in his tent when he was told that Xu You had come to offer his service. He was so excited that he rushed out barefoot to greet Xu You, saying "Very good! With your help I have a better chance of success."

After sitting down, Xu You said, "Yuan Shao is preparing a strong offensive. How do you plan to deal with him? How much do you have in the way of supplies?"

"We have enough for a year," Cao Cao replied.

Xu You laughed, "No, really?"

"No, we have just enough for six months," Cao Cao corrected himself.

Feigning anger, Xu You asked, "Don't you wish to defeat Yuan Shao? Why do you lie to an old friend?"

Cao Cao finally told the truth. "To be frank with you, our rations will only last a month. What do you think we should do?"

"I have heard about the critical plight you are in. I have come to you with valuable information. Yuan Shao has ten thousand carts of rations and weapons stored in Wuchao. They are maintained under lax guard by the troops of Chun Yuqiong. All you need to do is attack Wuchao with a light cavalry and torch all his rations. Within three days his force will crumble without a shot fired," Xu You replied.

After receiving this important intelligence, Cao Cao immediately summoned Xun You and Cao Hong. He gave them instructions to defend the barracks at Guandu while he himself led five thousand cavalrymen on a night march toward Wuchao. They carried flags and standards of the Yuan army, and whenever they were challenged by sentinels they would say they had been sent by Yuan Shao to reinforce Wuchao. The unsuspecting Yuan sentinels let them through.

Once in Wuchao, Cao Cao's troops surrounded the granaries and started a huge fire that destroyed ten thousand carts of grains. When Chun Yuqiong, the general guarding the granaries, arrived to engage the enemy, he was killed by the Cao troops.

When news of the blaze in Wuchao reached the Yuan troops in Guandu, they were thrown into a panic. Two of Yuan Shao's generals, Zhang He and Gao Lan, surrendered with their troops to the Cao camp. Emboldened by this success, the Cao troops launched a fierce offensive that routed the Yuan troops. Yuan Shao and his son Yuan Tan did not even have time to don their armor before they took the remaining eight hundred cavalrymen with them on a northward flight.

Yuan Shao's main force was annihilated in this decisive battle. Two years later, Yuan Shao died. After another seven years of fighting, Cao Cao finally wiped out Yuan Shao's remaining forces and unified north China.

66. Sun Ce Takes Control of Jiangdong

WHEN CAO CAO and Yuan Shao were slugging it out in the north, a separate regime rose and grew stronger under the brothers Sun Ce and Sun Quan in Jiangdong (in the lower reaches of the Yangtze River).

Sun Ce's father Sun Jian was governor of Changsha and had served under Yuan Shu. After Sun Jian's death, Sun Ce went over to Yuan Shu with his troops. Yuan Shu took a liking to this handsome young man and was often heard to say, "If I had a son like Sun Ce, I would ask no more of life."

Despite this professed good will, Yuan Shu did not particularly value Sun Ce's services. Sun Ce wished to become a commandery governor, but Yuan Shu would not promote him to this position. Sun Ce had a maternal uncle called Wu Jing, who had been governor of Danyang (today's Xuancheng in Anhui) in Jiangdong, but was forced out by Liu You, the governor of the region of Yangzhou. Sun Ce asked Yuan Shu's permission to go to Jiangdong to help his uncle fight Liu You. Yuan Shu agreed to assign one thousand soldiers to Sun Ce, but only because he had a personal grudge against Liu You.

As Sun Ce moved south with his troops, many people along the way offered their services to him. By the time they reached Liyang (today's He County in Anhui), their ranks had swelled to more than five thousand. Sun Ce's force was further augmented by the men brought in by Zhou Yu, a close friend of his since childhood.

Sun Ce's bravery in battle, his martial skills and the iron discipline he imposed on his troops earned him a lot of popular support. This enabled him to bring his troops across the river in good time not only to defeat Liu You's forces and recover Danyang, but also to capture the Wu and Guiji Commanderies. As a result of this action, Sun Ce succeeded in taking control of a vast area covering six commanderies in Jiangdong.

After gaining control of Jiangdong, the ambitious Sun Ce began a northward expansion. As Cao Cao and Yuan Shao were locked in a stand-off at Guandu, he began planning a sneak attack on Xudu to take Emperor Xian under his wing. When troop deployments and logistical preparations for the operation were under way, however, something unexpected happened.

It all began with Sun Ce's killing of Xu Gong, the governor of the Wu Commandery. The incident had earned Sun Ce the enmity of Xu Gong's retainers, who ambushed Sun Ce's hunting party in a heavily forested hill. Sun Ce was shot in the face by an arrow from one of the ambushers.

The wound proved serious and got worse despite treatment. Knowing he woud not survive much longer, Sun Ce called together a few close associates, including Zhang Zhao, and made a final request. "I have built up a power base here with enough people and territory to compete with my rivals. Please help my younger brother to take over from me."

Sun Quan was only 19 at the time, but already enjoyed great prestige among the officials in Jiangdong because of his natural inclination for cultivating friends, as well as the premium he put on talents. Sun Ce handed his tasseled seal to Sun Quan and made him put it on. "My brother!" he said to him. "On the battlefield you are no match for me, but in the ability to recognize and make good use of talented people I cannot hold a candle to you. Make sure you carry on what we've accomplished in Jiangdong." With those last words he breathed his last breath.

Sun Quan's long lament at Sun Ce's deathbed was interrupted by Zhang Zhao, who made him change immediately into official attire and ride through the barracks on an inspection tour in order to keep up the soldiers' morale. In the meantime, a messenger was dispatched with the latest news to Zhou Yu, who was camping in Baqiu (today's Yueyang in Hunan). That night, Zhou Yu returned with his troops to the Wuzhong area and, together with Zhang

Zhao, provided Sun Quan with all the support he needed.

Although Sun Ce had by that time taken control of all six commanderies of Jiangdong, there were still pockets of resistance in many remote areas. However, thanks to the devotion and help of Zhang Zhao and Zhou Yu, Sun Quan was finally able to cement his control.

Sun Quan took to heart his brother's last words and left no stone unturned in his quest for talented people to help his cause. Zhou Yu said to Sun Quan, "I have a friend called Lu Su, who is a knowledgeable and perceptive person. If you enlist his services, you will never regret it."

At Sun Quan's invitation, Lu Su arrived. The two men soon hit it off. On one occasion, Sun Quan asked Lu Su to stay after the other guests had left in order that they might talk in private.

"The Han dynasty is in decline and anarchy reigns in the country," Sun Quan began. "I want to carry on fighting for the cause my brother and my father fought for. I want to emulate the ancient Duke Huan of Qi and Duke Wen of Jin and help the emperor to project imperial power far and wide. What do you think?"

"I've carefully studied the situation in this country and have come to believe that it is no longer possible for the Han dynasty to return to its former glories," Lu Su replied. "Cao Cao has grown too powerful to be easily eliminated. I believe it is in your interest for the moment to consolidate your hold on Jiangdong and bide your time. Cao Cao is at the moment too busy dealing with enemies in the north to pay any notice to us. This is an opportunity to attack Liu Biao and capture Jingzhou. The conquest of the whole country will come later. It's a worthy cause that brings to mind Emperor Gaozu of the Han dynasty."

Sun Quan's spirit was lifted and his heart warmed by this analysis. Thanks to Sun Quan's ability to recognize and value talent, Jiangdong thrived under a meritocracy of numerous outstanding civil officials and military officers.

In order to court the support of Sun Quan, Cao Cao had the imperial court name him Zheng Lu ("the vanquisher of barbarians") General with double duty as the governor of Guiji. From then on, Sun Quan solidified his position as head of a de facto separate regime.

67. Liu Bei's Three Visits to the Thatched Hut

AFTER THE BATTLE of Guandu, Liu Bei fled to the region of Jingzhou for Liu Biao's protection. Liu Biao assigned some troops to him and then sent him to Xinye (today's Xinye County in Henan).

Liu Bei spent several years in Jingzhou. Despite the special treatment accorded him by Liu Biao, the ambitious Liu Bei never stopped fretting about his failure to accomplish what he had set out to do.

On one occasion he was overcome with emotion and was unable to hold back his tears. When asked by Liu Biao what was bothering him, Liu Bei replied, "I used to have powerful muscles in my legs because I was always riding in battle, but the sedentary life I now lead has added flab to my thighs. I am saddened to realize that as time flies and as I age I haven't accomplished much in life."

Liu Biao offered some soothing words, but Liu Bei could not take his mind from his plans for the future. He soon decided that he needed a good adviser.

As soon as he learned that a man of renown and learning called Sima Hui resided in Xiangyang, he paid him a personal visit. Sima Hui received him courteously and asked about the purpose of the visit.

"As a matter of fact I have come expressly to hear your analysis of the political situation in this country," Liu Bei said.

This triggered a burst of laughter from Sima Hui. "What is a very ordinary person like me to know about the state of the country? To achieve dominion of the country you need a topnotch mind and talents of the highest calibre."

Liu Bei begged Sima Hui to point him to such persons. "Where can I find the kind of talent you are referring to?"

"We have in this vicinity a Wolong (crouching dragon) and a Fengchu (fledgling phoenix). Either of them could help you gain control of the country," Sima Hui replied.

Liu Bei could not wait to know who this Wolong and Fengchu were. Sima Hui told him that the Wolong went by the name of Zhuge Liang, also known by the courtesy name of Kongming; the Fengchu was called Pang Tong, with the courtesy name of Shiyuan.

Liu Bei thanked Sima Hui and returned to Xinye, where a scholar came to visit him. The visitor's air of self-assurance and composure prompted Liu Bei to conclude that he must be either the Wolong or the Fengchu. The caller was therefore warmly received.

Some time into the conversation it was learned that the visitor's name was Xu Shu. He was a local intellectual and had come to offer his services to Liu Bei after learning that the latter was recruiting talented men.

Liu Bei gladly took him in as an adviser.

"I have an old friend called Zhuge Kongming, popularly known as the Wolong. Are you willing to meet with him?" Xu Shu asked.

From Xu Shu, Liu Bei found out details about Zhuge Liang's life. It turned out Zhuge Liang was not a native of that part of the country, but had come from Yangdu County (south of today's Yishui County in Shandong) of the Langya Commandery. His father had died when he was in his teens. His uncle Zhuge Xuan, who was a friend of Liu Biao, had decided to bring him to Jingzhou. Shortly after this, his uncle had also died. He settled down in a thatched hut in Longzhong (west of today's Xiangyang in Hubei), and spent his days farming and reading. He was then only 27 but was already admired by his friends for the breadth and depth of his learning and knowledge. He liked to compare himself to the legendary Guan Zhong and Yue Yi. Put off by the chaos in the country and realizing Liu Biao's inability to recognize and tap talent, he chose to lead the simple life of a recluse in Longzhong.

After hearing Xu Shu's account, Liu Bei said, "Since you know him so well, why don't you persuade him to come to me?"

Xu Shu shook his head. "That won't do. To get a person of his caliber, you must show your sincerity by going to him in person."

Having heard nothing but high praise for Zhuge Liang from both Sima Hui and Xu Shu, Liu Bei was convinced that Zhuge Liang must be greatly talented. He took Guan Yu and Zhang Fei with him to pay a visit to Zhuge Liang in Longzhong.

Informed of Liu Bei's impending visit, Zhuge Liang deliberately stayed away so that when Liu Bei arrived, he was greeted by an empty house.

Guan Yu and Zhang Fei, who accompanied Liu Bei on the visit, were much annoyed by the snub, but Liu Bei took Xu Shu's remark to heart and went back a second time, only for the same thing to happen again. Undeterred, he went back a third time, determined to obtain the services of Zhuge Liang.

Liu Bei's sincerity finally won over Zhuge Liang, who received Liu Bei in his humble thatched hut.

Liu Bei entered the hut to meet Zhuge Liang, leaving Guan Yu and Zhang Fei waiting outside. Once alone with Zhuge Liang inside the hut, Liu Bei got straight to the point. "The Han dynasty is in deep decline and power has now fallen into evil hands. I want to try to reverse the situation, only I don't have a good strategy. That's why I have come to you for enlightenment."

Moved by Liu Bei's humility in seeking his advice, Zhuge Liang made an exposé of his views, holding nothing back. "Cao Cao has defeated Yuan Shao and has one million troops under his command. He can issue commands in the name of the emperor, who Cao Cao is simply using as a pawn. Under the circumstances, you cannot expect to use force alone to compete with him. Sun Quan has ruled Jiangdong for three generations. He possesses the advantages of the forbidding terrain of Jiangdong, popular support and a large pool of talent to draw from. In my opinion, you should pursue an alliance with him instead of treating him as your next conquest."

Zhuge Liang went on to give an analysis of the situation in Jingzhou and Yizhou (covering parts of today's Sichuan, Yunnan, Shaanxi, Gansu, Hubei and Guizhou). According to him, Jingzhou was strategically important but Liu Biao would not be able to hold it for long. Yizhou boasted vast, fertile land and had for that reason long been known as a "Heavenly Country," but it was ruled by Liu Zhang, who was another weak and incompetent leader who was unpopular with his subjects.

"Honorable general, you are descended from Han royalty and well known across the country. If you succeed in taking control of Jingzhou and Yizhou, enter into an alliance with Sun Quan and ensure good government in areas under your control, then when the time comes you will be able to launch a two-pronged attack on Cao Cao from Jingzhou and Yizhou. You will be greeted with open arms by the people wherever your campaign takes you. When that happens, your vision will be realized and the Han dynasty will be revitalized."

"You have opened my mind," Liu Bei replied. "I will certainly follow your advice. I implore you to come down the mountain with me."

Liu Bei's enthusiasm and sincerity won over Zhuge Liang, who gladly followed Liu Bei to Xinye. This episode is historically known as the "Three Visits to the Thatched Hut" and Zhuge Liang's discourse as the "Longzhong Dialogue."

From then on, Liu Bei treated Zhuge Liang as his mentor and Zhuge Liang treated Liu Bei as his master, and their bond grew steadily stronger.

Guan Yu and Zhang Fei were very unhappy with this development and began to express private misgivings. In their estimation, Zhuge Liang was too young to have any major capabilities and they thought that Liu Bei overestimated his abilites.

Liu Bei admonished them for these feelings. "With Mister Kongming as my adviser I now feel like a stranded fish returned to water. I don't want to hear any of this nonsense from you in the future." This silenced Guan Yu and Zhang Fei, and the matter was laid to rest.

68. Zhou Yu's Fiery Attack at Red Cliffs

AFTER PACIFYING THE north, Cao Cao led a large force in 208 AD to attack Liu Biao in the south. Yet before the Cao army had even reached Jingzhou, Liu Biao died of illness. His son Liu Cong, petrified at the scale of the attacking force, sent an envoy to negotiate a surrender.

When Liu Bei, who was camped in Fancheng (today's Xiangfan City in Hubei), heard about the southward push of Cao Cao's army, he decided to pull his troops back to Jiangling (today's Jiangling in Hubei). The populace in Jingzhou decided to leave their land to follow Liu Bei because they had heard about his legendary generosity.

When Cao Cao arrived with his troops in Xiangyang, he learned that Liu Bei had withdrawn to Jiangling, where Liu Biao had reportedly stockpiled large quantities of grains and weapons. Concerned that these might fall into Liu Bei's hands, he personally led a light cavalry of five thousand troops to head him off. Loaded down with weapons, supplies and over a hundred thousand civilians who had chosen to follow him, Liu Bei's troops could advance only a dozen *li* a day, whereas Cao Cao's cavalry covered three hundred *li* in a single day and soon caught up with them at Changban Hills in Dangyang (northeast of today's Dangyang County in Hubei).

Liu Bei's army was soon routed by Cao Cao's cavalry. It was only Zhang Fei's rearguard action holding back the enemy for a while that enabled Liu Bei and Zhuge Liang, escorted by a small remnant force, to shake off their pursuers. However, by that time the road to Jiangling had been cut off by the Cao army and they were compelled to head instead to Xiakou (today's Wuhan City in Hubei).

Having captured Jiangling, Cao Cao's forces continued their march along the river toward the east. They were approaching Xiakou when Zhuge Liang said to Liu Bei, "We are in deep trouble. We have no choice but to seek help from Sun Quan."

It so happened that, worried by the prospect of Cao Cao's capture of Jingzhou, Sun Quan had sent Lu Su to lobby Liu Bei for an alliance against the Cao offensive. Zhuge Liang returned with Lu Su to meet with Sun Quan in Chaisang (southwest of today's Jiujiang in Jiangxi).

Zhuge Liang said to Sun Quan, "When Cao Cao takes Jingzhou, his next target will be the state of Wu in Jiangdong. If you are determined to put up a fight, you should sever your ties with Cao Cao now and join forces with us. The alternative is clearly to surrender to him. If you procrastinate, disaster will strike and it will be too late."

"Why doesn't General Liu surrender to Cao Cao?" Sun Quan retorted.

"General Liu is descended from the Han royalty and possesses superior abilities. He will never consent to debase himself by surrendering to Cao Cao," Zhuge Liang replied.

At these words Sun Quan became worked up. "I will not surrender Jiangdong and my hundred thousand troops either. But how will General Liu be able to defend himself against Cao's after his recent defeat?"

"Don't worry! Despite having lost one battle, General Liu still has twenty thousand navy men," Zhuge Liang reassured him. "Cao Cao may have a large force, but the long marches have tired his soldiers out. What's more, these northerners are not accustomed to naval battles and they face the hostility of the people of Jingzhou. If we are united, we will be able to defeat the Cao army."

Buoyed by Zhuge Liang's analysis Sun Quan immediately summoned his generals to draw up a plan of resistance against Cao

Cao's imminent attack.

In the meantime, a messenger had been sent by Cao Cao to deliver a letter of challenge, which read, "On the orders of the emperor of the Han dynasty, I am leading an expeditionary force on a southern campaign. I am challenging you to a battle against my 800,000-strong naval force."

Sun Quan showed the letter to his staff, all of whom suddenly became pale-faced and speechless.

Then Zhang Zhao, the most senior member of the Wu hierarchy, spoke, "Cao Cao is now campaigning in the name of the emperor. If we resist, it's already one strike against us as far as legitimacy is concerned. Besides, we used to have the natural barrier of the Yangtze on our side but we've lost that now. With Cao Cao's capture of Jingzhou and his armada of over a thousand battleships, we have no hope of resisting a joint land and naval attack. In my view, we have no alternative but to surrender."

His view was immediately echoed by others. Only Lu Su looked on dispassionately without uttering a word.

Sun Quan did not like what he was seeing and hearing, so he walked out, followed by Lu Su.

"Tell me what we should do." Sun Quan asked Lu Su.

"Zhang Zhao and the others don't know what they are talking about. Ignore them!" Lu Su replied. "It may be all right for me to surrender, but it is not for you. If I surrendered, I would at the worst go back to my hometown and renew my ties with scholars and intellectuals. I might even be able to get an official commission in the regional or commandery government. But if you, my esteemed general, surrendered, all six commanderies of Jiangdong would fall into Cao Cao's lap, and where would you go then?"

"I was really disappointed by what the others were saying just now. You alone have said what was on my mind," Sun Quan said with a sigh.

After the meeting, Lu Su urged Sun Quan to call General Zhou Yu back from Poyang without delay for consultation.

When Zhou Yu arrived in Chaisang, Sun Quan called another meeting of high officials. Zhou Yu made a passionate speech at the meeting. "Cao Cao is the Counselor-in-chief of the Han court in name, but in reality he is a traitor. He has now offered himself up to be killed, so why in the world should we surrender to him?" He went on to enumerate many disadvantages and handicaps Cao Cao had to contend with. His soldiers were northerners unaccustomed to naval warfare, and their long trek to an unfamiliar land almost guaranteed that they would suffer from stomach troubles. When that happened his natural advantages would evaporate.

Sun Quan, his nerves steeled by the reassuring words of Zhou Yu, got to his feet with his sword unsheathed, and with it he whittled off a corner of the table. "Whoever mentions surrender again will end up like this table," he declared.

That evening, Zhou Yu went to Sun Quan again for a private meeting. "I've found out that Cao Cao was just bluffing when he claimed to have 800,000 troops," he said. "The actual figure is more like 200,000, many of whom are from Jingzhou and therefore of questionable loyalty. Just give me fifty thousand of your best troops and I assure you I will defeat him."

The next day, Sun Quan made Zhou Yu Commander-in-Chief of 30,000 naval troops, with instructions to coordinate his actions with Liu Bei in a joint effort to resist Cao Cao's offensive.

Zhou Yu's troops ran into Cao Cao's forward sentinels at Red Cliffs (Chiji Mountains west of today's Wuchang County in Hubei). As predicted by Zhou Yu, many in the Cao army had been struck down with diarrhea. In the first skirmish the Cao troops were beaten back and had to withdraw to the north bank of the Yangtze. Zhou Yu and his naval force moored on the south bank opposite the Cao force.

Also as predicted by Zhou Yu, the northerners in the Cao force were ill-adapted to naval operations and got seasick whenever their battleships were buffeted by wind or waves. They decided to tie the ships together with steel cables to stabilize the river craft.

When Zhou Yu's staff officer Huang Gai saw what the enemy had done with the steel cables, he had an idea. "We are outnumbered by the enemy and it's not in our interest to prolong the stand-off. Now that the Cao army have tied their ships together, I think we might be able to defeat them by attacking with fire."

Huang Gai's idea sounded ingenious to Zhou Yu. The two formed a plan whereby Huang Gai would send word to Cao Cao stating his intention to abandon the state of Wu of Jiangdong and defect to Cao Cao's side. Convinced that the generals of the state of Wu were in awe of him, Cao Cao never had the slightest suspicion about the authenticity of Huang Gai's professed intention to defect.

In the meantime, Huang Gai had instructed his soldiers to load ten big vessels with dry twigs generously sprinkled with kerosene. The boats were then shrouded with sailcloth and adorned with numerous flags and standards. Smaller, lighter craft were tethered to the stern of the bigger boats to be used as getaways once the fire was started.

The November weather was abnormally warm, and a southeasterly wind began to blow. At nightfall, Huang Gai and some of his troops sailed in the ten big boats followed by the smaller craft, and when the flotilla reached midstream the sails were unfurled and the boats began to race toward the north bank.

Cao Cao's naval troops had heard about the imminent surrender of an enemy general and were crowded near the prows of their ships to gawk. When the flotilla of the Wu came within two *li* of the north bank, the ten big boats suddenly burst into flames. With the rising wind fanning the flames, the ten fiery boats rammed into the Cao troops' naval headquarters like ten fire-breathing dragons. The battleships moored there, having been tied together, could not break free and the blaze jumped from ship to ship, soon engulfing everything. Not only were the naval headquarters reduced to ashes, but the tents on the shore had also caught fire. Many soldiers were burned to death and many others who did not know how to swim drowned when they were jostled into the river.

When Zhou Yu saw the blaze on the north bank, he immediately crossed the river with his elite troops to press the attack. They made a sustained, loud racket on their war drums as they moved forward, confusing the Cao army into thinking that they were confronted by a large force. The panicked Cao army was quickly routed.

Cao Cao fled with his remnant troops toward Huarong (southwest of today's Qianjiang County in Hubei). They took a muddy back road that proved difficult for his cavalry to traverse. Cao Cao ordered the older and weaker soldiers to lay straw on the road to improve the surface. This enabled Cao Cao and his cavalrymen to finally ride ahead, but many of the soldiers covering the road with straw were trampled to death in the process.

Liu Bei and Zhou Yu relentlessly pursued Cao Cao's remnant forces on land and on the river until they came to the Nan Commandery (at today's Jiangling in Hubei), where Cao Cao found more than half of his hundreds of thousands of troops had either died in battle or of disease. Cao Cao entrusted the garrisons of Jiangling and Xiangyang to his generals Cao Ren, Xu Huang and Yue Jin, and then returned with his troops to the north.

The Battle of Red Cliffs was an early milestone in the division of the country into three separate kingdoms.

69. Guan Yu Swamps the Seven Armies

NOT LONG AFTER the Battle of Red Cliffs, Zhou Yu died of illness. At Lu Su's suggestion, Sun Quan ceded control of Jingzhou temporarily to Liu Bei.

In 214 AD, Liu Bei marched into Chengdu and declared himself governor of Yizhou.

When Sun Quan learned that Liu Bei had seized Yizhou, he demanded the return of Jingzhou, but Liu Bei refused. The two nearly had a falling-out over this issue. When Cao Cao was preparing to attack Hanzhong, thus also threatening Yizhou, Liu Bei and Sun Quan realized that Cao Cao was a formidable foe to both of them. They decided to make up with each other and agreed that the part of Jingzhou west of the Xiang River would go to Liu Bei and the eastern part would revert to the state of Wu.

With the question of Jingzhou out of the way, Liu Bei could devote his attention to dealing with Cao Cao. He left Zhuge Liang in charge of defending Chengdu and marched at the head of a large force toward Hanzhong, taking his adviser Fa Zheng along with him.

In response, Cao Cao readied his troops for battle againt Liu Bei. He went to Chang'an to personally direct the campaign in Hanzhong. The stand-off lasted a year until in a battle at Yangping Pass the army of the state of Shu (Liu Bei) finally defeated the Wei (Cao Cao) army, whose commanding general Xia Houyuan was killed in action. Cao Cao was forced out of Hanzhong and withdrew the Wei army to Chang'an.

In the aftermath of these battles, Liu Bei saw his position in Yizhou further consolidated. In 219 AD, with the enthusiastic support of his ministers and generals, Liu Bei declared himself King of Hanzhong.

The strategy mapped out by Zhuge Liang to deal with Cao Cao called for a two-phase approach. Now that the western campaign into Hanzhong had succeeded, Liu Bei should press his new military advantage by going east from Jingzhou to take the central plains.

The commander of the Jingzhou garrison was General Guan Yu, who though both intelligent and strong was also arrogant and conceited. After declaring himself King of Hanzhong, Liu Bei made him General of the Army of the Front, but Guan Yu remained unimpressed. It was only after the messenger bringing the appointment order and the official seal had painstakingly explained to him how the king of Hanzhong valued his service that he finally cheered up and accepted the appointment.

Liu Bei also made Guan Yu the Commander-in-Chief of the eastern campaign. Guan Yu left the defense of Jiangling and Gong'an to two of his men, while he led a large force to attack Fancheng.

Cao Ren, the commander of the Wei troops defending Fancheng, urgently appealed to Cao Cao for help. Cao Cao duly sent seven contingents under the command of generals Yu Jin and Pang De to reinforce the garrison of Fancheng. At the request of Cao Ren, these units set up defenses in the level terrain north of Fancheng and coordinated their operations with the city defenders. Guan Yu was thus prevented from storming the city.

As the stand-off continued, heavy rain began to fall in Fancheng, causing the Han River to flood. The flood water rose to ten feet above ground level and submerged the barracks of the seven contingents camping outside the city. Yu Jin and his troops had to swim to higher ground for safety.

Guan Yu had foreseen this vulnerability of the Yu Jin contingents camped on low ground. Taking advantage of the flood, he led a river force against the Cao troops. Guan Yu's forces surrounded Yu Jin, who was stranded on a mound of earth in the middle of the river, and called on him to surrender. The crestfallen Yu Jin had no alternative.

Guan Yu went on to attack Pang De, who had found refuge on a river dike with some troops. Archers on Guan Yu's ships showered the dike with arrows.

A frightened soldier said to Pang De, "Why don't we surrender?"

Pang De swung around and killed the officer with his sword. Their general's determination to fight inspired the soldiers to put up a stiff resistance. Pang De calmly picked up his bow and shot back at Guan Yu's ships. His accurate aims felled many Shu soldiers. The battle lasted from morning till late in the afternoon. When they had no more arrows left, Pang De told his soldiers to use their daggers in hand-to-hand combat. He said to the troops around him, "It is said that a good general will not run for his life and a brave soldier will not forfeit his honor just to save his skin. This is the day that I shall die."

As the flood water continued to rise, the emerged part of the dike kept shrinking. As Guan Yu's naval attack with big river craft gained in intensity, the Cao troops surrendered in droves. In the midst of the confusion, Pang De and three of his officers grabbed a small boat from the Shu troops and were trying to flee to Fancheng when a sudden wave flipped their boat over. Guan Yu's forces rushed to the scene and fished Pang De out of the water.

When Pang De was brought to Guan Yu's tent, where he tried to coax Pang De into surrender, Pang De retorted angrily, "The king of Wei has a million men under his command, and the entire nation bows before his authority. Your master Liu Bei is a puny figure in comparison with the king of Wei. I would rather die a martyr of the country than consent to be a general under your master!"

In a fury, Guan Yu waved his hand and his guards leapt forward and killed Pang De.

After decimating the seven armies of Yu Jin and Pang De, Guan Yu pressed his advantage and attacked Fancheng, which was awash with flood water and whose city walls had crumbled under the pressure of the rushing water. The troops under Cao Ren were thrown into a panic. Some of them approached Cao Ren to give him advice. "The city is undefendable under these circumstances. We should escape in small boats before Guan Yu's naval force closes the noose on us."

Cao Ren was also of the view that there was not much hope of holding the city. However, Man Chong, another general in charge of the defense of the city, told him, "The flash flood will recede in a few days. According to our intelligence reports, Guan Yu has sent troops north by another route. He has remained behind probably for fear of having his escape route cut off. If we flee now, the territories south of the Yellow River will likely no longer be ours. Let's hold on for a little longer!"

Conceding that Man Chong was right, Cao Ren encouraged his troops to continue the defense of the city.

In the meantime, Sun Lang, a resident of Luhun (northeast of today's Song County in Henan), led an uprising after killing the county officials and pledged his allegiance to Guan Yu. The uprising attracted a large following south of Xudu and helped to spread Guan Yu's reputation through the central plains.

After his arrival in Luoyang, Cao Cao was more than a little flustered by the spate of bad news. Alarmed at the recent turn of events, he gathered his officials to discuss his idea of temporarily evacuating Xudu to avoid a frontal confrontation with Guan Yu.

"Your Highness need not worry," his adviser Sima Yi said. "In my opinion, under the ostensibly close relationship between Liu Bei and Sun Quan lurks deep mutual mistrust. Now that Guan Yu has reason to feel good, Sun Quan is bound to be upset. Why don't we send someone to lobby Sun Quan and dangle before him the lure of recognizing his sovereignty over Jiangdong in return for his agreement to attack Guan Yu in coordination with us? This would relieve the siege of Fancheng."

Heeding Sima Yi's advice, Cao Cao sent an envoy to see Sun Quan.

70. Lü Meng Crosses the River in White

SIMA YI'S ANALYSIS was indeed on target. Their alliance notwithstanding, tensions were running high between Liu Bei and Sun Quan. When Lu Su was still alive, he had advocated a Wu-Shu alliance against Cao Cao. General Lü Meng, who took over from Lu Su did not share his approach.

Lü Meng was a renowned general of the state of Wu. His fine military skills enabled him to distinguish himself in numerous battles very early in his career, and he soon came to the notice of Sun Quan, who assigned important responsibilities to him.

On one occasion Sun Quan said to Lü Meng, "Since you have an important charge now, you should devote some time to reading."

"There are so many things that demand my attention in the army, I could hardly find time for books," Lü Meng replied.

"I do not mean for you to be versed in all the classics. I merely want you to read more on the arts of war and on history. You say you have too many things to attend to; I don't think you have more on your hands than I do. Some knowledge of the arts of war and history has helped me a lot. Why not give it a try?"

Following Sun Quan's advice, Lü Meng started to read whenever he had a chance.

When Lu Su passed through Lü Meng's garrison, he paid a visit to Lü Meng. He had thought Lü Meng was just another general, undistinguished by any great talents or grand vision. He was therefore surprised by the general's articulate and incisive arguments, as well as by his eloquence. He said to Lü Meng, "Your vision and insights are in sharp contrast to what I observed in you years ago."

"Remember the popular saying: you need to look with fresh eyes on a person every three days," Lü Meng replied with pride.

After taking over Lu Su's position, Lü Meng assumed garrison duty in Lukou (southwest of today's Jiayu in Hubei). Convinced of Guan Yu's intention to annex Jiangdong and the state of Wu, he petitioned Sun Quan to send troops against Guan Yu. "Both Liu Bei and Guan Yu are chameleons by nature; they can't be regarded as dependable allies," he argued.

Sun Quan also perceived Guan Yu as arrogant and conceited. Sun Quan had on numerous occasions sent matchmakers to Guan Yu in the hope of obtaining his consent to marry his daughter to Sun Quan's son. Not content with merely rejecting the idea, Guan Yu hurled insults at the messenger, to the great indignation of Sun Quan. The letter of petition from Lü Meng bolstered his resolve to eliminate Guan Yu.

Cao Cao's proposal of an alliance against Guan Yu was therefore greeted with agreement by Sun Quan.

Guan Yu had heard about Lü Meng's formidable qualities. He had accordingly made watertight deployments along the border of the Wu and the Shu.

Lü Meng, well known for the frequent relapses of his chronic illness, feigned another flare-up of his malady. Sun Quan acted his part and recalled Lü Meng for recuperation, sending the younger Lu Xun to take his place.

The news soon spread to Fancheng. Guan Yu was soon gloating about Lü Meng's deteriorating health and the fact that Lu Xun was an inexperienced scholar.

A few days later, Lu Xun sent an envoy from Lukou to pay a call on Guan Yu, carrying with him a letter and gifts. The letter said that news of Guan Yu's heroic feats had spread far and wide following the naval defeat of seven Cao armies and the capture of Yu Jin, that Cao Cao's latest setback was a cause for joint celebration, and that the letter writer was a mere scholar unqualified for the job he had been given and therefore counted on

General Guan Yu's support in the future.

Deeply impressed by the modesty exhibited in Lu Xun's letter, Guan Yu no longer saw any justification for his worries, and so began to redeploy his troops away from the Wu border to Fancheng. These troop movements were duly reported to Sun Quan and Lü Meng.

However, having accepted the surrender of several tens of thousands of Yu Jin's soldiers in Fancheng, Guan Yu was having difficulty ensuring enough food supplies, and so expropriated the grain stored by the state of Wu in Xiangguan.

When he learned that his supplies had been grabbed by Guan Yu, Sun Quan made Lü Meng Commander-in-Chief of an army sent to attack Guan Yu's troops.

At Xunyang (southwest of today's Huangmei in Hubei), Lü Meng disguised all his battleships as merchant ships, hiding his troops in their holds. The soldiers manning the oars and paddles were all dressed in white, as was customary for merchants of the time.

When the Shu troops guarding the north bank saw that the boats were filled with white-clad merchants, they allowed them to moor their crafts by the shore. At nightfall, the soldiers ensconced in the holds emerged and attacked the watchtowers near the shore, capturing all the Shu troops and taking control of the towers.

Lü Meng's army then marched on Gong'an. The generals responsible for the defense of Gong'an and Jiangling had never liked Guan Yu, so when Lü Meng urged them to surrender they readily submitted.

After Lü Meng's army entered a city, he would send messengers to reassure the families of the Shu troops and would impose strict discipline on his troops, forbidding them to harass the local people. In one instance a Wu soldier, who happened to be from Lü Meng's home village, took a bamboo hat from a local family to shield his armor from the rain. When Lü Meng heard about this, he had the soldier executed. This incident proved to be a deterrent for the rest of the troops.

In the meantime, reinforcements commanded by Xu Huang were approaching the front near Fancheng. Xu Huang had his archers fire copies of the letter in which Sun Quan promised Cao Cao to coordinate their attacks against Guan Yu into the latter's camp. Already in a quandary as to what to do about Lü Meng's attack, Guan Yu now faced a new attack by Xu Huang. He was defeated and forced to withdraw his troops laying siege to Fancheng.

Guan Yu then sent an envoy to Jiangling to gather information. The envoy was offered warm hospitality by Lü Meng and allowed to visit families of Shu troops, who told the envoy that the Wu people treated them decently. When the envoy returned to his camp, he relayed this information to the soldiers who inquired about their families behind enemy lines. When these soldiers heard about the decent treatment their relatives received at the hands of the Wu troops, they lost their will to fight and some soldiers even stole back to Jiangling.

By this time, Guan Yu had realized that he had underestimated the threat of the Wu, but it was already too late. He was forced to retreat with his troops to Maicheng (southeast of today's Dangyang in Hubei).

Sun Quan marched his army to Maicheng and urged Guan Yu to surrender. However, Guan Yu took a dozen cavalrymen with him and resumed his westward flight.

The ambushers pre-positioned by Sun Quan on a back road intercepted Guan Yu's party and captured Guan Yu alive. Knowing that Guan Yu would not surrender, Sun Quan had him summarily executed.

In recognition of Sun Quan's great contribution, Cao Cao made him Marquis of Nanchang. When Cao Pi ascended the imperial throne, he made Sun Quan the king of Wu.

THREE KINGDOMS (220 AD–280 AD)

71. Lu Xun Torches a 200-mile Chain of Barracks

IN 220 AD, Cao Cao had a relapse of a chronic illness, which would not respond to treatment. He died in Luoyang that year at the age of 66.

After Cao Cao's death, his crown prince Cao Pi succeeded him as both King of Wei and Counselor-in-chief to the emperor. In autumn of the same year his supporters and close associates signed a petition to Emperor Xian, urging him to cede the throne to the king of Wei.

By the end of 220 AD, Cao Pi had become emperor and founded the Wei dynasty, assuming the title of Emperor Wen of the Wei dynasty. This formally marked the demise of the Eastern Han dynasty.

When news of Cao Pi's accession to the imperial throne reached the state of Han, rumors were rife that Emperor Xian had been killed by Cao Pi. Liu Bei, the king of Hanzhong, even arranged a funeral for the emperor. Liu Bei's ministers believed that with

Emperor Xian's death, Liu Bei, a descendant of the Han royalty, should righfully succeed him as emperor. In 221 AD, the king of Hanzhong was formally made emperor in Chengdu with the title of Emperor Zhaolie of the Han dynasty. Since the geographical extent of his rule was largely confined to Shu (covering Sichuan, the bulk of Yunnan, Guizhou in its entirety, and parts of Shaanxi and Gansu), his kingdom was historically known as the Han of Shu or simply Shu.

The capture of Jingzhou and the slaying of Guan Yu had so rankled Liu Bei that his first order after becoming emperor was to avenge these humiliations by attacking Wu of Jiangdong.

His general Zhao Yun argued, however, that it was Cao Pi, not Sun Quan, who had usurped the imperial throne. If the Caos could be annihilated, the submission of Wu would follow as a corollary. He was therefore against attacking Wu while letting Wei off the hook.

Objections were also raised by a significant number of ministers, but they fell on deaf ears. Leaving Zhuge Liang in Chengdu to assist the crown prince Liu Shan, Liu Bei decided to lead a large expeditionary force against Wu.

As preparations were underway for the expedition, Liu Bei instructed Zhang Fei to join forces with him in Jiangzhou (today's Chongqing). Yet before the expeditionary force even began, Zhang Fei was murdered by mutinous soldiers, who then defected to Wu. The loss of two excellent generals in a row greatly weakened Liu Bei's fighting force, but his obsession with revenge continued to cloud his judgement.

Wu was alerted of the impending attack, and Sun Quan was alarmed when he was informed that Liu Bei was pitting a massive force against him. However, his offers of peace were spurned by Liu Bei.

Within a few days, Wu County (north of today's Wushan County in Sichuan) fell to the army of Han of Shu, which went on to take Zigui (in the south of Hubei). Sun Quan had no choice but to send Lu Xun as Commander-in-Chief of a 50,000-strong force to resist the advancing enemy.

After a few months, Liu Bei's army had penetrated 300 miles

into Wu territory. From Zigui he led his main force on a long march that took them across high mountains along the south banks of the Yangtze, until they eventually arrived near Xiaoting (northwest of today's Yichang in Hubei).

Every bite of Wu territory had whetted the Shu army's appetite for larger conquests, and as they pressed relentlessly onward, the soldiers began to long for battle. However, they were overridden by the Commander-in-Chief Lu Xun.

"The large expeditionary force led by Liu Bei on this eastern campaign has the advantage of high morale and robust combat capability. What's more, they are upstream and therefore control impregnable, strategic high ground. It would be foolhardy for us to risk our troops in a frontal confrontation. The wiser thing to do is increase our strength and take a long view. With time they will be tired out, and that will be our chance to attack."

The generals under Lu Xun were either veterans having served under Sun Ce, or members of the nobility of the Sun lineage, all of whom had been unhappy with Sun Quan's appointment of the young, scholarly Lu Xun as Commander-in-Chief. When Lu Xun vetoed their idea of engaging Liu Bei's army in battle, they believed that he was too cowardly to fight. Their growing resentment of him was reflected in their private grumblings.

The Shu army established several dozen large camps from Wu County all the way to Yiling (east of today's Yichang in Hubei), which were enclosed with fences made from tree trunks and branches, creating a chain of barracks that stretched for about two hundred miles. Liu Bei believed that this would act as a dragnet waiting to ensnare any Wu forces who attacked.

Yet still Lu Xun bided his time and made no move. The stand-off lasted from January until June of that year (222 AD).

Liu Bei began to lose his patience and sent his general Wu Ban with several thousand troops down the mountain to pitch tents on the plain and challenge the Wu forces. The Wu generals were also champing at the bit and demanded to be sent into battle.

Lu Xun told his troops, "I've studied the terrain. While it is true that the Shu soldiers camped in the plain are not numerous, there must be an ambush in the surrounding mountain valleys. They are trying to draw us in by clamoring for a fight, but we must not play into their hands by obliging them."

His troops remained unconvinced. Several days later, when the Wu troops still refused to come out for a fight, Liu Bei realized that Lu Xun must have seen through his ruse. When he ordered the withdrawal of the eight thousand Shu troops from the valleys, the Wu troops finally came to the realization that Lu Xun had been right all along.

One day, Lu Xun called an unscheduled meeting of his officers at which he announced his decision to launch an attack on the Shu army. However, his officers expressed doubts. "We have missed the opportunity to attack Liu Bei. Now that he has been allowed to penetrate three hundred miles into our territory and has taken control of strategic passes and roads, there's nothing to be gained by attacking him."

"When Liu Bei first arrived with his troops, they had high morale going for them and we could not have easily defeated them," Lu Xun explained. "But they have been tied down here for such a long time without making much progress that their soldiers are already tired out. This is the perfect time for us to defeat them."

He dispatched a small contingent to attack a Shu camp. As soon as his troops approached the wooden fence, Shu soldiers charged out from both sides. They were soon reinforced by troops from adjacent camps. The outnumbered Wu contingent, unable to withstand the robust counterattack and having sustained heavy casualties, beat a hasty retreat.

To the complaints of his generals, Lu Xun responded, "That was only a reconnaissance mission to probe the enemy's strengths and weaknesses. Now I have formed a plan to storm the Shu army."

That night, Lu Xun instructed every soldier to bring a bundle of straw and some kindling and hide themselves in the dense woods on the south shore. At midnight they were to charge out of their hiding places and torch the chain of Shu barracks.

At the appointed hour, four Wu generals led a charge of several tens of thousands of troops toward the Shu barracks and set the wooden fence on fire. The fire raced from one camp to the next, aided by the strong wind and the fact that all the camps were linked up by the wooden fences. The forty-odd large camps of Liu Bei's army were soon laid wide open to attack.

By the time Liu Bei realized there was a fire it was too late to put up a fight. Under the protection of his troops, Liu Bei broke out of the blaze and fled into the Ma'an Mountains.

Lu Xun ordered all his troops to surround the Ma'an Mountains and begin an all-out attack; the ten thousand Shu troops in the mountains were soon routed and suffered a huge number of casualties. The battle lasted into the night, when Liu Bei was finally able to breach the encirclement with a few remaining troops. When the Wu troops discovered his escape they immediately gave chase. The pursuing Wu troops were handicapped by the heavy pieces of equipment and armor thrown in piles in the middle of mountain passes by the successive post houses to help Liu Bei to escape to Baidi (in today's Fengjie County in Chongqing).

In this battle, the entire Shu army was decimated and all its riverine naval craft, materiel and equipment was captured by the Wu troops. This battle is historically known as the Battle of Xiaoting or the Battle of Yiling.

Following this debacle, Liu Bei ruefully remarked, "How did I lose to someone like Lu Xun? It must be my bad karma!" A year later he came down with an illness in Yong'an (today's Fengjie in Chongqing).

72. Meng Huo's Seventh Capture

AS HIS HEALTH continued to worsen, Liu Bei, the founder of the Han of Shu, summoned Zhuge Liang to Yong'an from Chengdu to leave instructions for after his death. He told Zhuge Liang, "You are ten times more able than Cao Pi, so I'm sure you will put the country on the right track. If you think my son Adou (infant name of the crown prince Liu Shan) can be helped, then by all means help him. Otherwise, I want you to take over from him as ruler."

Zhuge Liang had tears streaming down his cheeks and his voice was broken by sobs. "The only way to repay your trust, sire, is to give my best till my last breath."

Liu Bei called his youngest son Liu Yong to his bedside and said to him, "After my death you and your brothers must respect the Counselor-in-chief as you do your father."

Following Liu Bei's death, Zhuge Liang returned to Chengdu and with his assistance Liu Shan ascended the throne. He would later be known as the Last Emperor of the Han of Shu.

Following Liu Shan's accession, all matters of state, regardless of their gravity, were decided by Zhuge Liang, who worked diligently for the prosperity of the Han of Shu. Yet trouble soon started in several commanderies of the Nanzhong region (covering parts of present-day Sichuan, Yunnan and Guizhou).

A powerful local figure in the Yizhou Commandery by the name of Yong Kai had killed the governor after learning of Liu Bei's death, and had then started a rebellion. He switched his allegiance to the kingdom of Wu of Jiangdong and cultivated ties with Meng

Huo, the leader of an ethnic minority in Nanzhong, instigating him to rally other tribal groups in the southwest against the kingdom of Han of Shu.

At Yong Kai's instigation, Zhu Bao, the governor of Zangke (near today's Zunyi in Guizhou) and Gao Ding, a tribal chief in Yuexi (southeast of today's Xichang County in Sichuan) also rose in revolt. Half of Shu territory was thus lost, to the great consternation of Zhuge Liang.

The state of Han of Shu was then still recovering from the debacle of Xiaoting and the death of its founding emperor, and was therefore in no position to plunge back into war. Zhuge Liang brought about a reconciliation with the state of Wu of Jiangdong to ensure stability in the east. He implemented incentive measures to promote production, undertook irrigation works, accumulated surplus grain and intensified military training. When stability was restored two years later, Zhuge Liang decided to launch a southern campaign.

In March of 225 AD, Zhuge Liang set off at the head of a large army. Ma Su, the younger brother of Zhuge Liang's close friend Ma Liang, accompanied Zhuge Liang until they were miles out of the city.

When parting, Zhuge Liang took Ma Su's hands in his and said, "We have been friends for many years now. Do you have any good advice to offer me before we say goodbye?"

"Because of their inaccessible terrain and their geographical remoteness from the capital, the people of Nanzhong have long resisted the central government. Even if we subjugate them with overwhelming force, they are bound to make trouble in the future. I understand that the key to the art of war is winning hearts and minds. Military conquest is secondary to that. On your southern campaign make sure you win the hearts of the people of Nanzhong. That's the only way to solve the problem once and for all," Ma Su replied.

Ma Su had spoken Zhuge Liang's mind and the latter nodded approvingly. "Thank you for your helpful advice! I will do as you say."

The Shu expeditionary force led by Zhuge Liang scored a string of victories as it marched southward. With the large Shu force still halfway from their territory, Gao Ding (the chieftain of Yuexi) and Yong Kai were already in a pitched battle. Yong Kai was soon killed, yet when the Shu troops marched into Yuexi, they slew Gao Ding.

Zhuge Liang attacked in two prongs, led by his generals Li Hui and Ma Zhong respectively. In less than a fortnight, Ma Zhong broke the defenses of Zangke, wiping out all the rebels in the area. The rebellion of the four commanderies was thus put down in short order.

However, trouble was far from over. After absorbing Yong Kai's remaining troops, Meng Huo, a chieftain of Nanzhong, continued his resistance against the Shu army. Zhuge Liang found out that not only was Meng Huo a brave warrior but that he also enjoyed great prestige and authority among the tribes that inhabited Nanzhong.

Recalling Ma Su's parting advice, Zhuge Liang decided to try to win Meng Huo over. He ordered his troops to capture Meng Huo alive and to make sure that no harm was done to him.

With characteristic astuteness, Zhuge Liang directed his forces to beat a false retreat after a skirmish with the troops of Meng Huo, who sent his soldiers in hot pursuit of the fleeing enemy in the belief that his force enjoyed a numerical advantage. Yet it did not take him long to realize he had walked into an ambush; his troops dispersed in all directions and Meng Huo was subsequently captured alive.

When Meng Huo was bound and taken to Zhuge Liang's headquarters, he was sure he would be killed. To his surprise, Zhuge Liang ordered that he be untied as soon as he was brought into the commander's tent. Zhuge Liang began to try to regain Meng Huo's fealty to the Han of Shu, but Meng Huo would not change his position. "I walked into your trap only because of my carelessness. This is not fair."

Zhuge Liang did not insist, but instead rode with Meng Huo around his camp to show him the fortifications and the state of his troops. "What do you think of my troops?" He asked Meng Huo.

"I was defeated before because I was ignorant of the true state of your forces. I thank you for showing it to me. I am not impressed. I don't think it will be difficult to defeat you," Meng Huo replied.

Zhuge Liang had a good, hearty laugh. "Since that's how you think, I want you to go back and prepare for the next battle."

After his release, Meng Huo fled back to his tribe and rebuilt his force. Soon he launched another attack against the Shu troops. Brave but naive warrior that he was, Meng Huo proved no match for Zhuge Liang and was soon captured a second time.

Yet Zhuge Liang's eloquence still failed to win over Meng Huo, and he was set free once again.

The same events came to be repeated seven times. When Meng Huo was captured for the seventh time, Zhuge Liang intended to free him, but this time Meng Huo was reluctant to go. "You've captured me seven times and every time you've set me free again. You've done everything you could to be kind to me and I respect you from the bottom of my heart. From now on I can no longer bring myself to rebel against you."

Upon his return, Meng Huo secured the submission of all the tribes and the Nanzhong region once again reverted to Shu control.

Following the pacification of Nanzhong, Zhuge Liang decreed that Meng Huo and the other chieftains should administer their respective areas as they used to. Some of his generals said to Zhuge Liang, "The reconquest of Nanzhong has not been easy. Why do you leave the same old chiefs in power instead of appointing officials from the capital?"

"The cons far outweigh the pros in sending officials from the capital," Zhuge Liang replied. "If we send officials, they have to be accompanied by troops, which have to be fed. Besides, recent wars have inevitably left casualties in their wake. If we appoint our officials to administer the region, there is bound to be trouble. If we don't send officials, then we will not need to station troops here and we will not need to worry about sending supplies to the troops. When the tribes get their autonomy, there will be peace between the Hans and the other ethnicities. Surely this is an arrangement that suits everybody."

When Zhuge Liang returned to Chengdu, the emperor came

out of the city to welcome him. The pacification of Nanzhong was cause for national celebration.

Zhuge Liang then turned his attention to preparations for a major northern campaign. To this end he pursued a policy of accumulating national wealth and beginning intensive military training.

73. Ma Su Loses Jieting

IN THE WINTER of 227 AD, two years after the pacification of Nanzhong, Zhuge Liang was ready and fully prepared. He led a large garrison force into Hanzhong, which, by virtue of its proximity to the border between Wei and Shu, would be an ideal base from which he could invade the kingdom of Wei at the time of his choosing.

Before setting off from Chengdu, he presented a memorial to Liu Shan, the Last Emperor, in which he cautioned him against complacency and misplaced humility, and encouraged him to surround himself with sage counselors and to shun base-spirited persons. He also expressed his determination to take on the responsibility of restoring the Han dynasty. This is the historically famous "Chu Shi Biao" (memorial to the emperor on the occasion of the troops' send-off).

The following year, Zhuge Liang employed a feint: he leaked out information that he was targeting Meicheng (in what is now Mei County in Shaanxi) while actually dispatching his general Zhao Yun to lead a contingent into Ji Valley (north of what is now the city of Xibao in Shaanxi). When the leaked news reached the Wei army, it deployed the bulk of its troops to Meicheng, just as Zhuge Liang had planned. When the Wei army least expected it, the massive force led by Zhuge Liang advanced on Mount Qi (east of today's Li County in Gansu) from the west.

Years of rigorous training had made the Shu army into a well-organized and disciplined fighting force with high morale. Meanwhile, the uneventful years on the Shu front following Liu

Bei's death had lulled the kingdom of Wei into a false sense of security. Therefore, the Shu army's attack on Mount Qi caught the Wei garrison there totally off guard. The Wei troops retreated before the advancing Shu army, which seized the momentum generated by its fresh victory to press on. The Wei generals defending the commanderies of Tianshui, Nan'an and Anding north of Mount Qi defected and offered to surrender to Zhuge Liang.

Cao Pi, Emperor Wen of the Wei dynasty, also died around this time. So when the court officials of Wei heard about the massive campaign unleashed by Shu Han, they were thrown into great consternation. Cao Rui, the newly crowned Emperor Ming, immediately sent Zhang He with fifty thousand men to Mount Qi, in order to stop the advance of the Shu force. The emperor himself even traveled to Chang'an to direct the battle.

At Mount Qi, Zhuge Liang decided to send a contingent to take control of Jieting (southeast of what is now Zhuanglang in Gansu) as a base for further operations. Bypassing the veteran generals at his side he picked Ma Su to be commander of this contingent.

Ma Su was an avid reader of books on the art of war and enjoyed analysing military science. His good advice on war matters had earned him the trust of Zhuge Liang. Liu Bei, however, suspected Ma Su of being untrustworthy, and he had made a point of warning Zhuge Liang. "Ma Su tends to brag and is not fit for big responsibilities." Zhuge Liang did not pay much heed to this warning, and appointed Ma Su to the vanguard in this operation, with Wang Ping as his deputy.

As the troops led by Ma Su and Wang Ping reached Jieting, the Wei forces at the command of Zhang He were marching in from the east. After surveying the surrounding area, Ma Su said to Wang Ping, "We are protected by forbidding terrain here. There is a mountain near Jieting. We can camp on the mountain and prepare an ambush."

"The Counselor-in-chief left instructions to defend the city with fortifications. It is too risky to camp on the mountain," Wang Ping reminded him.

Ma Su, short on war experience but proud of his wide reading on the subject, ignored Wang Ping's advice and insisted on camping on the mountain. After several futile attempts to make Ma Su change his mind, Wang Ping gave up and asked Ma Su to assign one thousand men to him, who he set up camp with at the foot of the mountain.

When Zhang He arrived in Jieting he was delighted to find that Ma Su had not stayed within the city walls to defend it. He immediately proceeded to build fortifications and surround the mountain with troops.

Waves of soldiers charged downhill at Ma Su's orders, but were unable to breach the defenses built by Zhang He's troops. Many Shu soldiers were killed in the shower of arrows released by Wei archers.

With the mountain's water source cut off by the Wei army, the Shu troops were unable to cook their meals, and as the encirclement dragged on there was growing unrest in the Shu encampment. Zhang He chose this moment to launch a general attack. The Shu soldiers dispersed in all directions despite Ma Su's orders to stay grounded. He was forced to fight his way out of the encirclement and flee west.

In the meantime, Wang Ping was securely entrenched with his one thousand troops at the foot of the mountain. When he learned of Ma Su's rout, he ordered his soldiers to make a racket on their drums to simulate a charge. Zhang He, suspecting an ambush, kept his troops at safe distance from the noise. Wang Ping was thus able to assemble his troops and beat an orderly retreat without a single casualty, even picking up many of the deserters from Ma Su's army.

With the loss of Jieting, the Shu army was deprived of an important base and suffered heavy casualties. In order to cut his losses, Zhuge Liang decided to call his entire army back to Hanzhong.

Zhuge Liang conducted a thorough inquiry upon his return to Hanzhong, and found out that the loss of Jieting was entirely attributable to Ma Su's disregard for his orders. Ma Su was put in jail after being convicted of a capital offense.

In jail, Ma Su wrote a letter to Zhuge Liang. "You have

treated me like your own son and I've looked to you as a father. I've committed a capital offense. I hope you can treat my son in the way Emperor Shun of antiquity was able to give important responsibilities to Yu even after putting to death Yu's father Gun. This is my last request of you."

After the execution of Ma Su, Zhuge Liang fondly recalled the happy moments he had shared with Ma Su and, true to his promise, he took good care of Ma Su's son.

Wang Ping, who had tried to prevent Ma Su from making a mistake and had contributed to the preservation of his troops, was promoted by Zhuge Liang to a command of five divisions.

Zhuge Liang told his troops, "This military setback was admittedly a result of Ma Su's insubordination, but I cannot escape responsibility for not picking the right commander." He accordingly asked the emperor to demote him.

Liu Shan was at a loss as to what to do. A minister said, "Since this is what the Counselor-in-chief wants, you should grant his wish." Liu Shan issued an edict announcing the demotion of Zhuge Liang to General of the Right with de facto functions of Counselor-in-chief.

The officers and men of the Shu army were deeply moved by Zhuge Liang's example. They learned important lessons from the defeat and morale was heightened. That winter, Zhuge Liang's forces fought their way out of Sanguan Pass (southwest of what is now Baoji in Shaanxi) and encircled Chencang (east of Baoji), killing a Wei general; the next spring, his force recovered the commanderies of Wudu (today's Cheng County in Gansu) and Yinping (northwest of what is now Wen County in Gansu). In consideration of these achievements, Liu Shan the Last Emperor issued an edict reinstating Zhuge Liang as Counselor-in-chief.

74. Death of a Genius at Wuzhangyuan

IN APRIL OF 229 AD, Sun Quan, the king of Wu, was formally declared emperor. Most of the ministers of Shu Han believed that he had usurped and therefore demanded an end to Shu's alliance with Wu. Zhuge Liang, on the other hand, believed that the main threat came from Wei. He decided to maintain the alliance with Wu as he prepared for his northern campaign.

In 231 AD, Zhuge Liang launched his fourth northern expedition, marching his troops toward Mount Qi. To resist this offensive, the Kingdom of Wei immediately sent the generals Sima Yi and Zhang He with their troops toward Mount Qi. Leaving some of his troops near Mount Qi, Zhuge Liang led his main force to intercept Sima Yi.

Sima Yi was acquainted with Zhuge Liang's military strategies. In the belief that Zhuge Liang's force had penetrated too deep into enemy territory, carrying only a limited supply of grain, he instructed his troops to shield themselves behind strong defenses and refrain from engaging the opposing forces in battle.

The other Wei generals, thinking Sima Yi was afraid of Zhuge Liang, repeatedly asked for permission to engage the enemy. "You fear the Shu army as if it were a tiger. Aren't you afraid of being made a laughingstock?"

Against his better judgment, Sima Yi was pressured to throw his troops into battle. They suffered a crushing defeat. As a result of mishandling by supply officers, the Shu army soon depleted its grain supplies and had to withdraw. The Wei general Zhang He led his troops in hot pursuit of the retreating Shu army until they came to the vicinity of Mumen, an area crisscrossed with valleys, where he met his death in a volley of arrows shot by an ambush laid by Zhuge Liang.

Zhuge Liang had in several operations been forced to withdraw his troops as a result of running out of grain. Chastened by this experience, he devised two kinds of transport: one was called "*mu niu*" (wooden bullock) and the other "*liu ma*" (flowing horse) (both were new types of carts). These were used to convey grain to Xiegukou (southwest of modern Mei County in Shaanxi), where it was stored.

In 234 AD, after making thorough preparations, Zhuge Liang launched his last northern expedition with a massive force of one hundred thousand men. He sent an envoy to Wu to obtain Sun Quan's agreement to launch a parallel campaign so that they could subject Wei to an orchestrated attack on both its northern and southern flanks.

Zhuge Liang's army marched out of Xiegukou and arrived at Wuzhangyuan, on the south shore of the Wei River. Settling in for a long campaign, he had some of his troops build fortifications to get ready for combat and sent another contingent to Wuzhangyuan to set up a military agricultural zone, where the soldiers joined the local people in planting and farming. The excellent discipline of the Shu army fostered a congenial relationship between the troops and the people.

Emperor Ming of the Wei dynasty sent Sima Yi and his troops across the Wei River, where they also built fortifications opposite the Shu army.

After reading Zhuge Liang's letter, Sun Quan sent three contingents against Wei. In response, Emperor Ming personally led a large force to resist the attack from the south while ordering Sima Yi to hold his ground in Wuzhangyuan and to defend the city.

Zhuge Liang had been waiting for news from the Wu front, but was disappointed to hear that Sun Quan's attack had been repelled. He wanted a decisive battle with the Wei forces, but

Sima Yi stayed behind his fortifications, refusing to be provoked by Zhuge Liang's repeated challenges. The stand-off lasted over a hundred days.

To try and provoke him into battle, Zhuge Liang sent Sima Yi a woman's dress with the implication that he was not manly enough to come out and fight.

When the Wei troops saw that their Commander-in-Chief had been taunted in such an insulting fashion, they clamored for a fight with the enemy. Well aware that it was simply a trick to provoke a rash reaction, Sima Yi tried to calm his staff. "Very well! I will ask the emperor for permission to attack the Shu army."

A few days later a minister was dispatched by the emperor to the Wei camp, conveying the imperial order against engaging the enemy.

The officers of the Shu army were disappointed by the news, but Zhuge Liang understood Sima Yi's actions. "Sima Yi's query of his emperor was merely a show intended for the consumption of his officers and men. A top general commanding an army in the field at a great distance from the imperial court has no plausible reason to write all the way to the capital to seek permission to go into combat."

Zhuge Liang had understood Sima Yi, and Sima Yi was also trying to figure out Zhuge Liang. On one occasion, when Zhuge Liang sent a messenger to challenge the Wei army for a fight, he was courteously received by Sima Yi, who engaged the messenger in conversation. "Your Counselor-in-chief must be very busy. How is his health? And how is his appetite?"

Believing that these inquiries were made out of politeness, the messenger answered truthfully. "He is indeed very busy because he interests himself in everything, big or small, in the camp. He rises early and goes to bed late. His appetite hasn't been so good lately and he eats little."

After the messenger left, Sima Yi spoke to his staff, "You see! Zhuge Liang eats little and is weighed down by responsibilities. How long do you think he can hold up?"

As predicted by Sima Yi, the overworked Zhuge Liang soon fell ill in his camp.

On learning of Zhuge Liang's illness, Liu Shan the Last Emperor immediately sent his minister Li Fu to Wuzhangyuan to inquire after Zhuge Liang's health. After some discussion of matters of state and the military, Li Fu departed.

A few days later Li Fu returned to the camp for another visit. He cried when he found out that Zhuge Liang's health had deteriorated. Zhuge Liang opened his eyes and said to Li Fu, "I know what you want to know on this second visit. If I'm not mistaken, you want to know about Jiang Wan."

"You are right, Counselor-in-chief," Li Fu replied. "The emperor wants to know who can assume your responsibilities if you become too sick. Besides Jiang Wan, who else do you think would be a good candidate to succeed you?"

"Fei Yi will do," Zhuge Liang told him.

Although Li Fu asked more questions, Zhuge Liang closed his eyes and remained silent. Several days later, the 54-year-old Counselor-in-chief passed away in the camp.

Following his deathbed instructions, the generals of the Shu army kept his death a secret. They kept his body under cover in his carriage and started an orderly withdrawal of all the contingents.

When scouts of the Wei army found out about Zhuge Liang's death, it was reported to Sima Yi, who immediately led his troops in pursuit. Just past Wuzhangyuan, the standards and flags of the Shu army all of a sudden swung around and its soldiers began to charge at Sima Yi's troops, with war drums beating.

Sima Yi was caught by surprise and quickly turned his horse around and ordered a retreat.

While the Wei forces retreated, the generals of the Shu army moved all their troops to safety in an orderly fashion.

The incident prompted the populace to compose a ditty ridiculing Sima Yi. "A dead Zhuge scared away a live Zhongda!" (Zhongda being Sima Yi's style name.)

Yet Sima Yi did not take offense at the derision. "I could only go inside the mind of a live Zhuge. How can I be expected to do the same for a dead Zhuge?" When he later visited the Shu army campsite to survey Zhuge Liang's battle organization and fortifications, he was deeply impressed. "Zhuge Liang was truly a rare genius!" he announced.

Although Zhuge Liang failed to achieve his desire of unifying China, his strong character has become legenadary. He had also been revered as an incarnation of true wisdom. In the "Latter Chu Shi Biao" (second memorial before a military expedition) attributed to him, he wrote, "I put my nose to the grindstone, not stopping until exhaustion and death," which is considerd by many the epitome of his life and character.

75. Sima Yi Feigns Illness

FOR SEVERAL YEARS after Zhuge Liang's death, Shu Han maintained a defensive attitude toward Wei. Yet the growing power of Wei was accompanied by increasing internal unrest.

Sima Yi, one of Wei's top generals, came from a prominent landowning family of mandarins. In the early days of Cao Cao's rule, he had tried to draft Sima Yi into public service. Sima Yi was reluctant to accept an offer from a man of such lowly birth such as Cao Cao, but he didn't want to offend Cao Cao with an outright rebuff. He therefore decided to feign paralysis. Cao Cao suspected that this was simply a ruse and so he sent an assassin to visit Sima Yi's bedroom late one night.

The intruder was greeted by the sight of Sima Yi rigidly stretched out in bed.Unconvinced, he drew his sword and raised it against Sima Yi, making to bring it down on him. He believed that if Sima Yi was only feigning paralysis he would surely jump up in alarm. However, Sima Yi merely stared up at the assassin, his body not making the slightest movement. The assassin was satisfied that the illness was genuine and put away his sword to return to Cao Cao with his finding.

Knowing that Cao Cao would never give up, Sima Yi let some time pass before starting rumor that his paralysis had been cured. When Cao Cao drafted him a second time, he no longer resisted.

Sima Yi served in important capacities under both Cao Cao and Cao Pi. By the time of the reign of Emperor Ming, Sima Yi had become an elder statesman of Wei, largely controlling the military thanks to long years spent commanding troops fighting the Shu army in Guanzhong. When Gongsun Yuan, the governor of Liaodong, rebelled against Wei in collusion with the aristocracy of the Xianbei tribe, Emperor Ming sent Sima Yi to put down the rebellion.

When Sima Yi got ready to return to the capital following the pacification of Liaodong, a messenger arrived from Luoyang, bearing an urgent order from the emperor for him to rush back to Luoyang.

When Sima Yi arrived, he found that Emperor Ming's health had taken a turn for the worse. Emperor Ming summoned Sima Yi and Cao Shuang, a minister and member of the royal family, to his bedside to arrange their co-regency of Cao Fang, the crown prince.

Following the death of Emperor Ming, Cao Fang succeeded the throne as Emperor Shao of the Wei dynasty. Cao Shuang was made General-in-chief and Sima Yi became Defender-in-chief, each with a command of three thousand troops which took turns protecting the imperial palace. Although of royal descent, Cao Shuang was dwarfed by Sima Yi in ability and qualities and had to defer to him in the early days of their co-regency.

Yet Cao Shuang was bombarded with advice from his trusted associates, who reminded him that "power cannot be shared with outsiders." They came up with the idea of promoting Sima Yi to Grand Mentor in the name of the emperor with the intended effect of taking away his control of the army. Cao Shuang followed their advise and then put his close associates and brothers into positions of power.

When he had succeeded in concentrating power in his hands, Cao Shuang began a life of hedonistic pleasures. To establish his authority he led a force against Shu Han but was routed by the Shu army, nearly losing his entire expeditionary party.

Meanwhile, Sima Yi was privately making plans. His advanced age also gave him a handy pretext to excuse himself from the daily imperial audiences on account of ill health.

The news of Sima Yi's illness suited Cao Shuang perfectly. However, to have total peace of mind he needed to find out whether the Grand Mentor was really ill or merely faking it.

When Cao Shuang's trusted subordinate, Li Sheng, was appointed governor of Jingzhou and planned a visit to Sima Yi before departing for his new post, Cao Shuang gave him the task of finding out about the real state of Sima Yi's health.

When Li Sheng was ushered into Sima Yi's bedroom, he saw him lying in bed, being fed porridge by two servants. A few dribbles of gruel were dripping out of the corner of his mouth, wetting the front of his clothing. This sight made Li Sheng feel deeply sorry for Sima Yi.

"By the grace of the emperor, I've been appointed governor of my home region and I've come to bid farewell to the Grand Mentor," he said to Sima Yi.

"Oh, what a difficult mission," Sima Yi replied as he gasped for air. "Bingzhou in the north is very close to the northern Hu tribe. You must be on your guard. I'm very sick and I'm afraid this may be our last meeting."

"The Grand Mentor didn't hear me right. I said I'm going back to my home region of Jingzhou, not Bingzhou," Li Sheng said.

Sima Yi still didn't catch the name, prompting Li Sheng to repeat it at a louder register. Sima Yi finally had some idea of what was being said. "I'm old and hard of hearing so I didn't hear you correctly at first. It's wonderful that you've been made governor of Jingzhou!"

After taking leave of Sima Yi, Li Sheng made a full report to Cao Shuang. "The Grand Mentor is one breath away from death. You don't need to worry about him."

This put Cao Shuang in an excellent mood.

On the occasion of the spring festival in 249 AD, Cao Fang, Emperor Shao of the Wei dynasy, left the city to offer sacrifices at his ancestral tombs. Cao Shuang, his brothers and ministers loyal to him also attended. No one invited Sima Yi on account of his grave illness.

Yet no sooner had Cao Shuang and his cohorts left the imperial compound than Sima Yi had a complete recovery. In an exuberant mood, he donned his armor and, with his two sons Sima Shi and Sima Zhao in tow, led his troops to take control of the city gates and the armory. He also stripped Cao Shuang of all functions pertaining to his position of General-in-chief by faking an edict from the empress dowager.

When the news reached Cao Shuang and his brothers outside the city, they were thrown into great consternation. Some suggested that he flee to Xudu with the emperor as hostage and assemble a force to confront Sima Yi. But Cao Shuang and his brothers had no stomach for such a daring enterprise. When Sima Yi sent an envoy to urge him to surrender, promising lenient treatment as long as he handed over his control of the army, Cao Shuang promptly submitted.

A few days later, Sima Yi received denunciations of seditious plans made by Cao Shuang and his associated. They were therefore thrown in jail and soon executed.

While the Wei regime remained nominally in the hands of the Caos, real power was now exercised by the Simas.

76. The Ambitions of Sima Zhao

TWO YEARS AFTER he killed Cao Shuang, Sima Yi died and was succeeded by his son Sima Shi. Power in the kingdom of Wei was now firmly in the hands of the brothers Sima Shi and Sima Zhao. Any minister who stood in their way would be swiftly eliminated. Emperor Shao had the utmost hatred for Sima Shi, and had been urged to strip the two Sima brothers of their authority over the army. Yet before the emperor could do this, Sima Shi forced the empress dowager to depose Cao Fang and put Cao Mao, a grandson of Emperor Wen, on the throne instead.

Generals in some parts of Wei resented the Simas, and the removal of Cao Fang from the throne was the last straw. Wen Qin, the governor of Yangzhou, and General Guanqiu Jian raised arms against Sima Shi but were defeated. However, Sima Shi fell ill and died after returning with his troops to Xudu.

When Sima Zhao took over as General-in-chief he proved no less an autocrat and bully than his father and brother.

Cao Mao, the new emperor, found his tolerance stretched to breaking point. One day he summoned three ministers, including Wang Jing, the Imperial Secretary, to the court. "The ambitions of Sima Zhao are evident even to the people in the streets. I can't just sit here and wait for him to deal with me. With your assistance, I want to take action against him now."

Knowing that crossing Sima Zhao was akin to pitching an egg against a rock, the ministers advised patience and caution in order to avert disaster.

Cao Mao took out an edict he had prepared and threw it on

the floor. "I've made up my mind. I'll do it at the risk of death. Besides, I may yet come out alive." With those words, he went to inform the empress dowager of his plans.

Little did he know that two of the three ministers sneaked out to tip off Sima Zhao.

Cao Mao was only twenty years old, and had absolutely no idea of how to deal with Sima Zhao. He assembled the imperial guards and eunuchs, and the party headed forth from the palace with Cao Mao, wielding a sword, giving orders from his carriage.

Sima Zhao's trusted aide Jia Chong arrived with his troops to block the advance of the imperial guard. As the two parties scuffled, Cao Mao let out a sudden cry and charged into the fray with his sword raised. When Jia Chong's soldiers saw the emperor coming at them, they were understandably intimidated and unsure what to do.

Jia Chong's subordinate Cheng Ji asked, "What do you think we should do?"

"What has Sima Zhao paid you for? You know what to do!" Jia Chong replied sternly.

This emboldened Cheng Ji to lunge at Cao Mao with his lance. Caught by surprise, Cao Mao was stabbed in the chest and died almost instantly.

When news reached Sima Zhao that his people had killed the emperor, he rushed to the imperial hall to summon the ministers for consultation. "Tell me! What shall I do?" he asked them.

"To appease the country, we will have to execute Jia Chong," Chen Tai said.

Sima Zhao found this idea unpalatable. "Is there any alternative?"

"In my view, this is the smallest price to pay," Chen Tai replied.

Eventually, Sima Zhao issued, in the name of the empress dowager, an edict posthumously reducing Cao Mao to a commoner on account of his numerous crimes, glossing over the circumstances of his death.

Yet as public opinion began to turn against him for letting the killer off the hook, Sima Zhao knew he could not afford to hesitate any longer. He made a scapegoat of Cheng Ji, who was made to shoulder sole responsibility for the murder of the emperor, a crime that was punished by the wholesale execution of his entire clan.

With Cao Mao out of the way, Sima Zhao found from among Cao Cao's descendants a 15-year-old named Cao Huan to succeed the throne as Emperor Yuan.

77. Deng Ai Sneaks through Jian'ge

AFTER ENGINEERING THE death of Cao Mao, Sima Zhao no longer had to worry about internal unrest. He therefore decided to launch a massive campaign against Shu Han.

By that time both Jiang Wan and Fei Yi, who had succeeded Zhuge Liang, had died. The General-in-chief of Shu, Jiang Wei, committed to the continuation of Zhuge Liang's northern expeditons, launched nearly yearly raids against Wei. However, instead of winning any battle, Jiang Wei succeeded only in squandering his combat resources in these exercises in futility.

In 263 AD, Sima Zhao launched a three-pronged attack against Shu Han. This was led by his generals Deng Ai and Zhuge Xu, each commanding a force of thirty thousand, and Zhong Hui, commanding a force of over one hundred thousand.

Recognizing his inability to resist such an overwhelming force, Jiang Wei concentrated his troops in Jian'ge (today's Jian'ge County in Sichuan) in order to defend the strategic pass. When Zhong Hui's forces reached Jian'ge, his advance was temporarily blocked.

After finding out that the bulk of the Shu forces were deployed to defend Jian'ge, Deng Ai used a narrow footpath to sneak to the west of Jian'ge with an elite group of troops, before moving south. This elite band of soldiers traveled through territory where no human foot had previously trod, and had to blaze trails through mountains and build bridges to cross rivers. For four hundred miles they advanced undetected by the Shu army.

Their progress was blocked when they came to a sheer cliff

overlooking an abyss. Furthermore, they were also running out of rations. The officers began to panic.

In a bold, decisive act, Deng Ai wrapped himself in a blanket and tumbled down the steep slope. Deng Ai's officers and men followed his lead and went down the steep side of the abyss. Some carefully climbed down by grabbing onto tree trunks and branches. They were finally able to overcome the barrier to reach Jiangyou (today's Jiangyou County in Sichuan).

The Shu troops stationed in Jiangyou were caught by complete surprise by Deng Ai's attack. When the Wei troops appeared out of nowhere, the city defenders were unable to organize a timely resistance and soon capitulated.

Deng Ai pressed the attack toward Mianzhu (southwest of today's Mianyang in Sichuan), whose defenses were being manned by Zhuge Liang's son, Zhuge Zhan. Deng Ai sent Zhuge Zhan a letter urging him to surrender. "If you surrender, I will recommend to my emperor to create you Prince of Langya."

Enraged by this offer, Zhuge Zhan had Deng Ai's messenger killed. He drew up his troops and prepared for a fight to the finish. No match for Deng Ai, both Zhuge Zhan and his son, Zhuge Shang, were killed in combat.

After the capture of Mianzhu, Deng Ai raced toward Chengdu, the capital of Shu Han. The populace of Chengdu could not believe the speed with which the Wei army arrived at the capital, and they ran into the hills and forests for refuge. The court of Shu Han was in disarray, and the Last Emperor summoned his ministers for urgent consultation. Some suggested that the court move south; some advocated seeking protection from Wu of Jiangdong; others believed it would be wiser to submit without delay in the face of the overwhelming Wei force.

The Last Emperor of Shu Han was an indecisive man, but he had no wish to offer any resistance. When the force led by Deng Ai arrived at Chengdu, the Shu emperor had his arms voluntarily trussed behind him and left the city gate with his entire court to offer their surrender.

After he moved into the city with his troops, Deng Ai became so arrogant that he decided to bypass Zhong Hui to write directly to

Sima Zhao with a proposal to attempt to conquer Wu of Jiangdong by pressing the new military advantage. To his great chagrin, Sima Zhao issued an order to Deng Ai. "You cannot initiate any military action without authorization from your superiors."

The Shu general Jiang Wei was in the midst of battling Zhong Hui's troops when he learned of Deng Ai's attack on Chengdu. When he got ready to redeploy his troops to rescue Chengdu, an order arrived from the emperor instructing him to surrender to the Wei force.

This order provoked indignation and sadness among the Shu officers and men, some of whom drew their swords and struck at the rocks about them in their agitation.

Yet Jiang Wei remained calm. Following consultation with his men, the decision was made to surrender. Zhong Hui appreciated Jiang Wei's skills, and treated him as a friend; they often rode about in the same carriage and conversed about military matters together.

Playing on the frictions between Zhong Hui and Deng Ai, Jiang Wei persuaded Zhong Hui to write secretly to Sima Zhao accusing Deng Ai of plotting a rebellion.

When Sima Zhao receiced Zhong Hui's letter of accusation he issued an edict in the name of Emperor Yuan to order that Deng Ai be arrested in Chengdu and taken back to Luoyang in a pillory cart. To preempt any resistance on Deng Ai's part, he ordered Zhong Hui to move his troops into Chengdu.

Once in Chengdu, Zhong Hui had a contingent of troops take Deng Ai to Luoyang. Deng Ai met his death on the way to the capital. After engineering the elimination of Deng Ai, Zhong Hui had gained total control of the army, and began plotting a rebellion in earnest.

Zhong Hui discussed his idea with Jiang Wei, who enthusiastically supported it. However, Jiang Wei had his own hidden agenda: he wanted to let Zhong Hui eliminate the top military brass of Wei, and then do away with Zhong Hui himself. He therefore secretly wrote to Liu Shan, "I ask Your Majesty to be patient for a few days more. I will revive the country."

Zhong Hui, meanwhile, took it for granted that Jiang Wei

was a sincere ally. He issued an order, allegedly from the empress dowager, that instructed him to lead an expedition against Sima Zhao. To preempt any opposition from the generals, he had them placed under house arrest inside the palace grounds.

The Wei military had doubts about the authenticity of the order from the beginning. Rumor soon circulated that Zhong Hui and Jiang Wei were planning a wholesale slaughter of all the officers and men from the north. This provoked a disturbance in which fires were set on the periphery of the palace and leaderless soldiers surged into the palace compound. Jiang Wei and Zhong Hui were both killed by the riotous soldiers as the situation spun out of control.

78. Adou Revels in a Foreign Court and Forgets His Home Country

AFTER SHU HAN was extinguished in the wake of Deng Ai's attack, the Last Emperor Liu Shan (infant name: Adou) stayed in Chengdu. In the aftermath of the rebellion of Zhong Hui and Jiang Wei, Sima Zhao came to question the wisdom of allowing the Last Emperor to stay so far away, so he sent his trusted associate Jia Chong to bring Liu Shan to Luoyang.

Liu Shan had always been an incompetent leader. When Zhuge Liang was alive, he left all military, administrative and political decisions to Zhuge Liang because he did not trust his own judgment. Although he was able to rely on top aides (notably Jiang Wan, Fei Yi and Jiang Wei) to assist him after Zhuge Liang's death, he was not as careful as when Zhuge Liang had been around. Following the death of Fei Yi and Jiang Wei, and with the eunuch Huang Hao wielding increasing power, the political situation was becoming increasingly unsteady.

Following the downfall of Shu Han, Jiang Wei was killed and the other ministers either died or abandoned the court, leaving only two low-ranking officials, Xi Zheng and Liu Tong, to accompany the emperor to Luoyang. Unfamiliar with the ways of the world, Liu Shan depended on Xi Zheng's guidance down to the smallest detail. Until now, Liu Shan had not thought much of Xi Zheng, but in the new circumstances, he came to see Xi Zheng as a loyal aide.

When Liu Shan arrived in Luoyang, Sima Zhao made him Duke

of Anle and conferred the title of marquis on his progeny as well as on more than fifty ex-ministers of Shu Han. Sima Zhao did all this to win hearts and minds, thereby consolidating his authority over the old dominion of the now-defunct Shu Han. However, Liu Shan considered it the greatest honor.

Sima Zhao gave a lavish banquet for Liu Shan and his former ministers. A troupe of singing girls was brought in to perform songs and dances originating from Shu country.

These songs and dances from their home country were, to some former Shu ministers, a painful reminder of the tragic loss of their country and brought them to the brink of tears. Liu Shan meanwhile, in sharp contrast, was so absorbed by the performance that his jaw dropped, seemingly oblivious of the fact that he was in a foreign court.

This did not escape the notice of Sima Zhao. "Liu Shan is really a heartless creature. Shu Han would not have survived even if Zhuge Liang, a counselor of much higher caliber than Jiang Wei, had been alive and had done his best to help him," he said to Jia Chong after the banquet.

When Liu Shan was received a few days later by Sima Zhao, he asked him, "Do you still feel nostalgia for Shu?"

"I am quite happy here," Liu Shan replied contentedly. "No, I don't miss Shu anymore." (This is the origin of the Chinese phrase "le bu si shu," literally "so happy one no longer yearns for his home country Shu.")

Xi Zheng, who was present at the meeting, was outraged by Liu Shan's reply. When they returned to Liu Shan's residence, Xi Zheng said, "You should not have answered the way you did to the question of Sima Zhao."

"How do you think I should have answered?" Liu Shan asked.

"If he asks the same question again, you should say with tears in your eyes: my ancestral tombs are in Shu; I have a heavy heart and I miss my home country all the time. We may then have a chance to be allowed to go home," Xi Zheng replied.

Liu Shan nodded his approval, "You are right. I will remember that."

On another occasion Sima Zhao did ask Liu Shan the same

question again, "You seem to be enjoying our warm hospitality here. Do you still miss your home country?"

Remembering what Xi Zheng had coached him to say, Liu Shan regurgitated it word for word. He tried to put on a sad face, but the tears simply wouldn't come, so he had to keep his eyes closed.

Observing Liu Shan's effort, Sima Zhao guessed what had happened. "This sounds like Xi Zheng speaking."

Liu Shan reopened his eyes with a start and admitted as much. "You are right! You are right! It is Xi Zheng who coached me to give this reply."

Sima Zhao couldn't help bursting out laughing, as did the attendants.

This convinced Sima Zhao that the addle-brained Liu Shan posed no threat to him and therefore he saw no need to eliminate him.

People have since used the expression "Adou the Unhelpable" to describe someone who is hopelessly faint-hearted and incompetent.

JIN DYNASTY (265 AD–420 AD)

WESTERN JIN DYNASTY (265 AD–316 AD)

79. Shi Chong and Wang Kai in a Wealth Contest

BEFORE HE HAD time to launch an attack against Wu of Jiangdong following his conquest of Shu Han, Sima Zhao fell ill and died. His son, Sima Yan, deposed the nominal emperor Cao Huan, and declared himself emperor of Jin, a new dynasty. He gave himself the title of Emperor Wu of Jin. From 265 to 316 AD, the Jin dynasty had its capital at Luoyang and is therefore historically known as the Western Jin.

Long before the founding of the Western Jin dynasty, Wu of Jiangdong, the only kingdom remaining from the Three Kingdoms period, had begun to decline. In 279 AD, Emperor Wu of Jin launched an attack on the Wu capital Jianye (today's Nanjing in Jiangsu) with a 200,000-strong force. The last emperor of Wu, Sun Hao, with his back against the wall and all options closed, bared his upper torso and had his arms trussed behind him in order to surrender to Wang Jun.

This marked the end of the Three Kingdoms period, which began with Cao Pi's accession to the throne in 220 AD. The country was thus reunified under the Jin dynasty.

After unifying the country, Emperor Wu became complacent and turned his attentions instead to wealth and pleasure. Following his example, the high officials of the court vied to enhance their prestige by flaunting the trappings of wealth.

In the imperial capital of Luoyang, the three richest men were Yang Xiu (the Capital Protector), Wang Kai (the emperor's uncle and General of the Rear), and Shi Chong (the Cavalier Attendant-in-ordinary).

Yang Xiu and Wang Kai were related to the royal house by marriage and possessed greater power than Shi Chong. However, Shi Chong was far richer than they were, and no one could put an exact figure on Shi Chong's wealth. He had amassed his vast wealth during his tenure as governor of Jingzhou, where he was renowned for his corruption. When foreign legations or merchants passed through Jingzhou, Shi Chong would send his henchmen to extort money from them or even to openly rob and kill them. He had therefore become the richest man of the realm.

Upon his arrival in Luoyang, Shi Chong heard of Wang Kai's impressive wealth. To put Wang Kai's wealth to shame he instructed his culinary staff to use candles in lieu of firewood because he had heard that Wang Kai's household used sweetwater from maltose to wash pots and pans. Thus a wealth contest began between Shi Chong and Wang Kai.

Wang Kai responded by commissioning the construction of a twenty-mile-long stretch of screens made of purple silk along both sides of the road leading to his house. Anyone visiting the Wang residence would have to pass between these twenty miles of screens. This lavish fencework created a sensation in Luoyang.

Not to be outdone, Shi Chong used more expensive and more elegant satin to construct screens that extended for twenty-five miles before his own home.

Wang Kai, however, refused to concede defeat. He sought the help of his nephew, Emperor Wu of Jin. Intrigued by the contest, the emperor gave a two-foot-tall coral tree in his imperial collection to Wang Kai, so that the latter could show it off to the public.

The emperor's help gave a boost to Wang Kai's determination to continue the contest. He then invited Shi Chong and a large number of officials to a dinner at his home.

At the banquet, Wang Kai announced with glowing pride, "I have a rare coral tree in my house. Do you want to have a look?"

Wang Kai had a maid bring out the coral tree, which had symmetrical branches and bright, pink flowers. His impressed guests lavished praise on the rare plant.

Yet Shi Chong simply looked on with a sneering expression. Seeing an iron *ruyi* (ornamental back-scratcher) on the table, he grabbed it and lightly tapped the coral tree with it. With a loud crash, the coral tree shattered into tiny pieces.

The invited officials were stupefied and Wang Kai's face turned red with anger. "What on earth are you doing?"

"Don't be so upset, I'll give you another one," Shi Chong replied.

"Yes, give me another one! Give me another one then!" Wang Kai shouted.

Shi Chong sent his attendant home to fetch all the coral trees in his collection for Wang Kai to choose from.

A group of attendants returned with dozens of coral trees, including six or seven that were three to four feet tall, every one of them elegantly shaped and brightly colored.

All those present were dazzled by the display. Wang Kai conceded defeat, finally realizing that the wealth of Shi Chong was many times that of his own.

That brought to a close the farce of a wealth contest and Shi Chong's fabulous wealth became known throughout Luoyang. A minister, Fu Xian, complained to Emperor Wu, criticizing this extravagance and squander and describing it as even more devastating than natural disasters. He expressed a fear for the future if this kind of one-upmanship continued to confer prestige instead of being actively discouraged.

Emperor Wu ignored these complaints. Like Shi Chong and Wang Kai he went on supporting his extravagant lifestyle by redoubling his plunder of the country. This corruption and decadence signalled impending disaster.

80. Imbecile of an Emperor

IT WAS WELL known that the crown prince, Sima Zhong, was not blessed with much in the way of intelligence. There was concern both in and outside the court about what disaster might be in store for the country once Emperor Wu died and was succeeded by the crown prince.

Some ministers wanted to advise the emperor to establish another son as crown prince, but were afraid to come out and say so. One day, at a banquet hosted by the emperor, the minister Wei Guan stumbled and fell in front of the throne in feigned drunkenness. "What a waste of this chair!" He mumbled as he stroked the seat of the throne.

Emperor Wu immediately understood the drift of the complaint but decided to play dumb. "What is this nonsense? You must be drunk," he said, and told his attendants to help Wei Guan up and take him home.

From then on no one dared mention the topic again.

However, Emperor Wu began to have doubts. To test how intelligent the crown prince was, he sent a dossier to the prince and asked him to deal with a few pieces of official business in it.

The wife of the crown prince, the princess consort Jia, was an astute lady. When she saw the dossier, she immediately sent for a court official to help answer all the questions for the prince. The official was an erudite man, and the report he ghostwrote was well-reasoned and contained numerous classical allusions and references.

The princess consort Jia read the report and was quite happy with it. However, a eunuch reminded her, "This is indeed a well-written piece, but the emperor knows perfectly well that the prince has never been a particularly intelligent person. An excellent report like this would only awaken his suspicions, and the whole thing could come back to haunt us if he should order an inquiry."

"You are right. That was a timely reminder. Why don't you redraft it? If your draft does the job, we will not fail to reward you," the princess consort replied.

The eunuch wrote an unpolished, plain report, which was recopied by the prince and passed on to the emperor.

Emperor Wu read the report. Though it was not an exemplary piece of writing, it did provide an answer to every question asked, and thus proved that the crown prince was clear-headed after all.

In 290 AD, Emperor Wu fell critically ill. The crown prince was then in his thirties and should in normal circumstances have been mature enough to take over the reins of state. Yet Emperor Wu was not convinced; he left deathbed instructions for Yang Jun (the Queen's father) and Sima Liang (Prince of Ru'nan and the emperor's uncle) to act as co-regents. At Emperor Wu's death, only Yang Jun was by his bedside. In order to take sole control of imperial power, Yang Jun in collusion with his daughter the queen rewrote the emperor's last edict to designate Yang Jun as sole regent.

Upon his death, Emperor Wu was succeeded by the crown prince Sima Zhong as Emperor Hui.

After his accession to the throne, Emperor Hui proved incapable of making any decisions concerning the running of the state and on numerous occasaions he made a laughingstock of himself.

One early summer day, as he was amusing himself in the imperial garden with the usual retinue of eunuchs, he heard a chorus of croaking toads.

"Are these little fellows singing for the government or for some private citizens?" the emperor asked the eunuchs.

The eunuchs looked at each other, not knowing how to answer. A eunuch with a quick wit said with a straight face, "They sing for the government if they are located on government land and sing for private citizens if located on private land."

Emperor Hui nodded with an air of uncertain comprehension.

In a year of widespread famine, local officials reported to the central government that many civilians had starved to death. When Emperor Hui was made aware of the situation, he asked his ministers, "How can people starve to death?"

"As a result of natural disasters people in some areas have run out of grain," the ministers replied.

Emperor Hui had a sudden idea. "Why don't they adjust their diet to eat more meat porridge?"

With such a person on the throne, plotters of all stripes began to come out of the woodwork.

81. War of Eight Princes

EMPEROR WU ATTRIBUTED the downfall of the Wei dynasty to the isolation of the royal house resulting from failure to distribute power to its members. After his accession to the throne, he accordingly created 27 princes. Each of these principalities had its own army and its prince had the power to appoint his own civil and military officials. He believed that with so many empowered blood relations supporting the central government, the House of the Simas would be solidly entrenched in power.

After the accession of Emperor Hui, Yang Jun, a relative on his mother's side, became the sole regent. A number of princes naturally begrudged this monopoly of power, but they had no opportunity to act against him.

Emperor Hui had a ruthless, scheming wife Queen Jia, who had no intention of letting Yang Jun monopolize power. She sent secret emissaries to contact Sima Liang, Prince of Ru'nan, and Sima Wei, Prince of Chu, inviting them to advance on the capital to topple Yang Jun.

Prince Wei of Chu set out from Jingzhou with his troops and entered Luoyang. With the backing of Prince Wei, the queen publicly accused Yang Jun of plotting a rebellion and had him killed after surrounding his residence with troops.

Following Yang Jun's death, Prince Liang of Ru'nan returned to Luoyang as regent. He also wanted to monopolize power, but the army was still controlled by Prince Wei of Chu. Tensions developed between them. Queen Jia believed that Prince Liang of Ru'nan was a liability, and so she counterfeitd a secret order from Emperor Hui, authorizing Prince Wei of Chu to arrest and execute Prince Liang of Ru'nan.

Although Prince Wei was Queen Jia's ally, the queen was worried that after killing two princes in a row he would become too powerful. That same evening, she accused Prince Wei of forging an imperial edict to kill Prince Liang without cause or authorization. This was a capital offense. It dawned on Prince Wei of Chu that he had been duped by Queen Jia, and he cried foul, but it was too late.

From then on, there was no regent in the court; though Emperor Hui was the nominal ruler, it was Queen Jia who wielded all the power.

Queen Jia's eight years in power were notorious for her overbearing, arbitrary decisions. She was not the biological mother of the crown prince Yu, and feared losing her power once the crown prince grew stronger, so she worked diligently for his removal.

On one occasion, Queen Jia had a letter written in the name of the crown prince pressuring Emperor Hui to abdicate. She then invited the crown prince for a few drinks and when he became drunk she somehow persuaded him to copy out the letter in his own hand.

The next day, Queen Jia asked Emperor Hui to summon his ministers. She showed them the crown prince's letter and accused him of plotting a rebellion. The ministers expressed doubts that the letter had been written by the prince. When Queen Jia asked them to check it closely, they found that it was indeed the prince's handwriting. Queen Jia thus succeeded in deposing the crown prince.

The ministers' resentment of Queen Jia's ruthlessness was now intensified by her role in deposing the crown prince, and they privately voiced angry criticism of her. Sima Lun, the Prince of Zhao, who controlled the imperial guard, sensed a good opportunity to raise arms against Queen Jia. However, he was concerned that an empowered crown prince would be one more obstacle to deal with. He began to spread rumors that the ministers were secretly planning the reinstatement of the crown prince. When the rumors reached Queen Jia's ears, she became apprehensive and had the crown prince poisoned. This gave Prince Lun of Zhao the excuse he needed. He sent the Subcommander of the Imperial Guard, Sima Jiong, to arrest Queen Jia in the imperial palace.

When she saw Sima Jiong entering the palace at the head of his troops, Queen Jia asked with great astonishment, "What do you want?"

"I am here to arrest you on orders of the emperor," Prince Jiong of Qi replied.

"All imperial edicts pass through my hands. I haven't seen any such order," Queen Jia said.

Queen Jia kicked up a fuss in the hope of getting Emperor Hui to rush to her rescue. However, Prince Lun of Zhao had her arrested and executed.

Once he had a taste of power, Prince Lun of Zhao's ambitions grew. He was no longer content to be a mere prime minister. A year later, he placed Emperor Hui under house arrest and declared himself emperor. He immediately proceeded to confer official titles of varying ranks on his supporters, be they civil or military officials, attendants or soldiers. In that era, the hats worn by officials were ornamented with an ermine's tail. The new officials appointed by Prince Lun of Zhao were so numerous that they soon used up all the ermine tails in the government's storehouse. Many had to content themselves with dog tails on their hats. There was a popular ditty lampooning the phenomenon that went "Dog tails are in when ermine tails run out."

When the other princes heard that Prince Lun of Zhao had declared himself emperor, they all began to vie for the same throne. A period of strife started as Sima Lun (the Prince of Zhao), Sima Jiong (the Prince of Qi), Sima Ying (the Prince of Chengdu), Sima Yong (the Prince of Hejian), Sima Yi (the Prince of Changsha) and Sima Yue (the Prince of Donghai) all jostled for power. If Sima Liang (the Prince of Ru'nan) and Sima Wei (the Prince of Chu), who had been killed, are counted, there were eight princes who were embroiled in this battle for the throne. This period is therefore known as "the War of the Eight Princes" in Chinese history.

The War of Eight Princes went on for sixteen years until 306 AD, when seven of the eight had died, leaving only Prince Yue of Donghai. He killed Emperor Hui of Jin with poison and established Emperor Hui's younger brother Sima Chi as Emperor Huai of the Jin dynasty.

82. A Xiongnu (Hun) Declares Himself Emperor of Han

IN 304 AD, Liu Yuan, a member of the Xiongnu (Hun in Western terminology) aristocracy in the north, stopped paying homage to the Jin dynasty and declared independence, naming himself the king of Han.

Toward the end of the Western Han dynasty, Xiongnu tribes were scattered in remote commanderies and counties in the north. After prolonged contact and interaction with people of Han stock, they had integrated with Han culture. Members of the Xiongnu aristocracy considered themselves related to Han royalty by virtue of the several intermarriages between the Xiongnu and the Han royal families in previous generations. They even changed their name to Liu, the surname of the Han emperors. After unifying the north of China, Cao Cao had grouped the thirty thousand Xiongnu tribes into five leagues, each led by a League Commander. Liu Bao, a Xiongnu aristocrat, was one of the League Commanders.

Liu Yuan, a son of Liu Bao, had read many Han books. He had great physical strength and carefully-honed combat skills. It is even said that he could manipulate a 300-pound bow. On Liu Bao's death, Liu Yuan took over his father's position. He later served as a general under Sima Ying, Prince of Chengdu of Western Jin (one of the Eight Princes). He stayed in Yecheng, in charge of the troops of five Xiongnu leagues.

When the War of the Eight Princes started, some Xiongnu noblemen called a meeting in Zuoguo (north of today's Lishi in

Shanxi). An elderly Xiongnu nobleman addressed the tribesmen, "The Xiongnu have been like brothers to the Han people since the time of the Han dynasty. Through the Wei and the Jin dynasties the descendants of our Chanyus have been granted titles of nobility by the Chinese emperors, but we do not possess any land that we can call our own. In this regard we are no different from the common people. Now that the Jin dynasty has collapsed into civil war, the Xiongnu have a great opportunity to restore our old glory."

The other noblemen agreed—but who was going to lead them on the path to glory? After some deliberation, they agreed that Liu Yuan possessed the necessary ability and authority.

The noblemen sent an envoy to Yecheng to convey the consensus of the meeting to Liu Yuan and to invite him to return to them. Liu Yuan embraced the proposal and submitted a leave request to Sima Ying, claiming he needed to attend his father's funeral. However, the request was denied and Liu Yuan had no choice but to send the envoy home. In the meantime he instructed the troops of the five Xiongnu leagues in his charge to join forces and move south.

Some time later, Sima Teng (governor of Bingzhou) and General Wang Jun, both officials of the Jin dynasty, aided by the Xianbei minority, launched an attack on Sima Ying, who was defeated and forced to flee to Luoyang. Liu Yuan asked Sima Ying for permission to go back home and return with Xiongnu reinforcements. This time, Sima Ying granted the request.

In 304 AD, Liu Yuan returned to Zuoguo and was unanimously made Chanyu. He put together a force of fifty thousand and personally led it on a southward march, in order to help the Jin troops fend off the Xianbei army.

One of his men asked him why he did not seize the opportunity to overthrow the Jin dynasty instead of helping them.

"To extinguish the Jin would be as easy as snapping dead branches from a tree, but there is no way of telling whether the people of the Jin would support us. In my view, since the Han dynasty enjoyed the longest reign, it continues to exert the strongest grip on the popular imagination. Besides, the Xiongnu of the last generation were brothers to the Han royalty. If we take over the name of the defunct Han dynasty, we may yet win over the people," Liu Yuan replied.

This was found to be a good idea and Liu Yuan subsequently declared himself King of Han.

After proclaiming himself King of Han, Liu Yuan went from strength to strength, quickly capturing the commanderies of Shangdang, Taiyuan, Hedong and Pingyuan. Some lesser rebel forces of various minorities challenging Jin rule also gave their allegiance to Liu Yuan.

In 308 AD, Liu Yuan declared himself Emperor of Han. The following year, he moved his capital to Pingyang (southwest of today's Linfen in Shanxi) and concentrated his forces to attack Luoyang. For all their hatred of the corrupt Western Jin dynasty, the people of Luoyang were loath to submit to Xiongnu rule. Twice Liu Yuan attacked and twice he was forced to retreat in the face of resistance from the civilians and the troops defending Luoyang.

During this time, the last of the eight princes still alive, Sima Yue (the Prince of Donghai), was involved in bloody infighting with many court ministers, thus sapping what little fighting strength the Jin still possessed.

When Liu Yuan died, his son Liu Cong succeeded him as Emperor of Han. Liu Cong sent his generals Liu Yao and Shi Le to attack Luoyang once again. Its civilian and military defenders put up a heroic resistance, but were outnumbered by the Xiongnu. In 311 AD, Luoyang fell and Emperor Huai of the Jin dynasty was taken prisoner.

After entering Luoyang, Liu Cong massacred large numbers of Jin officials and civilians. At a banquet hosted by Liu Cong, Emperor Huai was made to wear a servant's blue uniform and pour wine for the guests. Some ex-ministers of the Jin burst out crying at the sight. Maddened by this display of deep affection by the former Jin ministers for their monarch, Liu Cong had Emperor Huai killed.

After the death of Emperor Huai of Jin, the Jin officials in Chang'an established his nephew Sima Ye as Emperor Min of the Jin dynasty.

In 316 AD, Liu Cong captured Chang'an. Emperor Min fared no better than his predecessor: he was killed after being put through unspeakable humiliations. That marked the end of the Western Jin dynasty, which had lasted fifty-two years.

After the fall of the Western Jin dynasty, the northern peoples (principally the Xiongnu, the Xianbei, the Jie, the Di and the Qiang minorities) started rebelling. Their leaders took advantage of the chaos to raise arms and, like Liu Yuan, to establish their own regimes. This period saw the emergence of a total of sixteen separate regimes, and is therefore known in Chinese history as the "Sixteen Kingdoms" period (another term used is the "Sixteen Kingdoms of the Five Hu," hu being a term used in ancient times to collectively describe the northern nomadic tribes).

83. Sword Practice at the First Crow of the Rooster

THOUGH THE REBELLIONS staged by Xiongnu noblemen in the north were threatening the very existence of the Western Jin dynasty, there were still some Jin generals who fought fiercely to uphold the dynasty. Liu Kun was one such general.

In Liu Kun's youth he had a good friend named Zu Ti. When they both served in the regional government of Sizhou (northeast of today's Luoyang) in the early years of the Western Jin, they often engaged in serious discussions about the general state of the country late into the night.

One night, Zu Ti was awoken by the crowing of a rooster. He looked out of the window and found a sliver of moon still hanging over the horizon, the eastern sky still uncoloured by dawn.

Not feeling like going back to sleep Zu Ti awoke Liu Kun. Liu Kun rubbed his eyes and asked what the matter was. "Listen! That was a timely alarm! The rooster just sounded a wakeup call!" Zu Ti replied.

The two got out of bed in high spirits, took down their swords which were hanging on the wall, and headed outside to begin their sword practice.

As a result of this daily practice of martial skills, as well as their diligent study of the arts of war, they eventually became famous generals.

In 308 AD, Emperor Huai appointed Liu Kun governor of

Bingzhou. At that time, Bingzhou was plagued by the plundering, looting and murderous incursions of Xiongnu warriors, which produced waves of refugees. Liu Kun raised an army of over a thousand men, which he led into combat.

Within the city walls of Jinyang (southwest of today's Taiyuan in Shanxi) they were greeted by a forlorn scene of houses burned to the ground and abandoned ruins everywhere around them. The few residents they occasionally ran into were doubled over with hunger.

Liu Kun was deeply saddened by what he witnessed. He instructed his men to bury the dead and rebuild the houses and city walls and he personally oversaw the construction of city defenses against Xiongnu attacks. As a result of his policy of sowing dissension among the Xiongnu tribes, more than ten thousand Xiongnu soldiers surrendered to Liu Kun. Even Liu Yuan, the self-styled King of Han, was deterred from further incursions into his territory.

Liu Kun encouraged the refugees to return to replant the fallow fields. Within less than a year, the city was once again alive with the sounds of domesticated animals, and soon found its way back to the bustling prosperity of years before.

After Liu Cong breached the defenses of Luoyang, the Western Jin's military efforts in the north largely collapsed. Only Liu Kun kept up the fight in the region of Bingzhou. After his accession in Chang'an, Emperor Min conferred the title of General-in-chief on Liu Kun, who was put in charge of all military matters in Bingzhou.

General Shi Le of the Kingdom of Han, having gained control of the county of Xiangguo (southwest of today's Xingtai in Hebei), was poised to take Bingzhou with a force of hundreds of thousands of troops. Liu Kun was trapped, with Liu Cong attacking from the south and Shi Le threatening from the north. Undeterred by this dire situation and unyielding in his resistance, he wrote to Emperor Min. "Liu Cong and Shi Le are my sworn enemies. I will only return to the capital after putting down their rebellion."

When Jinyang was surrounded by the huge crowds of Xiongnu cavalrymen, the seriously outnumbered defenders of the city panicked. However, Liu Kun maintained his composure. When night fell, he mounted the watchtower and emitted a loud mournful cry in the moonlight. When the Xiongnu horsemen heard it, they returned the cry. Later that night, Liu Kun had musicians play Xiongnu tunes on Xiongnu reed pipes, which evoked nostalgia among the Xiongnu soldiers and moved them to tears. Shortly before daybreak, when the reed pipes sounded again, the Xiongnu soldiers deserted and dispersed.

Liu Kun's later attack on Liu Cong by allying himself with Xianbei chieftains did not succeed. When Shi Le subsequently attacked Leping (southwest of today's Xiyang in Shanxi), Liu Kun sent his forces to the rescue but nearly lost all of them when they were ambushed by Shi Le's elite troops. In the meantime, news arrived that Chang'an had been taken by Liu Cong. Under the circumstances, no amount of tenacity on Liu Kun's part was enough to enable him to hold on to Bingzhou. He therefore took his remaining troops to seek sanctuary in Youzhou.

EASTERN JIN DYNASTY (317 AD–420 AD)

84. House of the Simas and the Wangs

AFTER LIU CONG captured Chang'an, the south remained in the control of Jin officials. Before his capture, Emperor Min left instructions for Sima Rui, Prince of Langya, who was defending Jiankang (formerly known as Jianye, and now as Nanjing in Jiangsu), to succeed his throne.

Sima Rui did not enjoy a high status as a member of the royal house of the Western Jin dynasty. During the reign of Emperor Huai, he was dispatched to Jiangnan (the coastal regions south of the Yangtze) on garrison duty. Of the northern mandarins he took with him, the most renowned was Wang Dao. Sima Rui valued Wang Dao's advice and considered him a close friend.

After Sima Rui's arrival in Jiankang, the large landowning families of mandarins in Jiangnan slighted him because of his low status, and did not even deign to pay him a courtesy call. Sima Rui was unsettled by this treatment and asked Wang Dao to come up with a solution.

Wang Dao had a cousin named Wang Dun, who was then governor of Yangzhou and was therefore an influential man. Wang

Dao invited Wang Dun to Jiankang and together they came up with an idea.

The third day of the third month of the year was by local tradition the Xi Festival (the bathing to cleanse sin festival). This was a day when civilians and officials would flock to the river to "pray for good fortune and for bad luck to be averted." On this particular day, following Wang Dao's advice, Sima Rui rode in an elegant sedan chair to the bank of the river, preceded by a guard of honor clearing the way by striking gongs, and followed by Wang Dao, Wang Dun and high officials from the north, all riding on large horses. This created a dramatic and imposing sight.

The Xi Festival traditionally attracted large crowds to the riverside to take part in the festivities. This unprecedented display of power created an instant sensation in the city.

When members of the local high society, including Gu Rong, learned of the procession, they all came to see what was happening. They were surprised by the respect that powerful figures such as Wang Dao and Wang Dun showed to Sima Rui. Eager not to be thought of as lacking in respect, they all came out of their residences and lined up on the street to pay homage to Sima Rui.

As a result, Sima Rui's prestige rose among the rich and powerful families of Jiangnan. Wang Dao subsequently offered another piece of advice to Sima Rui. "Gu Rong and He Xun are well-known intellectuals in this part of the county. If we have these people on our side, others will follow."

Following Wang Dao's advice, Sima Rui sent him to Gu Rong and He Xun, to offer them high positions in his administration. The two soon came to see Sima Rui, who received them with warm hospitality and appointed them to the promised posts.

Thereafter, all the prominent families in Jiangnan offered their allegiance to Sima Rui, who was thus able to establish his authority there.

In the aftermath of the anarchy in the north, a large number of families of mandarins and landowners sought refuge in Jiangnan. Wang Dao once again advised Sima Rui to enlist the best and brightest of them to serve in his administration. Sima Rui took this advice to heart and appointed 106 talented people to various positions.

Thanks to Wang Dao's guidance, Sima Rui was able to further consolidate his position both by winning local support and by using the talents of the northern diaspora in the region. The deeply greateful Sima Rui once said to Wang Dao, "You are indeed my Xiao He!"

In 317 AD, Sima Rui acsended to the throne in Jiankang and thus revived the Jin dynasty, taking the name Emperor Yuan. He also made Jiankang the imperial capital. To distinguish this dynasty from the Western Jin founded by Sima Yan, historians have called it the Eastern Jin dynasty.

On the day of his ascension to the throne, the empeor recieved Wang Dao and the rest of the court.

When Emperor Yuan saw Wang Dao, he rose from the throne and took hold of him, insisting that he should share the throne with the emperor to receive the homage of the court.

Wang Dao was startled by this unexpected gesture, since the occupation of the throne by anyone other than the emperor was something that had never been heard of. Wang Dao was quick to decline this unusual honor. "I must decline. If a common organism is placed too close to the sun, it will be deprived of the possibility of basking in the sunshine."

Emperor Yuan was greatly pleased by Wang Dao's metaphor. He was deeply conscious of the fact that the help of the brothers Wang Dao and Wang Dun had been instrumental in his accession to the throne and therefore held them in great esteem. He made Wang Dao the Imperial Secretary, in charge of overseeing the administration of the court, and he put Wang Dun in charge of the army. Many other members of the Wang family also received important commissions.

A popular saying circulated in that period. "Wang and Ma rule in the same house," reflecting the fact that power was shared by the Wang family and the royal house of the Simas in the Eastern Jin dynasty.

With control of the army, Wang Dun grew arrogant and conceited and soon began to take the emperor for granted. Wang Dun's arrogance prompted Emperor Yuan to shift important responsibilities to Liu Kui and Diao Xie and to distance himself from the Wang brothers. In this way, the newly founded Eastern Jin dynasty was already riven by internal rifts.

85. Shi Le Enjoys Han Books

IN THE SECOND year of the reign of Emperor Yuan, Liu Cong, the Xiongnu King of Han, died, leaving a kingdom filled with strife. His nephew Liu Yao, who took over as king, believed that taking the name of the old Han dynasty had not been useful, so in 319 AD he changed the name of the dynasty to Zhao. Shi Le, general of the Xiongnu Kingdom of Han, who had expanded his military force in the campaign against the Jin, no longer wanted to play second fiddle to Liu Yao and named himself the king of Zhao as well.

Shi Le had descended from a family of minor chieftains of a Jie tribe. When Bingzhou was ravaged by a famine, the young Shi Le got separated from his tribe and only survived by selling himself into servitude as a slave. He was also once captured by rebels and put in a prisoner transport cart. It was only thanks to the sudden appearance of a herd of deer, drawing the rebel soldiers away on a deer hunt, that Shi Le was able to escape.

After going through a series of trials and tribulations, Shi Le assembled a group of peasant refugees and molded it into a strong fighting force. After Liu Yuan raised a rebellion, Shi Le offered his allegiance to the Kingdom of Han, serving as a general under Liu Yuan.

The members of the Jie minority were, in general, less educated than the Xiongnu. Unlike Liu Yuan, Shi Le had never received a Han education and was therefore illiterate. After being appointed general, he came to realize that to achieve greater things he needed more than military capabilities. On the advice of a Han intellectual

Zhang Bin he implemented numerous political reforms. He also took under his wing a group of impoverished Han scholars and organized them into a "Division of Gentlemen."

The bravery and ability demonstrated by Shi Le in warfare, and the policy guidance provided by advisers such as Zhang Bin, made Shi Le increasingly powerful. By 328 AD, he finally succeeded in toppling Liu Yao and two years later Shi Le proclaimed himself emperor in the county of Xiangguo, retaining the dynasty name of Zhao. Historians call the Zhao of the Liu lineage the "Former Zhao" and Shi Le's Zhao the "Later Zhao."

Although he was illiterate, Shi Le had high regard for scholars and intellectuals. After becoming emperor of the Later Zhao, he gave explicit orders to his troops that they were forbidden to kill any educated people captured by them, who were instead to be transported to Xiangguo for his personal attention.

Following Zhang Bin's advice, he founded a number of schools and put the children of his military officers into these schools to receive an education. He also found talent for public service by instituting a system of recommendations and examinations. Persons recommended by local authorities for public service would be appointed if found qualified after evaluation and appraisal.

Shi Le strictly forbade the mention of the words "Hu" (meaning northern barbarians) and "Jie" (the name of his minority) by his subordinates. However, in the interest of humoring intellectuals of Han stock the prohibition was sometimes waived.

On one occasion, Fan Tan, a newly appointed Han official, arrived at the palace to attend an imperial audience dressed in tattered clothes. "How did you become so impoverished?" Shi Le asked in astonishment.

Fan Tan, momentarily forgetting the prohibitions, replied, "A band of Jie bandits just cleaned out my house; that's why I couldn't find any appropriate clothes to wear to the audience."

Shi Le realized that the official had been wronged. "These Jie bandits cause a lot of trouble! Allow me to recompense you on their behalf," he said.

Suddenly realization that he had violated an imperial taboo, Fan Tan began to shake with fright and quickly asked Shi Le for forgiveness.

"My prohibition is intended for ordinary people. I am not going to hold senior scholars to account," Shi Le said with a smile.

As promised, Fan Tan received compensation for his losses and was even given a horse and carriage as a bonus.

Shi Le loved books. He asked others to read and explain the books to him and would give his opinions and comments as the reading went on.

Once, when someone was reading from the *History of Han* and came to the part about Emperor Gaozu being advised to confer titles on the remaining members of the nobility of the former six states, Shi Le commented, "Liu Bang was wrongheaded to do that. How could he expect to control the country with a misguided policy like that?" The reader hastened to explain to him that as a result of Zhang Liang's objection, Emperor Gaozu did not go down that path. At this, Shi Le nodded in approval. "That's more like it!"

On the occasion of a feast organized by Shi Le for his ministers, he asked one of the ministers, "What emperors of antiquity do you think I can be compared to?"

The minister came up with a fawning reply. "Your Majesty is superior to Emperor Gaozu in wisdom and might. None of the others could even come close."

"You exaggerate," Shi Le said with a laugh. "If I had been alive in Gaozu's time, the most I would have been qualified for was being one of his ministers, maybe in the league of Han Xin and Peng Yue. However, if I had been born in the time of Emperor Guangwu, then there's no telling which of us would have come out the winner."

As a result of Shi Le's ability to nurture talent as well as his relatively enlightened politics, the Later Zhao witnessed an initial period of prosperity.

86. Zu Ti Knocks His Oar against the Gunwale in Mid-crossing

AFTERE THE XIONGNU gained control of the central plains of China, massive waves of refugees began to migrate southward from the north. Liu Kun's close friend Zu Ti also brought hundreds of families from his home town to the Huai river basin. Zu Ti volunteered to direct the entire exodus. He offered his own carriage and horses to the elderly, frail and sick in the group, and shared his food and clothing. Commanding the respect of all, he was made leader by popular demand.

By the time the group reached Sikou (southwest of today's Huaiyin in Jiangsu), Zu Ti had already assembled a large number of warriors, who were all northerners forced to flee their homes and who hoped Zu Ti would lead them in the fight to take back the central plains which would allow them to return to their homeland.

At that time, Sima Rui had not yet acsended to the throne. Zu Ti crossed the river into Jiankang, where he explained his idea to Sima Rui, Prince of Langya. "The anarchy in the Jin dynasty is mainly the result of conflicts between members of the royal house, which gave the Hu barbarians an opening to attack the central plains. The people of the central plains have been brutally oppressed and persecuted by the enemy and so are eager to fight back. All it takes is an order from you and we will begin wresting back the territory we lost. When that happens, the people in the north will rise up in arms to follow us into combat."

The recovery of the central plains had not been part of Sima Rui's plans, but finding no good excuse to reject Zu Ti's well-argued proposal he gave a grudging consent. He appointed Zu Ti governor of Yuzhou (covering the eastern parts of today's Henan and the northern parts of Anhui) and allotted him enough food for a thousand men as well as three thousand *pi* of cloth, though he made it clear that Zu Ti had to raise his own army and find his own weapons.

Zu Ti organized the hundreds of families he had led on the southward exodus into a fighting force and took them across the Yangtze. When the boats reached midstream, Zu Ti made a pledge by hitting the gunwale with an oar. "If I, Zu Ti, cannot wipe out the enemy that seized the central plains from us, I will never cross this river again." His impassioned speech roused the warriors and steeled their will to fight.

In Huaiyin, they paused in their march in order to manufacture weapons and recruit more fighters. By the time they resumed their northward advance their force had expanded to more than two thousand men.

Zu Ti's army received popular support along the way and was able to recover a lot of lost territory. At the time, many powerful local families and landowners had taken advantage of the chaos in the area to engage in turf wars from their private fortresses. Zu Ti was able to persuade many of them to stop their fighting and join his northern expedition. Insubordination was severely punished, and Zu Ti's authority continued to grow.

Liu Kun, who had remained in the north, was delighted that his friend Zu Ti had launched a northern expedition. "Every night I sleep with my head resting on my sword because I'm committed to defeating the enemy. Now, Zu Ti has acted ahead of me," he said.

In 319 AD, following the submission of Chen Chuan (a powerful landowner in Chenliu) to Shi Le (King of the Later Zhao), Zu Ti decided to attack Chen Chuan. The fifty thousand troops sent by Shi Le to reinforce Chen Chuan were swiftly routed by Zu Ti. Subsequently Tao Bao (general of the Later Zhao) and Han Qian (one of Zu Ti's men) fought for control of the city of Pengpi (near today's Kaifeng in Henan). Both sides began to see their rations running out as the battle raged for over forty days without an apparent winner.

One day, Zu Ti sent a thousand soldiers carrying bags filled with earth to the Jin camp, in order to give the impression that their camp still had plenty of rations. He then sent out a number of soldiers carrying bags of rice, instructing them to pause for a rest en route to their destination.

When Tao Bao saw the Jin soldiers carrying rice, he sent a large number of troops to grab the rice from the Jin soldiers taking a rest. The Zhao camp had long run out of food and the rice seized from the Jin soldiers lasted only a few days with the strictest rationing. The impression created of plentiful supplies of food in the Jin camp started to affect the morale of the Zhao troops, and Tao Bao urgently appealed to Shi Le for help.

A few days later, Shi Le sent a thousand donkeys carrying food for Tao Bao's troops. Having found out about the shipment ahead of time, Zu Ti's forces ambushed the convoy and intercepted all the food. As a result, Zhao Bao was unable to hold out any longer and abandoned his position that very night.

Under Zu Ti's leadership, the Jin forces were able to regain all the lands south of the Yellow River and large numbers of Later Zhao troops surrendered to them. Emperor Yuan named Zu Ti "Zhen Xi General" for his outstanding achievements.

Despite the harsh wartime conditions, Zu Ti lived a frugal life, using his savings to help out his men. He offered incentives to promote crop cultivation and was not averse to offering positions to people who had recently transferred allegiance to him. Even people outside his circle of friends and acquaintances, as well as people of low standing, were received with warm hospitality by him, which earned him a large amount of popular support.

At a feast organized by Zu Ti for the elderly, the partygoers sang and danced with great joy. "Though we are all getting on in years, we can go with peace now that we have been able to see our loved ones again," many old people were heard to say.

Zu Ti kept training his soldiers and expanded recruitment of new blood in preparation for the next stage of the northern expedition, which was aimed at regaining lands north of the

Yellow River. Emperor Yuan, however, was becoming paranoid about Zu Ti's loyalty, and feared that an overpowerful Zu Ti would be hard to rein in. He therefore appointed Dai Yuan as "Zheng Xi General" (zheng xi literally means conquest of the west) overseeing the military affairs of the six regions in the north, meaning that Zu Ti was under his command. Zu Ti was naturally unhappy about this attempt by the central government to clip his wings after he had fought so hard to reclaim so much territory for it.

Soon after this, Zu Ti learned that his friend Liu Kun had been killed in Youzhou by one of Wang Dun's henchmen. As a result of excessive worry and anger he fell ill and died. His death was greaty mourned.

Although Zu Ti did not get to fully accomplish his vision of recovering the central plains of China, his heroic pledge made with an oar knocking against the gunwale in mid-crossing has become a popular legend that has echoed down the ages.

87. Wang Xizhi Writes His Famous "Preface to the Poems Composed at the Orchid Pavilion"

IN THE EASTERN Jin dynasty, the prominent Wang clan, having provided generations of high ranking mandarins, exercised a powerful influence in court politics. The descendants of Wang Dao and Wang Dun held public office at varying ranks, though most of them remained mediocre bureaucrats. One, however, stood out from the rest. He was Wang Xizhi, one of China's best known calligraphers.

Wang Xizhi enjoyed writing since he was a child. It is said that even while walking he would practice writing on his clothes with his finger, so much so that they became threadbare in some spots. With hard work and assiduous study, Wang Xizhi soon became a highly accomplished calligrapher.

The fact that he came from a prominent family of mandarins and possessed an unusual talent earned him recommendations for public office from ministers and high officials in the imperial court. He became a regional governor and the Right Leader of Court Gentlemen (hence the nickname Wang the Right Leader), and he later served in the commandery government of Guiji. In fact, he preferred the quiet beauty of Guiji to the bustling and opulent imperial capital. In Guiji, whenever he could spare some time he would often travel to various scenic spots with his friends. On one such occasion, Wang Xizhi and his friends had a feast at the Orchid Pavilion in Shanyin, where they composed poetry over wine. The feast culminated with Wang Xizhi wielding his brush to compose an essay in memory of the occasion. This is the famous "Preface to the Poems Composed at the Orchid Pavilion." The original, written in Wang Xizhi's hand, has been called the "Finest Piece of Calligraphy in Running Script." Unfortunately it has been lost, and only later imitations have survived.

As Wang Xizhi's fame as a calligrapher grew, his works became avidly sought after by his contemporaries. Legend has it that Wang Xizhi once visited a student's home, and spotted a brand new table with a smooth and clean surface. This put him in a mood for some brushwork, and so he asked his student for a brush and some ink. The student was overjoyed and immediately brought him his tools. After writing a few lines on the table surface as souvenir, Wang Xizhi left.

A few days later, the student had to leave his home to attend to some business. When his father entered the study to tidy it up, he noticed that the new table was covered in ink, so he scraped off the stain with a knife. When the student returned to find the calligraphy gone from the table surface, he became beside himself with anger.

Another story relates what happened when Wang Xizhi met an old woman at a country fair. She was hawking hexagonally shaped bamboo fans which she carried in a basket. The fans had a simple, crude design, obviously quite unappealing to the passers-by, and the woman had a sinking sense of not being able to sell any fans that day.

Wang Xizhi was sympathetic. "The fans are not selling because they are not adorned by a painting or calligraphy. Do you mind if I write something on them?"

The old woman did not know Wang Xizhi, but she gave the bamboo fans to him anyway because of his friendly offer of help.

Wang Xizhi wrote five characters on each fan in his "dragons-flying-and-phoenixes-dancing" flowing style before returning them to the old, illiterate woman, who was quite put off by the apparently careless scribblings.

Wang Xizhi sensed her disappointment. "Don't worry! Just tell the prospective buyers that this is the work of Wang the Right Leader."

After Wang Xizhi left, the old woman did as instructed. Her new customers, recognizing the handwriting of Wang the Right Leader, snapped up the fans in no time.

Wang Xizhi had a particular interest in geese. Whenever he heard of a fine specimen of a goose he would go and inspect it, with a view to buyinig it in order to take it back home.

A Taoist priest in Shanyin (today's Shaoxing in Zhejiang) had always entertained the idea of asking Wang Xizhi to copy a chapter of the *Tao Te Ching* (*The Book of the Way and Its Virtue*, attributed to Laozi) in his exquisite handwriting. However, he knew that Wang Xizhi rarely agreed to such requests. So, having found out about Wang Xizhi's predilection for geese, the priest bred a batch of fine-pedigreed white geese.

When Wang Xizhi learned of the fine geese kept by the *Taoist* priest, he visited him to take a look. As he approached the Taoist's dwelling, he was greeted by the captivating sight of a gaggle of geese swimming in the river, their glowing plumage snow white and their bright red crowns held high in the air.

Wang Xizhi paused, transfixed, on the river bank, loath to take his eyes from the beautiful creatures. He sent someone to ask the priest if he would sell the geese to him.

"Since Mr. Wang likes them so much, I will give the entire batch of geese to him free of charge. But I have a little request: I'd like to ask him to copy a chapter of the *Tao Te Jing* for me," the *Taoist* priest said with a smile.

Without hesitation, Wang Xizhi granted him his wish and then took the geese home with him.

88. Huan Wen on a Northern Expedition

THE DEATH OF Shi Hu, king of the Later Zhao and son of Shi Le, was followed by a period of enormous internal upheaval, with a general of the Later Zhao, Ran Min, claiming the throne and founding the kingdom of Wei (historically known as the Wei of Ran). This in turn was conquered by the kingdom of the Former Yan, founded by Murong Huang of the Xianbei nobility. In 352 AD Fu Jiàn of the Di nobility, also took advantage of the anarchy to gain control of Guanzhong and establish the Former Qin.

When the kingdom of the Later Zhao fell, Huan Wen (a general of the Eastern Jin) presented a petition to Emperor Mu (the fifth monarch of the Eastern Jin dynasty), asking for permission to lead a force on a northern expedition. Huan Wen was known for his military talent and ability; during his governorship of Jingzhou he had rendered great service to the Eastern Jin through his military achievements.

However, the Eastern Jin was racked by internal conflicts. Although Emperor Mu had promoted Huan Wen, he harbored suspicions about the general. Therefore, Emperor Mu did not grant Huan Wen permission to lead an expeditionary force to the north; instead he gave the mission to Yin Hao.

Yin Hao was a civilian who, despite his military title, had no real military ability. In a crushing defeat by the Qiang minority at Luoyang, his forces suffered over ten thousand casualties and forfeited all their food supplies and weapons.

In the wake of this debacle, Huan Wen presented another petition to the emperor, this time asking that Yin Hao be stripped of his position and charged with dereliction of duty. Emperor Mu had no choice but to agree; he sacked Yin Hao and authorized Huan Wen to lead the expedition to the north.

In 354 AD, the forty-thousand-strong Jin force led by Huan Wen set out from Jiangling on a three-pronged attack against Chang'an. The fifty thousand troops sent by the king of the Former Qin, Fu Jian, to encounter the expeditionary force at Yao Pass were soon scattered by the Jin army. Fu Jian was forced to flee back with his six thousand old, weak and wounded soldiers to Chang'an, where he had deep trenches dug in preparation for a long siege.

When Huan Wen's victorious force reached Bashang, many officials of the commanderies and counties around Chang'an instantly surrendered. Huan Wen put out public announcements that urged the populace to continue to go about their normal business. The inhabitants were delighted by this policy and came of their own accord with gifts of cattle and wine to the troops.

Since the fall of the Western Jin, the people of the north had suffered enormously in the interdynastic wars. "We never expected to see Jin troops again in our lifetime," they said to the Jin troops of Huan Wen.

Huan Wen camped in Bashang, in the expectation of replenishing his troops' food supply with the local wheat crop when it became ready for harvesting. However, Fu Jian quickly caught on to Huan Wen's intentions and had the wheat crop harvested before it was ripe to deprive Huan Wen of the bounty.

With his hope of locally restocking his food supply dashed, Huan Wen was no longer able to maintain his troops there and had to pull them back. Despite this setback, the major battle won by him in the expedition prompted Emperor Mu to promote him to Commander-in-Chief of the Punitive Expedition.

Huan Wen led two more northern expeditions. The last of these, targeted at the Former Yan, reached as far as Fangtou (southwest of today's Xun County in Henan), but eventually failed because the troops' supply route was cut off by the Former Yan.

Huan Wen's ambitions grew in proportion to the length of time he exercised sole control over the army. He was once overheard to mutter to himself, "If a man could not leave a lasting legacy of virtue and honor, it would be nice if his name could at least live forever in infamy."

A trusted supporter who was well aware of his ambitions suggested to him that in order to bolster his authority he should follow the example of Huo Guang in the time of the Western Han, and replace the incumbent emperor with one of his own choosing.

By that time, Emperor Mu had died and been succeeded by Sima Yi. Huan Wen marched his troops to Jiankang, where he deposed Sima Yi and established Sima Yu as Emperor Jianwen. Huan Wen became Counselor-in-chief and was stationed with his troops in Gushu (today's Dangtu in Anhui).

Two years later, the seriously ill Emperor Jianwen designated Sima Yao as his successor in last will. Sima Yao duly became Emperor Xiaowu. Huan Wen, who had expected Emperor Jianwen to leave the throne to him, was bitterly disappointed by this turn of events and once again marched his troops into Jiankang.

The court officials who turned out to greet Huan Wen turned pale with fright at the ominous sight of his troops, who were dressed in full battle gear and armed to the teeth.

Huan Wen invited two of the most prominent mandarins, Wang Tanzhi and Xie An, for a meeting at his official residence. They had been tipped off that Huan Wen planned to kill them by placing soldiers in ambush outside the meeting room, and Wang Tanzhi consequently arrived with his clothes soaked with sweat.

Xie An, on the other hand, retained his composure. "I understand that just-minded generals since antiquity have always deployed their troops on the frontiers to defend the country from foreign aggression. Therefore, I wonder why Lord Huan has hidden his troops behind these walls?" he said to Huan Wen.

Huan Wen was a little embarrassed by this remark. "I just wanted to take some extra precaution," he said, and swiftly ordered the ambushers to withdraw.

Sensing strong opposition to him among the prominent

mandarin families in Jiankang, Huan Wen bided his time—however, he soon died of illness.

Upon Huan Wen's death, Xie An became Couselor-in-chief and Huan Wen's brother Huan Chong became governor of Jingzhou. The two worked closely together to support Emperor Xiaowu. In this way, a new-found unity began to take hold in the Eastern Jin.

89. Wang Meng Discusses National Politics While Picking Lice

WHEN HUAN WEN billeted his troops in Bashang during his first northern expedition, a scholarly man dressed in a ragged short tunic came to the camp one day and asked to see him. Huan Wen, who had recently been on the lookout for new talent, greeted the scholar with open arms.

The scholar, whose name was Wang Meng, had grown up in an impoverished family that eked out a living by selling bamboo dustpans. Nonetheless, he was an avid reader and possessed a keen intellect. The families of mandarins in Guanzhong snubbed him because of his humble origins, but that did not bother him in the least. He declined offers of low-ranking positions in the government of the Former Qin and eventually chose to live a recluse's life on Mount Huayin. News of Huan Wen's advance into Guanzhong brought him to Bashang to request a meeting.

To test Wang Meng's knowledge and abilities, Huan Wen asked him to comment on the situation in the country.

Wang Meng gave a clear analysis of the political and military situation in both the south and the north, and Huan Wen marveled at his insights.

As he held forth on national politics, Wang Meng frequently reached inside his tunic to pick lice. The soldiers at Huan Wen's side nearly burst out laughing at the sight, but Wang Meng kept up his lively discussion with Huan Wen, oblivious of the spectacle he was making of himself.

"I've led a massive expeditionary force to Guanzhong on the emperor's orders to help the people there. Therefore, I am baffled by the fact that the local elite have not deigned to pay me a visit," Huan Wen said.

"You've come all this way, deep into enemy territory, but have stopped short of crossing the Ba River into Chang'an, which is clearly within reach. People are unsure what you have in mind—that's why they have not yet come to call on you," Wang Meng replied.

Wang Meng's assessment was correct, since the hidden agenda behind Huan Wen's northern expedition was to cement his authority in the court of the Eastern Jin and to subdue his political rivals. The act of stationing his troops in Bashang and taking his time in capturing Chang'an was designed to preserve his strength.

Huan Wen fell silent in recognition of Wang Meng's unusual talent. When he withdrew his force from Guanzhong, he invited Wang Meng to accompany him to the south, even promising him high office. Wang Meng, however, was well aware of the deep rifts inside the Eastern Jin dynasty and declined the offers, and returned instead to his hermitage in Mount Huayin.

Fu Jiàn, the emperor of the Former Qin, was succeeded upon his death by his son Fu Sheng, a cruel man, who was soon overthrown by his cousin Fu Jian.

Fu Jian took his new position extremely seriously. He looked for a capable aide and Wang Meng was recommended to him.

Wang Meng was invited for a meeting with Fu Jian, and the two hit it off immediately. Their views on the rise and decline of past dynasties turned out to be identical. Fu Jian was elated, comparing the experience to Liu Bei's good fortune in finding Zhuge Liang to advise him.

Following Fu Jian's accession as the self-styled Son of Heaven of the Great Qin, Wang Meng became his most trusted minister, and was promoted five times in a year until he occupied a position of unrivaled power.

Members of the old guard of the Di ethnicity in the Former Qin were naturally resentful of Fu Jian's trust in Wang Meng, since Wang Meng was then only 36 years old, and of Han stock to boot. On one occasion Fan Shi, a minister of the Di minority who had fought shoulder to shoulder with Fu Jiàn in the conquest of Guanzhong, angrily denounced Wang Meng to his face, "We tilled the soil and planted the crops so that you can have free lunches!"

"In the future, you will not only plant crops but also cook my meals!" Wang Meng retorted.

Incandescent with anger, Fan Shi said, "I will not rest until I have cut off your head and hung it on the gate of Chang'an."

A few days later, Fan Shi and Wang Meng had another argument, this time in front of Fu Jian, where Fan Shi tried to attack Wang Meng. Fu Jian found this behavior unacceptable, and had Fan Shi executed. After that, Wang Meng was rarely criticized by officials of Di ethnicity, at least in front of Fu Jian.

With the help of his trusted adviser Wang Meng, Fu Jian was able to subdue powerful local interests and undertake political reform. At this time, a man named Qiang De (brother of the empress dowager and Grand Master of Splendid Happiness) often got into drunken brawls and was involved in the forcible taking of property and women from others. One of the first things Wang Meng did upon becoming Metropolitan Governor of the capital was to arrest Qiang De. Though Fu Jian was informed of the arrest straight away, by the time he had sent a messenger with an imperial pardon, Qiang De had already been executed. In the next couple of months, more than twenty members of rich and powerful families, as well as some in the royal clan, were either put to death, sentenced to prison terms or dismissed from office. The entire court was in shock and frightened would-be criminals were consequently dissuaded from action. "Now I understand how important it is to have the rule of law in the country," Fu Jian said with admiration.

Owing to Fu Jian and Wang Meng's reforms, the strength of the Former Qin grew steadily, enabling it to subdue the three minor kingdoms of the Former Yan, the Dai and the Former Liang, thus achieving the unification of the part of the country in the Yellow River basin.

In 375 AD, Wang Meng fell critically ill. When Fu Jian visited him, Wang Meng said to him, "Although the Eastern Jin is in

Jiangnan far in the south, it has inherited the legitimacy of the Jin dynasty and its imperial court enjoys relative peace. It is my earnest hope that you will not attack the Jin after my death. Our enemies are the Xianbei and the Qiang tribes. They would be an ever present threat if allowed to grow in strength. The security of the Qin can be ensured only with their elimination."

90. Strong-willed Fu Jian

THOUGH FU JIAN had closely followed Wang Meng's advice when he was alive, he paid no heed to his deathbed admonition.

While Wang Meng considered the Xianbei and the Qiang to be the enemies of the Former Qin, Fu Jian placed his trust in the Xianbei aristocrat Murong Chui and the Qiang aristocrat Yao Chang, who had come to offer their services. Wang Meng advised him not to attack the Eastern Jin, but Fu Jian was bent on annihilating it in the belief that it was his sole enemy.

In the third year after Wang Meng's death, Fu Jian sent his son Fu Pi, Murong Chui and Yao Chang with a 100,000-strong force to attack Xiangyang in the Eastern Jin. The Jin general Zhu Xu put up a valiant fight and hostilities lasted for almost a year before Xiangyang finally fell to the Qin army.

Zhu Xu was captured by Fu Pi and sent to Chang'an. Fu Jian, impressed by Zhu Xu's integrity and loyalty to the Jin in his heroic defence of Xiangyang, invited him to join his government.

Fu Jian then sent another 100,000-strong force east to attack Huainan. The generals of the Eastern Jin defending the city, Xie Shi and Xie Xuan, led a two-pronged operation on land and water against the Qin army, and subsequently dealt it a crushing defeat.

However, Fu Jian refused to give up. In 382 AD, he decided that it was time to lauch a major campaign against the Eastern Jin.

In October of that year, Fu Jian summoned his court to Taiji Palace for a consultation. "I've been on the throne for nearly 30 years and have succeeded in pacifying most of the country. Now only the Jin in the southeast refuses to submit. We possess an elite fighting force of 970,000 men, which it is my intention to personally lead on a punitive raid against the Jin. What do you think?" Fu Jian asked.

Most of those gathered expressed strong disapproval of his plans. "Despite the weakness of his kingdom, the ruler of the Jin has committed no offense and has the loyal support of top civilian and military officials like Xie An and Huan Chong. This is not the time for a major military action against the Jin," the minister Quan Yu argued.

Fu Jian was displeased by Quan Yu's remarks. "The Jin have the natural barrier of the Yangtze in their favor. Besides, the people there are no doubt united in their determination to put up a stiff resistance. A victory would by no means be certain," a general commented.

Getting angrier, Fu Jian began to shout, "Huh! What's so formidable about the natural barrier of the Yangtze? We have a massive army. If our cavalrymen threw their whips into the river, its flow would be interrupted. Where would be their barrier then?"

The meeting went on for a long while without coming to any conclusion. Finally Fu Jian became impatient and said, "You are all dismissed. I will make the decision without you."

Realizing that Fu Jian was in a foul mood, the ministers left the palace, and only the emperor's brother Fu Rong stayed behind.

"Since antiquity it has always been one or two persons who have made the important decisions for the country. Today's discussion was fruitless. Let's make the decision between you and me," Fu Jian said to him.

"I am afraid that it's also my view that the planned action against the Jin is fraught with difficulties. Moreover, long years of military action has tired the troops out and dampened their will to keep fighting. Those who spoke out against military action did so out of their loyalty and devotion to you. I hope Your Majesty can heed their advice in that spirit," Fu Rong replied with a heavy heart.

Fu Jian was surprised by Fu Rong's opposition. "I am disappointed that such defeatist talk should come from you of all people. With my mighty force, as well as my mountains of military hardware and supplies, there is no conceivable reason why I can't wipe out such a feable foe as the Jin."

Fu Jian's stubborn persistence brought Fu Rong to the brink of tears. "Leaving aside the fact that a war against the Jin is not assured of victory, you must realize that in our capital there are many residents of other minorities such as the Xianbei, the Qiang and the Jie. If they exploit your absence to raise a rebellion while you are away on a long campaign, you would be in serious trouble. Has Your Majesty forgotten Wang Meng's deathbed advice?" He said imploringly.

Yet Fu Jian ignored all subsequent objections to his planned attack on the Jin. When the Metropolitan Governor, Murong Chui, came to the palace asking for an audience with Fu Jian, he asked him to give his view on the matter. "It is a law of nature that the strong gobble up the weak and big powers devour small ones. A strong and wise ruler like Your Majesty, who has a million valiant fighters under his command and a court stuffed with able generals and excellent advisers could easily snuff out an insignificant power like the Jin. It's Your Majesty's call—there's no need to consult others about it," Murong Chui said.

Fu Jian's face lit up at Murong Chui's words. "It appears that you are the only person prepared to help me achieve my dreams." He immediately ordered his attendants to reward Murong Chui with five hundred bolts of silks and satins.

At Murong Chui's incitement, Fu Jian has become too worked up to sleep that night. The imperial concubine Lady Zhang, aware of widespread opposition both inside and outside the government to the war, tried to dissuade him from the enterprise. "You womenfolk should stay out of war matters!" Fu Jian told her.

His favorite son Fu Xian also tried to talk Fu Jian out of it. "Uncle Fu Rong is most devoted to Your Majesty. Why won't Your Majesty heed his advice?"

"You are too young to have a say in affairs of state," Fu Jian replied dismissively.

Rebuffing all advice from officials and family members, Fu Jian decided to attack the Eastern Jin.

He sent Fu Rong and Murong Chui to lead a vanguard and appointed Yao Chang Longxiang General, ordering him to head the troops of Yizhou and Liangzhou in preparation for a march on the Jin.

Two of Murong Chui's nephews privately said to him, "The emperor is much too cocky. This war seems to be a perfect opportunity for us to restore the kingdom of Yan."

91. Xie An Makes a Comeback

IN AUGUST OF 383 AD, the leader of the Former Qin state, Fu Jian, led a massive force of 870,000 out of Chang'an. This juggernaut, composed of infantry, cavalry, carts, horses and provisions, stretched for thousands of *li*, kicking up a storm of dust in its wake as it marched south towards the Jiangnan region (the region south of the mouth of the Yangtze River).

A month later, Fu Jian's main army arrived at Xiangcheng (south of modern-day Shenqiu, Henan Province). The Former Qin navy in Yizhou traveled east, propelled by the currents of the Yangtze. Meanwhile, troops from north of the Yellow River reached Pengcheng (modern-day Xuzhou, Jiangsu Province). On land and by water, Former Qin forces were amassed opposite the Jiangnan region on a front stretching more than ten thousand *li* from east to west.

When this ominous news reached Jiankang, Emperor Xiaowu of the Eastern Jin and his entire court were thrown into a panic. The populace and the military of the Eastern Jin, not wanting to see the Jiangnan region fall into the hands of the Former Qin, looked to their Counselor-in-Chief, Xie An, for a way out of the crisis.

Xie An was born into a family of scholar-officials in the town of Yangxia (modern-day Taikang, Henan Province) of the Chen Prefecture. In his youth, Xie An was good friends with Wang Xizhi. They frequently met on Mount Dongshan in Guiji to recite poetry and engage in literary discussions while taking in the natural beauty surrounding them. Xie An was highly regarded by his literary contemporaries for his admirable qualities, but he preferred to live as a recluse on Mount Dongshan rather than to take up a career in government. Once, he did accept a post as a government official, but ended up quitting one month into his tenure. Most intellectuals held that Xie An's refusal to hold a public office was a great loss for the nation.

He finally returned to government service in his forties. This is the origin of the Chinese saying "dong shan zai qi," literally meaning, "to re-emerge out of Mount Dongshan," where he had spent a good many years of his life as a recluse. Nowadays, this saying can best be paraphrased as "to stage a comeback."

As the Former Qin army under Fu Jian's reign grew in strength, Former Qin troops began harassing the northern border areas of the Eastern Jin with increasing frequency. Facing this, the government desperately needed a general with administrative and military capabilities to take charge of border defense. Xie An recommended his nephew Xie Xuan for this post. The emperor gave Xie Xuan the rank of General and sent him to garrison Guangling (modern-day Yangzhou, Jiangsu Province), putting him in charge of all the troops stationed north of the Yangtze.

Xie Xuan was a gifted military leader. After taking up his post in Guangling, he started immediately to expand his armed force by recruiting more soldiers. Many refugees from the north responded to the recruitment effort. Among them was a native of Pengcheng by the name of Liu Laozhi, who had trained as a warrior since a child and had acquired impressive martial skills, distinguishing himself by his valor in battle. Xie Xuan made him Adjutant with command of an elite force. After being put through rigorous training by Xie Xuan and Liu Laozhi, this elite force evolved into an invincible fighting machine, called the Beifu Army because it was normally stationed in Beifu, another name for the city of Jingkou (modern-day Zhenjiang, Jiangsu Province).

To repel the million-strong invading army unleashed by Fu Jian against the Eastern Jin, Xie An decided to stay in Jiankang to defend the capital. He appointed his younger brother, Xie Shi, as Zhengtao ("Punitive Expedition") Area Commander-in-Chief, and Xie Xuan as Vanguard Commander-in-Chief. They were given 80,000 troops, and were ordered to engage the Former Qin army in battle in the Jiangbei region (the region north of the mouth of the Yangtze River). Xie An also dispatched General Hu Bin, with 5,000 water-borne troops, to Shouyang (modern-day Shou County, Anhui Province) to support the land operation.

Although the Beifu Army was an elite combat unit, Xie Xuan was outnumbered 10 to 1 by the Former Qin forces. Justifiably apprehensive, before setting out he paid a visit to Xie An at his residence to bid him farewell and to consult with him on tactics. Surprisingly, when Xie Xuan voiced his concerns, Xie An was nonchalant. He answered laconically, "Everything has been taken care of."

Xie Xuan expected Xie An to follow up with more detailed instructions, but Xie An apparently had nothing more to say. Xie Xuan waited fruitlessly for Xie An to break his studied silence, then returned home feeling unsettled. A day later, he had his friend Zhang Xuan call on Xie An in the hope of getting more details. However, instead of discussing military matters with Zhang Xuan, Xie An invited him immediately to his country home in the mountains. There, many intellectuals had already gathered, and so Zhang Xuan could not find an opening to ask the questions he had in mind.

Xie An had Zhang Xuan join him in a game of chess. Jokingly, he told Zhang Xuan that he would wager his house on the outcome of the game. Zhang Xuan was an excellent chess player, usually winning most of his matches with Xie An. However, that day he found himself preoccupied by events and unable to focus his mind on the game, so he lost. Following the chess game, Xie An took his guests on a day-long tour of the mountains. It was already nightfall when the party broke up.

That night, Xie An summoned Xie Shi, Xie Xuan and the other generals to his home, giving each of them detailed instructions concerning their respective missions. Their confidence boosted by Xie An's self-assurance and composure, they returned in good spirits to their barracks.

At the same time, learning of the critical situation, Huan Chong deployed 3,000 elite troops from his Jingzhou garrison to Jiankang in order to bolster the defence of the capital. However, Xie An told these troops, "Everything has been taken care of here. You should go back to reinforce the western front."

When the troops returned to Jingzhou and told Huan Chong what had come to pass, Huan Chong became worried. He said to his troops, "While I admire Lord Xie's generosity, he has no military sense. How can he be so carefree and careless in the face of an impending attack? With many fewer troops and green commanders, how can we hope to win?"

92. The Battle of Fei River

AS XIE AN'S general Hu Bin led his waterborne troops up the Huai River towards Shouyang, he learned that Shouyang had fallen to a Former Qin vanguard led by Fu Rong. Consequently, Hu Bin had to fall back to Xiashi (southwest of modern-day Fengtai, Anhui Province), where he camped, waiting for the main army led by Xie Shi and Xie Xuan.

Now in control of Shouyang, Fu Rong sent his second-in-command, Liang Cheng, with 50,000 troops to attack Luojian (east of modern-day Huainan, Anhui Province) in order to cut off Hu Bin's escape. After the Eastern Jin troops were encircled, their food supplies began to dwindle ominously with each passing day. The situation was dire.

Hu Bin sent a messenger through the blockade to inform Xie Shi of the bleak situation: "The enemy is on a fierce offensive and our rations are running out. I'm afraid we won't be able to join forces with you." The messenger was captured by Former Qin troops as he tried to sneak through their encampment, allowing the urgent message to fall into Fu Rong's hands. It was forwarded posthaste to Fu Jian in Xiangcheng. His ego and conceit inflated by the Former Qin's string of victories, Fu Jian left his main army behind in Xiangcheng, and rushed with 8,000 cavalrymen to Shouyang, eager to gobble up the Eastern Jin troops in one mouthful.

After consultation with Fu Rong in Shouyang, Fu Jian came to the conclusion that the Eastern Jin troops were in a very vulnerable situation, so he sent an envoy to the Eastern Jin camp, urging surrender. This envoy was none other than Zhu Xu. A few years earlier, Zhu Xu had fought against the Former Qin armies, making a heroic stand against them before being captured. After his capture, Zhu Xu was brought by Fu Jian into the government of the Former Qin as Imperial Secretary. However, in his heart, he remained loyal to the Eastern Jin dynasty. Therefore, when he met Xie Shi and Xie Xuan in the Eastern Jin camp, it was like he was coming home. Instead of carrying out Fu Jian's instructions demanding surrender, he handed over intelligence about the Former Qin army to Xie Shi, "Fu Jian has mobilized a 1,000,000 men for the campaign against the Eastern Jin. If he unleashes the entire army in the operation, the Eastern Jin army probably wouldn't stand a chance of stopping the onslaught. You should launch an attack and defeat their vanguard now, before all their forces have time to assemble. This will sink their morale and hasten the collapse of the Former Qin campaign."

When Zhu Xu departed, Xie Shi mulled over the situation long and hard. Finally, he came to the conclusion that he could not have full confidence in his ability to defeat the strong Former Qin force in Shouyang, and that a defensive posture was the more prudent route. Xie An's son Xie Yan, on the other hand, urged Xie Shi to heed Zhu Xu's advice and act without delay.

After further discussion, Xie Shi and Xie Xuan decided to send Liu Laozhi, the renowned commander of the Beifu Army, with 5,000 of his elite troops in a surprise attack against the Former Qin detachment in Luojian. Living up to their fame, members of this elite force, full of spirit, flew across the Luojian gorge like winged tigers. No match for them, the Former Qin troops defending Luojian crumbled after a token resistance. In the rout, their general, Liang Cheng, was killed in battle. Most of the Former Qin men and officers not killed in battle drowned in the Huai River while scrambling to escape.

The victory at Luojian boosted the morale of the Eastern Jin army tremendously. Consequently, Xie Shi and Xie Xuan sent Liu Laozhi on to Xiashi to relieve the Eastern Jin troops there. Meanwhile, pressing their new military advantage, they brought up their main force to the east bank of the Fei River (south of Shou

County, Anhui Province). They set up their encampment at the foot of Mount Bagong, across the river and in direct sight of the Former Qin army occupying Shouyang.

After he had sent Zhu Xu with his ultimatum to the Eastern Jin army, Fu Jian had spent his time gloating, waiting for their surrender to materialize. Therefore, when he received the shocking news of the fall of Luojian, he was shaken and suddenly lost his smug over-confidence. He and Fu Rong ascended the watchtower of the Shouyang city gate and surveyed the situation across the river. Looking out from the tower, Fu Jian was greeted by the sight of neat rows of tents in the Eastern Jin camp, regularly patrolled by well-disciplined, fierce-looking squads of Eastern Jin soldiers. He could vaguely make out untold numbers of more Eastern Jin soldiers on Mount Bagong in the background. In reality, there were no Eastern Jin soldiers on Mount Bagong. Fu Jian, in his agitated state and with his blurred vision, saw an Eastern Jin soldier in every tree and every shrub on its hills. This is the origin of the Chinese saying "cao mu jie bing," literally meaning, "seeing every tree and bush as a soldier." It is used in everyday speech to describe a jittery state of mind.

Fear growing in his heart, Fu Jian turned towards Fu Rong and said, "There's a frightening enemy in front of us. How could you tell me they were weak?"

Immediately, Fu Jian ordered his army to tighten their defenses and security. The Former Qin army's lines strengthened, the Eastern Jin army was prevented from safely crossing the Fei River. This made Xie Shi and Xie Xuan anxious: if things dragged on, the several strands of Former Qin troops would be able to join forces, putting the Eastern Jin army at a great disadvantage.

Xie Xuan sent a messenger with a letter to Fu Jian reading, "You have brought a massive force deep inside Eastern Jin territory. However, now you have arrayed your troops on the bank of the Fei River for the purpose of holding off any real action. Are you really here to do battle? Why don't you pull back your army some distance from the river to create a battlefield? Then my army can cross the river and we can finish this in battle. Isn't that the manly thing to do?"

Fu Jian knew that if he declined this offer, it would be taken as an admission that he was afraid of the Eastern Jin army. Therefore, he immediately summoned his generals and said to them, "They asked us to free up a battlefield. Let's oblige them by pulling back a distance. But when they are mid-river, we can stage a cavalry charge and make mincemeat of them."

When the reply came that Fu Jian had agreed to pull back, Xie Shi and Xie Xuan quickly assembled their army to prepare for the crossing.

At the appointed time for the crossing, Fu Jian ordered his army to fallback, intending to immediately turn his troops around and launch an all-out attack. He had no clue that many of his Former Qin soldiers, partly out of battle fatigue and partly out of fear of the enemy, might quickly run and never stop running as soon as the order for retreat order was given.

No sooner had the pullback begun than Xie Xuan, at the head of his 8,000 cavalrymen, quickly crossed the Fei River and started fiercely attacking the Former Qin army. At this time, Zhu Xu who was at the rear of the Former Qin camp, started to cry out, "The Former Qin army is routed! The Former Qin army is routed!" The soldiers in the rear, not knowing what was happening at the front, and seeing only the Former Qin soldiers turning and running toward the rear, also turned their backs and ran while shouting the same cry of alarm.

Fu Rong wielded his sword in a desperate attempt to restore some order and control, but the tidal wave of retreating Former Qin soldiers was unstoppable. In the confusion, Fu Rong's horse lost its footing and fell to the ground in the face of stampeding Former Qin soldiers. He struggled to get up, but Eastern Jin troops closed in on him and finished him off. Once their chief general was killed, the Former Qin troops, like startled horses having broken free of their reins, dispersed in all directions.

Surveying the scene from the rear, Fu Jian saw that the situation was untenable, so he jumped on a horse and fled as fast as he could. However, he was hit in the shoulder by a stray arrow. Braving the pain, he continued to prod his horse on a frenzied gallop, only able to breathe more easily when he reached Huaibei.

With the Eastern Jin army in hot pursuit, the Former Qin troops continued their desperate flight, leaving behind trampled comrades whose bodies littered the fields and roads. Those who escaped with their lives were too terrified to stop running. They imagined the howling of the wind and the honking of cranes along the way to be the battle cries of the pursuing Eastern Jin army. This is the origin of the Chinese expression "feng sheng he li," literally meaning, "the wind howls and the cranes honk," used in common speech to describe a sense of being hounded.

The successful recovery at Shouyang was reported posthaste by Xie Shi and Xie Xuan to the capital Jiankang. News of the victory caught Xie An at home in the middle of a chess game with a guest. After impassively reading the report, he left the paper on his sofa and resumed the game.

Realizing that Xie An had just received a report from the front, the guest could not resist asking, "How is the war going?"

Xie An replied in an even tone, "The kids have done it. They have defeated the Former Qin after all."

Buoyed by the good tidings, the guest lost his desire to play chess, and left in a hurry to spread the word. After seeing his guest to the door, Xie An returned to his room. Unable to contain the excitement he was feeling any longer, as he stepped unsteadily over the threshold he broke the heel off his wooden clog.

The mighty Former Qin emerged from this major battle considerably weakened. By the time Fu Jian arrived at a safe haven, Luoyang, he had only a little over a 100,000 troops remaining with him. Meanwhile, the army of his underling, Murong Chui, was left intact. Wang Meng's prediction proved prophetic: in the end, Murong Chui (of Xianbei ethnicity) and Yao Chang (of Qiang ethnicity) betrayed the Former Qin and founded their own kingdoms—the Later Yan and the Later Qin—and Fu Jian would be killed by Yao Chang.